Contents

P9-DGP-521

Introduction

THE ANCIENT OLYMPIC GAMES, 776 B.C.-393 A.D.

While the exact origin is unknown, the Ancient Olympic Games were held in a sacred valley at Olympia in Elis, near the western coast of Greece. The earliest recorded Olympic competition was in 776 B.C. although religious festivals in honor of Olympian Zeus had been observed in the sacred valley centuries before. Over a period of time, the Olympic Games became the greatest festival of a mighty nation. Once every four years trading was suspended, the continuously warring states and the fighting tribes laid down their arms, and all of the people went forth in peace to pay tribute to the manhood of the nation.

The immediate site of the Games, the Stadium of Olympia, consisted of four sloping heights, two at the sides and two at the ends. The grassy slopes could accommodate 40,000 spectators. For the first 13 Olympiads the "Games" consisted of a single race of about 200 yards (approximately the length of the stadium). The race was called the "Stade" from which our word "stadium" was derived.

The first recorded victor in 776 B.C. was Coroebus of Elis, a cook. The athletes of Elis maintained an unbroken string of victories until the 14th Olympiad at which time a second race, two lengths of the stadium, was added.

The early rewards were simple crowns of wild olive, but by the 61st Olympiad, it was permitted in Olympia to erect statues in honor of the victors. After Greece came under the domination of the Romans in the second century before Christ, the Games were allowed to continue but the Romans had little interest in them. Finally, in 393 A.D. Roman Emperor Theodosius forbade the Games altogether.

BARON DE COUBERTIN AND THE MODERN OLYMPIC GAMES

Full credit for the revival of the Olympic Games in the modern era must be accorded Baron de Coubertin. He saw in the Olympic Games an opportunity for the French to develop as individuals. In the Spring of 1894, Coubertin gathered together a blue ribbon panel of sportsmen and diplomats who voted unanimously to revive the Games in 1896.

Coubertin believed that the Olympic Games must be contests between individuals, not tests of a nation's strength, or indicative of the superiority of certain political philosophies or ideologies. This conception has not been exactly maintained in all of its original fervor.

ORGANIZATION OF THE WORLD-WIDE OLYMPIC MOVEMENT

The International Olympic Committee, a self-perpetuating body of worldly wise individual sportsmen elected by themselves, is charged with establishing overall policies, determining the rules of athletes' eligibility, negotiating and approving all important contracts in connection with the Games, and selecting the host cities at least six years in advance of the Games. The current president is Lord Michael Morris Killanin of Ireland. He succeeded the late Avery Brundage who served as fifth IOC president for the period 1952–1972. The approximately 90 members of the IOC regard themselves as ambassadors from the IOC to their own countries. They pledge to remain free from all pressures, including those from the National Olympic Committees in their own countries.

The International Sports Federations are in full charge of each of the sports approved for the Games—generally a separate body for each sport. They are in charge of the conduct of the competitions and, with the approval of the IOC and the host city's Organizing Committee, draw up and schedule the events.

The National Olympic Committee of a country is the only organization with authority to enter athletes in the Olympic Games. In the USA that body is the United States Olympic Committee, one of the almost 140 similar committees scattered throughout the world. They must be independent, autonomous and in a position to resist all political, religious, or commercial pressure.

The IOC encourages National Olympic Committees to accept financial help from national governments, provided those governments don't dominate the organization and operation of the group.

THE UNITED STATES OLYMPIC COMMITTEE

The task of arousing American interest to compete in the first modern Olympics in Athens, in 1896, was accepted by James E. Sullivan, longtime secretary of the Amateur Athletic Union. The U.S. Olympic Committee was formalized at a meeting at the New York Athletic Club, in 1921. It was incorporated in 1950 when the 81st Congress enacted Public Law 805.

There are 44 national sports organizations holding memberships in the USOC. It is funded mainly by contributions from the general public and a number of national corporations whose products or services are identified with the USOC or the Olympic Team. This current "Olympiad" has a budget goal of 26 million; up 100% over the previous 4 year period.

The USOC funds the full expenses of all members of the Olympic and Pan American teams, including trips to the Games, in addition to expenses of all athletes for final training sessions and special pre-Games training sessions.

The U.S. is the only country which selects all team members on the basis of results of the announced final selection trials which bring together the top athletes of the nation. Also the U.S. is the only country which enters athletes in every sport and every event within a sport for which we are eligible.

Athletes are eligible for the Olympic Games if they have not competed or coached for money or appeared in commercial products' advertisements, whether they received compensation or not.

In December, 1976, the USOC Executive Board adopted the National Training Center Concept. This provides centralized and supervised training facilities at no expense to the athletes selected by the national sports governing bodies. The two training centers in operation thus far are located at Colorado Springs, Colo., and Squaw Valley, Cal.

The first USOC National Sports Festival was inaugurated at Colorado Springs in July, 1978. Almost 2,200 athletes selected by 25 different sports organizations participated. All costs are underwritten by the USOC. Such festivals will be conducted annually except in the Olympic years.

The USOC *House of Delegates,* consisting of representatives of all member organizations and current and past officers, meets annually to establish overall policies. All members of the USOC must serve without pay under IOC regulations.

The current headquarters of the United States Olympic Committee, is Olympic House, Colorado Springs, Colo. and is under the direction of Col. F. Don Miller, USA (ret.).

THE OPENING CEREMONY

Those athletes who have been there share a bond unparalleled in competitive athletics—the thrill of marching in the parade of nations at the Olympic Games. This is the parade of athletes, with a minimum number of officials from each of the National Olympic Committees, into the main Olympic Stadium.

Can anyone name a single other ceremony of any kind in the world which quadrennially attracts the Chief of State of the host nation? There is none on record! President Jimmy Carter already has accepted the invitation of the Lake Placid Olympic Organizing Committee to take the internationally-recognized "eyes right" salute during the Opening Ceremony for the XIII Olympic Winter Games, February 13, 1980. Likewise, the Chief of State of the Union of Soviet Socialist Republics will be on hand for the Games of the XXII Olympiad in Leningrad Stadium, Moscow, July 19, 1980.

Those who have witnessed the parade of athletes unanimously agree that there is not a more colorful demonstration anywhere else in the world—many of the nations in their native dress, the teams from East Germany, the USSR and France sporting the latest in the fashion circles, and the United States athletes always smartly attired in clothes featuring our nation's colors—red, white, and blue. Each delegation is preceded by a young lady bearing the official name of the country, in the language of the host country. For example, in Montreal the U.S.A. delegation marched behind a banner reading in the French language, "Etats Unis."

The line of march is fixed by the language of the host country, except the privilege of leading the parade is always accorded to Greece, in recognition of that nation's role in inaugurating the Ancient Olympic Games and hosting the first of the Modern Olympic Games. Also, protocol dictates that the host nation will bring up the rear.

Each delegation selects its own standard bearer—the foremost honor to be accorded an active athlete. For the U.S.A., representatives of each of the men's and women's teams meet two days before the Opening Ceremony to elect the active athlete for this honor. In two of the last three Olympic Games our representatives have chosen women. At Mexico in 1968 it was Janice York Romary, a member of six U.S.A. Olympic fencing teams. Four years later the honoree was Olga Figatova Connolly, a former Czechoslovakia discus champion (1956) who later married an American hammer throw champion, Harold Connolly.

After the nations have taken their place in the center of the stadium the ceremony begins.

The President of the host city's Olympic Games Organizing Committee, accompanied by International Olympic Committee president, The Lord Killanin, then escorts the Chief of State. The IOC President says, "I have the honor to invite _____ (Chief of State) to proclaim open the Games of the __ Olympiad of the modern era, initiated by Baron Pierre de Coubertin in 1896."

The Chief of State responds, "I declare open the Games of _____ celebrating the __ Olympiad of the modern era."

With the Games "proclaimed open" the band plays the sacred Olympic Hymn, composed in 1896 by Spirou Samara with words by Costis Palamas of Greece, while the official Olympic flag (five interlocked rings on a plain white background) is slowly raised. A second official flag is then presented by the mayor of the immediate previous host city to the mayor of the city celebrating the Games. This flag shall fly daily at the local City Hall until the next Olympic Games.

This simple ceremony immediately precedes the arrival of the Olympic torch which was lit by rays from the sun at ancient Olympia and then carried by a relay of runners. The runner (or runners) circles the field once, climbs special stairs erected for the occasion to light the cauldron or flame which will burn without cease during the celebration of the Games.

Two highlights of the Opening Ceremony immediately follow—an active athlete of the host country and a representative of the judges and officials swear an oath to uphold the highest traditions of Olympism.

It is customary for the formal ceremony to close with the release of a number of doves of peace signifying the spirit of the Games. After which release of doves, the athletes leave the stadium.

THE CLOSING CEREMONY

In recent years it has been customary for the Closing Ceremony in the main Olympic stadium to be preceded by the magnificent competition of the **Prix des Nations** team jumping equestrian event. The International Olympic Committee has decreed that each national Olympic committee may designate six athletes to participate in the parade. Again, the U.S.A. athletes select these representatives (including a flag bearer) from the most outstanding members of the team in the Games.

Unlike the Opening Ceremony, the athletes march in, eight to ten abreast, without distinction of nationality, united only by the friendly bonds of Olympic sport. It is an emotional experience for athletes and spectators, alike.

The flag bearers of the participating nations form a semi-circle behind the main rostrum.

In a simple ceremony, to the strains of the Greek national anthem, the Greek flag is raised on a flag pole to the right of the center flag pole, after which the flag of the host country is raised and, finally, the national flag of the city selected to organize the next Games on the left hand flag pole. Thus, at Lake Placid the flag on the left will be that of Yugoslavia which will host the XIV Olympic Winter Games in 1984, and in Moscow the spectators and one billion television viewers will thrill to Old Glory being run up on this flag pole on the far left.

The Lord Killanin closes the Games with a simple statement, closing with the words, "I call upon the youth of all countries to assemble four years from now at _____, there to celebrate with us the Games of the __ Olympiad (or the __ Olympic Winter Games)."

As the band plays a short musical fanfare, the Olympic flame is extinguished, followed by the Olympic hymn as the Olympic flag is slowly lowered to be carried from the stadium by a group of eight men in uniform.

The program closes with a five-gun salute, a short choral selection, and the exit of the flag bearers and competitors. At the recent Olympic Games the exit of the athletes often has been a happy and joyous occasion as the athletes in unrestrained glee wave to the cheering spectators. The "march off" at both Mexico City (1968) and Montreal (1976) were superb, with the Montreal Games also staging a beautiful pageant for the benefit of spectators and athletes, alike.

What a wonderful way to close down the joyous celebration of the single most significant athletic happening.

These are the dates:	July 19	July 20	July 21	July 22	July 23	July 24
Opening Ceremony	■					
Archery						
Athletics Track and Field						■
Basketball		■	■	■	■	■
Boxing		■	■	■	■	■
Canoe and Kayak						
Cycling		■		■	■	■
Diving		■	■	■	■	
Equestrian						■
Fencing				■	■	
Field Hockey		■	■		■	■
Gymnastics		■	■	■	■	
Judo						■
Modern Pentathlon		■	■	■	■	■
Rowing		■	■	■	■	
Shooting		■	■	■	■	■
Soccer Football		■	■	■	■	■
Swimming		■	■	■	■	■
Team Handball		■	■	■		■
Volleyball		■	■	■	■	
Water Polo		■	■	■		■
Weightlifting		■	■	■	■	■
Wrestling		■	■	■	■	■
Yachting			■	■	■	■
Closing Ceremony						

July 25	July 26	July 27	July 28	July 29	July 30	July 31	Aug. 1	Aug. 2	Aug. 3

1

Archery

Event Days:

Wednesday,
July 30, 1980

Thursday,
July 31, 1980

Friday,
August 1, 1980

Saturday,
August 2, 1980

Contributors:

Judi Adams
Richard Lee Bednar
Irene Daubenspeck
Lynette R. Johnson
Richard L. McKinney
Darrell O. Pace
Scott Page

Archery was a part of the Olympic Games in 1900, 1908, and 1920 and then disappeared from the program until the 1972 Olympic Games. In both 1972 and 1976 the United States of America captured the gold medals in the men's and women's competitions. The United States has been recognized as pre-eminent in this discipline since World War II and has captured many world and international competitions.

Although not regarded as a big spectator sport, the skills of these modernday Robin Hoods are remarkable when considering the high percentage of bulls' eyes scored. In the Olympic Games 288 shots are shot on two separate days of competitions, 144 arrows each day. Both the men and women shoot arrows from four different distances. The women shoot two series of 36 arrows each from 70-60-50-30 meters each; for the men the distances are 90-70-50-30, also 36 arrows in two series.

The 1976 Olympic Champions were Miss LuAnn Ryon, Riverside, California, and Airman Darrell Pace, USAF, Cincinnati.

Contributors	Recipes

Judi Adams

Residency: Phoenix, Arizona
Age: 19
Height: 6'
Weight: 110
School: Glendale Community College
Training hours per week: 9

Spiced Nuts

1 cup sugar
1/2 cup water
2 teaspoons allspice
2 cups pecan halves

In a medium pan, combine sugar and water. Bring to a boil and cook to soft ball stage. Stir in allspice. Stir in nuts. Pour out onto waxed paper. Separate nuts immediately. Makes about 2½ cups nuts.

Richard Lee Bednar

Residency: Suffield, Ohio
Age: 21
Height: 5'10"
Weight: 160
School: University of Akron Graduate
Training hours per week: 14

Fly-Off-The-Plate Rolls

2 packages dry yeast
1/2 cup warm water
1 cup warm milk
1/4 cup melted butter or margarine
2 tablespoons sugar
1 teaspoon salt
1 egg, beaten
1½ cups flour
18 marshmallows
1 cup melted butter
1 cup sugar
1 teaspoon cinnamon

Dissolve yeast in warm water. Combine milk, butter, sugar, salt and egg in a large bowl. Add yeast mixture and beat for four minutes at medium speed. Stir in enough flour to form a soft dough. Turn out onto a floured surface and knead until smooth and elastic, working in more flour if necessary. Place in a greased bowl, cover, and let rise in a warm place until double, about 30 minutes. Punch down, and divide dough into 18 pieces. Flatten each piece and wrap around a marshmallow, pinching to seal. Place on a greased cookie sheet and let rise for 30 minutes. Dip balls in melted butter and roll in a mixture of sugar and cinnamon. Bake at 350° for 30 minutes on a greased cookie sheet. Makes 18 rolls.

Cheese Dip

2 8-ounce packages cream cheese, softened
2 tablespoons catsup
1 tablespoon dried onion flakes
1/2 cup Western salad dressing
1/8 teaspoon garlic salt

In a medium bowl, beat all ingredients until blended. Chill. Makes about 2½ cups dip.

Irene Daubenspeck

Residency: Phoenix, Arizona
Age: 25
Height: 5'5"
Weight: 160
Training hours per week: 8

Cherry Delight

1 16-ounce can cherry pie filling
1 16-ounce can crushed pineapple
1 package yellow or white cake mix (two-layer size)
2 cups melted butter or margarine
Nuts and/or coconut (optional)

Mix cherry pie filling and undrained pineapple in a 13x9-inch baking pan. Sprinkle dry cake mix over fruit. Drizzle with melted butter. If desired, sprinkle with nuts and/or coconut. Bake at 350° for 40 to 50 minutes. If desired, top with whipped cream or ice cream. Serves 12.

Lynette R. Johnson

Residency: Cypress, California
Age: 21
Height: 5'6"
Weight: 145
School: Glendale Community College
Training hours per week: 25

Hot Bean Dip

2 cups refried beans
1 cup canned tomatoes, drained and chopped
1 tablespoon instant minced onion
1 teaspoon Worcestershire sauce
1 clove garlic, minced
1 teaspoon chili powder
3/4 cup grated Colby or Cheddar cheese
Corn chips

Combine all ingredients except corn chips in a medium saucepan. Over medium heat, stirring occasionally, heat until cheese melts. Serve warm, sprinkled with additional grated cheese, if desired. Use as dip for corn chips. Makes about three cups.

Snowcaps

1/2 cup magarine
4 squares semi-sweet chocolate
2 cups sugar
4 eggs
2 teaspoons vanilla
2 cups flour
2 teaspoons baking powder
1/4 teaspoon salt
Powdered sugar

In a small saucepan, over low heat, melt margarine with chocolate, stirring constantly. In a medium mixing bowl, beat sugar with eggs. Stir in chocolate mixture and vanilla. Combine flour, baking powder and salt; add to chocolate mixture. Mix well. Chill overnight. With hands, roll into small balls. Roll balls in powdered sugar. Bake on a greased baking sheet at 350° for 10 minutes. Makes about four dozen.

Fruit Slush

1/2 cup sugar
2 bananas, mashed
2 cups gingerale or white soda
1 15½-ounce can crushed pineapple with juice
1 46-ounce can orange-pineapple drink or orange drink
1 12-ounce can frozen orange juice concentrate
1 12-ounce can frozen lemonade concentrate

Combine all ingredients in a one-gallon covered container. Stir well to combine. Store in freezer. To serve, remove from freezer, stir well and spoon into punch cups or cocktail glasses. Serves 12 or more.

Richard L. McKinney

Residency: Muncie, Indiana
Age: 25
Height: 5'6"
Weight: 120
Training hours per week: 2

Baked Stuffed Squash

1 medium acorn squash
Water
3/4 teaspoon seasoned salt
1 cup diced cooked ham
3/4 cup applesauce

Cut squash in half lengthwise; scoop out seeds and pulp. Place cut-side-down in about 1/2-inch of water in a baking dish. Bake at 350° for about 30 minutes or until tender. Sprinkle cut sides of squash with seasoned salt. Discard water and set squash cut-side-up in baking dish. Combine ham and applesauce. Spoon into cavities in squash. Bake at 350° for 20 to 30 minutes or until heated through. Serves two.

Sesame Seed Cookies

1 cup brown sugar
3/4 cup butter or margarine
1 egg
1 teaspoon almond extract
2 cups whole wheat flour
1 teaspoon baking powder
1/2 teaspoon baking soda
1/2 teaspoon salt
1 cup sesame seeds
1/2 cup unsweetened flaked coconut

Cream butter and sugar in a medium bowl. Beat in egg and almond extract. Mix in remaining dry ingredients until well blended. Roll into balls the size of a small walnut. Place on a lightly greased cookie sheet. Flatten with a fork or drinking glass, lightly greased and dipped in granulated sugar. Bake at 350° for 10 to 15 minutes. Makes about four dozen cookies.

Darrell O. Pace

Residency: Cincinnati, Ohio
Age: 22
Height: 6'
Weight: 150
School: Reading Community High School/Scarlet Oaks Career Development Center
Training hours per week: 30

Cincinnati Chili

2 pounds ground beef
1 quart water
2 medium onions, grated
2 8-ounce cans tomato sauce
5 whole allspice
1½ teaspoons red pepper
1 teaspoon ground cumin
4 tablespoons chili powder
1/2 ounce unsweetened chocolate
4 cloves garlic, minced
5 whole cloves
2 teaspoons Worcestershire sauce
1½ teaspoons salt
2 tablespoons vinegar
1 large bay leaf
1 teaspoon cinnamon

In a four-quart pot, crumble ground beef into water. Stir until beef separates to a fine texture. Boil slowly for 30 minutes. Add remaining ingredients. Stir well and bring to a boil. Reduce heat and simmer, uncovered, for about three hours. (It may be covered during the last hour if the desired consistency is reached.) Refrigerate overnight. Skim fat. Reheat. Serve over spaghetti or over hot dogs on buns. If desired, add chili beans or sprinkle with chopped onions or grated cheese. Serves six to eight.

Darrell O. Pace

Fantasy Fudge

3 cups sugar

3/4 cup margarine

1 5⅓-ounce can evaporated milk

1 12-ounce package semi-sweet chocolate chips

1 7-ounce jar marshmallow creme

1 cup chopped nuts

1 teaspoon vanilla

Combine sugar, margarine and milk in a heavy 2½-quart saucepan. Bring to a full rolling boil, stirring constantly. Continue boiling over medium heat for five minutes, stirring constantly. Remove from heat. Stir in chocolate chips until melted. Add marshmallow creme, nuts and vanilla. Beat until well blended. Pour into a greased 13×9-inch pan. Cool to room temperature. Cut into squares. Makes about five dozen pieces.

Butter Pecan Turtle Cookies

Crust:

2 cups flour

1 cup brown sugar

1/2 cup butter, softened

1 cup pecan halves

Caramel layer:

2/3 cup butter, softened

1/2 cup brown sugar

1 cup milk chocolate chips

Combine flour, brown sugar and butter in a large mixing bowl. Beat with electric mixer until mixture resembles coarse meal. With hands, pat firmly into an ungreased 13x9-inch baking pan. Arrange pecan halves over unbaked crust. To prepare caramel layer, combine butter and brown sugar in a heavy one-quart saucepan. Cook over medium heat, stirring constantly, until entire surface begins to boil. Boil 30 to 60 seconds, stirring constantly. Pour caramel mixture evenly over pecans and crust. Bake near center of a 350° oven for 18 to 20 minutes or until caramel is bubbly and crust is golden brown. Remove from oven. Sprinkle with chocolate chips. Allow chips to melt slightly. Swirl chips over surface with spatula. Cool completely. Cut into small bars. Makes about four dozen bars.

Scott Page

Residency: Fallbrook, California

Age: 23

Height: 5'10"

Weight: 145

School: San Diego State University

Training hours per week: 18

Avocado Salad

2 medium avocados

1/4 cup diced celery

Seasoned salt

Lettuce

Cottage cheese

Peel and cut avocado into bite-size pieces. Combine with celery. Add seasoned salt to taste. Serve on a lettuce leaf with a scoop of cottage cheese. Serves three.

Contributors	Recipes

Scott Page

My Daily Smoothie

1 banana

3 slices pineapple, fresh or
    canned and unsweetened

1 cup of your favorite fruit juice

1/3 cup apple juice

1 cup crushed ice

1 egg (optional)

2 tablespoons honey

Combine all ingredients except honey in electric blender. Blend well. Add honey and blend again. Serves two.

2 Athletics

Track and Field

Event Days:

Thursday,
July 24, 1980

Friday,
July 25, 1980

Saturday,
July 26, 1980

Sunday,
July 27, 1980

Monday,
July 28, 1980

Wednesday,
July 30, 1980

Thursday,
July 31, 1980

Friday,
August 1, 1980

Contributors:

Mark Belger
Paula Darcel Girven
Wendy Koenig Knudson
Martin Liquori
Steve Riddick
Alberto Salazar
Steven Michael Scott
Michael L. Shine

This premier sport on the Olympic program ranks second only to soccer in attracting spectators. In the revival of the Olympic Games in 1896 in Athens, the first event to be decided was the triple jump won by James B. Connolly, USA.

In the 18 Olympic Games no country has ever won as many Olympic titles in the men's events as the United States of America. Since 1952 the women's events have been dominated by the athletes from Eastern Europe. The last individual gold medals won by USA women were in 1968: Wyomia Tyus in the 100 meters and Madeline Manning Jackson, 800 meters.

There have been 225 USA men who have won Olympic titles. Among the noteworthy achievements are the following, alphabetically:

Harrison Dillard, 1948, 100 meters; 1952, 110-meters hurdles.
Dr. Clarence Houser, 1924, shotput and discus; 1928, discus.
Alvin Kraenzlein, 1900, only man to win four individual events in track and field.
Bob Mathias, 1948 and 1952, decathlon.
Alfred A. Oerter, Jr., 1956, 1960, 1964, and 1968, discus.
Jesse Owens, 1936, winner of the 100 meters, 200 meters, long jump, and ran on the winning sprint relay.
Mel Sheppard, 1908, 800 and 1,500 meters.

Perhaps the three most noteworthy women for the USA have been, alphabetically:

Mildred (Babe) Didrikson, 1932, winner of the 80-meter hurdles and the javelin throw, second to teammate Jean Shiley in the high jump.
Wilma Rudolph, 1960, winner of the 100 and 200 meters, member of the winning sprint relay.
Wyomia Tyus, 1964, 100 meters; 1968, 100 meters, sprint relay.

Mark Belger

Residency: Arlington, Massachusetts
Age: 22
Height: 5'11"
Weight: 150
School: Villanova University
Training hours per week: 27½

"The Morning After" Breakfast

1/2 fresh melon, in season (such as cantalope, honeydew, etc.)

2 scoops vanilla ice cream

1 banana, sliced

1/4 cup blueberries

2 to 3 tablespoons honey

1 tablespoon wheat germ

Fill melon with ice cream. Top with sliced bananas and blueberries. Drizzle with honey and sprinkle with wheat germ. Serves one.

Fruit "Cereal"

1 apple, cored and cut in chunks

1 orange, peeled and cut in chunks

1 grapefruit, peeled and cut in chunks

1 banana, sliced

1 16-ounce can pineapple chunks in natural juice, or equivalent amount of fresh pineapple, cut in chunks

1 cup fresh blueberries

2 cups melon balls or chunks (cantaloupe, watermelon or honeydew)

Orange juice

Combine fruits in a large bowl. To serve, spoon fruit into cereal bowls. Serve juice on the side to pour over fruit. (Any combination or quantity of fruits and juices may be used.) Serves four.

Paula Darcel Girven

Residency: Dale City, Virginia
Age: 21
Height: 5'9"
Weight: 136
School: University of Maryland, College Park
Training hours per week: 12

P. G.'s Roast Beef

1 4-to-6-pound sirloin tip or rump beef roast

Garlic salt

Salt and pepper

2 teaspoons lemon juice

5 medium onions, quartered

1 4-ounce can sliced mushrooms

1 cup water

3 potatoes, peeled and cut up

3 carrots, peeled and sliced

Rub roast with garlic salt, salt and pepper. Sprinkle with lemon juice. Place roast on a large sheet of heavy-duty foil or in a roasting bag, fat side up. Place onions and mushrooms in bag with roast. Add half the water to the roast. Place the remaining water in a roasting pan. Seal foil or bag. Place in pan. Roast at 325°, allowing 30 minutes per pound. One hour before roast is done, open bag or foil and add potatoes and carrots. (Increase amount of vegetables if desired.) Make gravy from pan drippings. Serves eight to 12.

Contributors	Recipes

Paula Darcel Girven

P. G.'s Stew

2 pounds beef stew meat

Seasoned flour

3 tablespoons butter or margarine

1 onion, chopped

3 carrots, peeled and sliced

4 potatoes, peeled and cut in chunks

1 10-ounce package frozen peas

Dredge meat in seasoned flour. In a large heavy kettle or Dutch oven, brown meat in butter. Add onion and water to cover. Cover and simmer for 1½ hours, stirring occasionally. Add vegetables and additional water if necessary. Simmer for 30 more minutes or until vegetables are done. If desired, thicken gravy with a paste made of water and flour or cornstarch. Serves four to six.

Wendy Koenig Knudson

Residency: Logan, Utah

Age: 23

Height: 5'7 1/2"

Weight: 122

School: Colorado State University, B.S., M.S.

Training hours per week: 24

Whole Wheat Bread

3/4 cup warm water

2½ teaspoons honey

2 packets dry yeast

1/3 cup vegetable oil

2¼ cups warm water

1/2 cup honey

1½ tablespoons salt

8 to 9 cups whole wheat flour

In a small bowl, dissolve yeast with honey and warm water. In a large bowl, mix oil, warm water, honey and salt. Stir yeast mixture into large bowl. Stir in flour to form a stiff dough. Turn out onto a floured surface and knead until smooth and elastic, adding more flour as necessary. Place in an oiled bowl and let rise in a warm, draft-free place until doubled. Punch down and let rise a second time. Meanwhile, grease three medium loaf pans. Punch dough down, divide into three parts and shape into loaves. Place in greased pans, brush with oil and bake at 400° for 10 minutes. Reduce heat to 350° and bake for 45 minutes. Makes three medium loaves.

Green Tomato Mince Meat

3 pints chopped, peeled apples

3 pints chopped green tomatoes

4 cups brown sugar or honey

3 cups raisins

3 teaspoons cinnamon

1 teaspoon cloves

1 teaspoon allspice

1 teaspoon nutmeg

1/2 teaspoon pepper

2 teaspoons salt

1⅓ cups vinegar

In a large kettle, combine all ingredients and mix well. Simmer for three hours, stirring frequently. Seal in pint jars; adjust lids; process in a boiling water bath, 20 minutes for pints or 30 minutes for quarts. Serve as a relish, or add butter and use as pie filling, crepe filling or coffee cake filling. Makes about six pints.

Contributors	Recipes

Wendy Koenig Knudson

Crock Pot Barbecued Chicken

1 cup catsup

4 tablespoons lemon juice

2 tablespoons honey

2 tablespoons Worcestershire sauce

2 tablespoons vinegar

2 tablespoons Dijon mustard

Salt and pepper to taste

6 frozen broiler-fryer chicken thighs, or any favorite chicken parts

Mix all ingredients except chicken in crock pot. Add frozen chicken. Cook on high for eight to 10 hours with lid on. Serve over rice. If desired, thicken sauce with cornstarch. Serves four.

Martin Liquori

Residency: Gainesville, Florida
Age: 29
Height: 6'
Weight: 145
School: Villanova University
Training hours per week: 21

Veal Scaloppini With Marsala

1/2 pound fresh mushrooms, sliced

4 tablespoons butter

1½ tablespoons lemon juice

1½ pounds veal cutlets

1/4 cup flour

1 teaspoon salt

1/4 teaspoon pepper

3/4 cup Marsala

1 tablespoon minced parsley

In a large skillet, saute mushrooms with 2 tablespoons butter and lemon juice. Remove mushrooms with slotted spoon and set aside. Cut veal into strips and dredge in flour seasoned with salt and pepper. Melt remaining butter in skillet and brown meat on both sides at high heat. Remove meat to heated platter. Add Marsala to skillet and scrape to loosen browned bits. Add mushrooms and bring to a boil. Pour over veal. Sprinkle with parsley. Serves four.

Steve Riddick

Residency: Philadelphia, Pennsylvania
Age: 27
Height: 6'3½"
Weight: 175
School: Norfolk State College
Training hours per week: 16

Quick Meatball Casserole

1/3 cup flour

1 teaspoon salt

1/4 teaspoon pepper

4 cups thinly sliced potatoes (about 4 medium)

1 10-ounce package frozen green beans, thawed

1½ cups shredded Cheddar cheese

1 16-ounce can tomato sauce

1/2 teaspoon sage

1 pound ground beef

1/2 cup fine dry bread crumbs

1/3 cup milk

1/4 cup minced onion

1 egg, beaten

Combine flour, salt and pepper: set aside. Layer half the potatoes and beans in a 13x9-inch baking pan. Top with 1/4 of the cheese. Sprinkle with half the flour mixture. Repeat layers. Combine tomato sauce and sage. Pour half the sauce over the casserole. Bake uncovered at 350° for 20 minutes. Meanwhile, mix the remaining cheese with the remaining ingredients. Shape into 24 meatballs. Arrange meatballs over top of casserole. Pour on remaining tomato sauce. Return to oven and bake for 45 minutes or until potatoes and meatballs are done. Serves six.

Contributors	Recipes

Steve Riddick

Halibut Stroganoff

1½ pounds halibut fillets

1/4 cup butter or margarine

1 medium onion, sliced

1/4 pound fresh mushrooms, sliced

1/4 cup dry white wine

1 teaspoon salt

2 teaspoons lemon juice

1/2 teaspoon Worcestershire sauce

1/2 teaspoon Dijon mustard

Dash of pepper

1½ cups sour cream

Chopped parsley

Cooked green noodles

Cut fish into bite-size chunks. In a large skillet, saute onions and mushrooms in half the butter until tender. Remove with a slotted spoon. Add remaining butter to skillet and saute fish until flesh turns white. Blend wine, salt, lemon juice, Worcestershire sauce, mustard and pepper with sour cream. Return onions and mushrooms to skillet. Add sour cream mixture and stir gently to blend. Cook over low heat, stirring frequently, until just heated through. Serve over noodles. Sprinkle with parsley. Serves four.

Alberto Salazar

Residency: Eugene, Oregon
Age: 20
Height: 6 '
Weight: 142
School: University of Oregon
Training hours per week: 20

Cuban Chicken With Rice

3 tablespoons vegetable oil

3 medium onions, minced

2 green peppers, minced

4 cloves garlic, minced

1 2½ to 3-pound broiler-fryer chicken, cut up

1 6-ounce can tomato paste

1 bay leaf

6 cups water or chicken broth

Pinch of saffron

3 cups raw rice

1/2 cup white wine

1 17-ounce can small peas

1 4-ounce can pimientos, diced

Salt and pepper

In a heavy skillet, saute onions, peppers and garlic in oil until soft. Add chicken and brown. Transfer to a heavy kettle or covered casserole. Add tomato paste and bay leaf and stir well. Cover with water mixed with saffron. Cover, bring to a boil, reduce heat and simmer until chicken is fork-tender, about 45 minutes. (Or, cover and bake at 350° for about 45 minutes.) Add rice, wine, peas and pimientos. Season to taste with salt and pepper. (Water should cover rice by about one inch. Add more water if necessary.) Cover and continue to cook until rice is done, about 30 minutes. Garnish with additional pimiento, if desired. Serves four to six.

Contributors	Recipes	

Steven Michael Scott

Residency: Irvine, California
Age: 22
Height: 6'1"
Weight: 160
Training hours per week: 23

German Blueberry Cake

1/3 cup butter, softened
3 tablespoons sugar
1 egg
1 cup flour
1 teaspoon baking powder
3 tablespoons milk
3 16-ounce cans blueberries
Cinnamon
2 tablespoons cornstarch
2 tablespoons sugar

In a medium bowl, cream butter with sugar. Beat in egg. Combine flour and baking powder. Add flour mixture alternately with milk to creamed mixture until well blended. (Batter will be stiff.) Turn into a greased 9 to 10-inch pie pan. Flour hands and shape dough into a shell. Prick all over with a fork. Drain berries, reserving two cups juice. Fill shell with berries and sprinkle with cinnamon. Bake at 350° for one hour. Just before cake is finished baking, combine cornstarch and sugar in a small pan. Gradually stir in blueberry juice and cook, stirring constantly, until thick. Pour over cake. Serve warm or cold. Serves six to eight.

Michael L. Shine

Residency: Youngsville, Pennsylvania
Age: 25
Height: 6'
Weight: 168
School: Penn State University, C. W. Post
Training hours per week: 10

Country Stew

2 pounds beef for stew
2 cups dry red wine
1/2 teaspoon rosemary
1 bay leaf
1/2 teaspoon basil
1/2 teaspoon thyme
1/2 pound salt pork or bacon, diced
1 cup water
2 medium onions, chopped
2 cloves garlic, minced or pressed
2 tablespoons bottled steak sauce
1 teaspoon cinnamon
1/2 teaspoon ground cloves
4 to 6 carrots, sliced
1 cup fresh mushrooms, whole or sliced
1 cup peeled, chopped tomatoes
4 large potatoes, cut into chunks

Early in the day, combine meat with wine and herbs in a covered glass or stainless steel container in the refrigerator. Marinate for four to five hours, stirring occasionally. Drain meat, reserving marinade. In a large skillet or Dutch oven, brown salt pork or bacon. Drain off excess fat. Add meat and brown. Add water and strained marinade and stir to loosen browned bits. Add remaining ingredients except mushrooms, carrots, tomatoes and potatoes. Add water to cover. Bake, covered, at 300° for two to three hours or until meat is tender. Add carrots, mushrooms, tomatoes and potatoes. Bake one more hour. Remove meat and vegetables to a heated platter. If desired, thicken pan juices and serve separately. Serves four to six.

Spinach Onion Dip

1 10-ounce package frozen chopped spinach
1 cup mayonnaise
1 1⅞-ounce packet dry onion soup mix

Cook spinach according to package directions. Drain well. Combine all ingredients, mix well and chill. Serve as dip with raw vegetables, such as fresh mushrooms, carrot and celery sticks, sliced cucumbers and cauliflowerets. Makes two cups dip.

3
Basketball

Event Days:

Sunday,
July 20, 1980

Monday,
July 21, 1980

Tuesday,
July 22, 1980

Thursday,
July 24, 1980

Friday,
July 25, 1980

Saturday,
July 26, 1980

Sunday,
July 27, 1980

Monday,
July 28, 1980

Tuesday,
July 29, 1980

Wednesday,
July 30, 1980

Contributors:

Genia Gail Beasley
Carol Blazejowski
Michael Thomas Gminski
Albert King
Nancy Lieberman
Clifford Trent Robinson
Darnell Valentine
Ernest "Kiki" Vandeweghe
Holly Warlick

Basketball was not added to the Olympic program until the 1936 Berlin Olympics where the U.S. team defeated Canada in the final game. The USA has won 69 out of 70 games which it has played in the Olympics, losing a highly questionable decision to the USSR in 1972 in Munich.

Recently the U.S. Amateur Basketball Association has arranged for summer exhibition tours to Europe and South America to familiarize some of the top eligible athletes with international rules.

The greatest team ever assembled was the 1960 squad which included—Ralph Bellamy, Bob Boozer, Terry Dischinger, Burdette Haldorson, Darrall Imhoff, Les Lane, Jerry Lucas, Oscar Robertson, Adrian Smith and Jerry West under coach Pete Newell.

Women's basketball competition was introduced at Montreal in 1976 when host Canada, world champion USSR and four teams chosen from an all-comers tournament prior to the Games met in a round robin series. The USSR won all five games, including a 112–77 triumph over the USA. The U.S. team, led by Lusia Harris, Pat Head, Patricia Roberts and Ann Myers, came back from an opening game loss to Japan and defeated Canada, Bulgaria and Czechoslovakia to win the silver medal. The coach of the 1980 team is Sue Gunter of Stephen F. Austin College and the ass't. coach is Pat Head, U. of Tennessee.

Contributors	Recipes

Genia Gail Beasley

Residency: Benson, North Carolina

Age: 20

Height: 6'2"

Weight: 155

School: North Carolina State University

Training hours per week: 20

Chewy Bars

2¼ cups brown sugar

1/2 cup butter or margarine

3 eggs

2 cups self-rising flour

2 cups chopped pecans

1 teaspoon vanilla

In a medium bowl, cream sugar and butter. Add eggs one at a time, beating well after each addition. Add flour; mix well. Stir in nuts and vanilla. Spread into a greased 11x8-inch pan. Bake at 350° for 30 to 35 minutes. Cool. Cut into bars. Makes about three dozen bars.

Italian Cream Cake

1/2 cup butter

1/2 cup vegetable shortening

2 cups sugar

5 egg yolks

2 cups cake flour

1 teaspoon baking soda

1 cup buttermilk

1 cup chopped pecans or walnuts

1 cup flaked coconut

1 teaspoon vanilla

5 egg whites

Cream Cheese Frosting (see directions)

In a large bowl, cream butter and shortening with sugar. Add egg yolks. Beat well. Combine flour and soda and add to creamed mixture alternately with buttermilk, beating well after each addition. Stir in nuts, coconut and vanilla. In a medium bowl with clean beaters, beat egg whites until stiff. Fold into batter. Pour into three greased and waxed paper-lined 9-inch layer cake pans. Bake at 350° for 30 to 35 minutes. Cool. Remove from pans. Frost with Cream Cheese Frosting and sprinkle with additional chopped nuts, if desired. Serves 12.

Cream Cheese Frosting: Beat 1 8-ounce package of cream cheese with 1/4 cup butter or margarine until smooth. Mix in 3 to 4 cups powdered sugar and 1 teaspoon vanilla until mixture is of spreading consistency. Makes enough to frost a three-layer cake.

Spiced Pecans

1 egg white

3 tablespoons water

1/4 teaspoon salt

1 teaspoon cinnamon

1/2 cup sugar

1 quart pecan halves

In a medium bowl, beat egg white with water until foamy. Beat in salt, cinnamon and sugar. Fold in pecans. Pour into a large buttered heavy skillet. Bake at 250° for one hour, stirring every 15 minutes. Cool. Store in tightly covered container in a cool, dry place. Makes one quart spiced nuts.

Carol Blazejowski

Residency: Fairview, New York
Age: 22
Height: 5'10"
Weight: 150
School: Graduate School
  Montclair State College
Training hours per week: 15

Veal Saute

2 pounds veal stew meat
Seasoned flour
1/4 cup olive oil
1/4 cup butter
3 shallots, finely chopped
1 cup dry white wine
1/2 cup chicken stock or
  bouillon
12 small white onions, peeled
6 to 8 small carrots, peeled
1/2 pound fresh mushrooms,
  sliced
1/4 cup parsley, chopped
  (preferably flat Italian type)

Dredge veal in seasoned flour. In a large skillet, heat olive oil and butter. Brown veal quickly. Reduce heat and add shallots, wine and stock. Bring to a boil and reduce heat to a simmer. Add onions and carrots. Cover and simmer for about 45 minutes. Add mushrooms and continue simmering until meat is tender. Add parsley. Remove meat and vegetables to a heated serving dish and pour on the sauce. If desired, thicken the sauce with small balls of blended butter and flour. Variation for Red Veal Saute: for carrots, substitute 3 or 4 medium tomatoes, peeled, seeded and chopped. Serves six.

Michael Thomas Gminski

Residency: Monroe,
  Connecticut
Age: 19
Height: 6'11"
Weight: 245
School: Duke University
Training hours per week: 24

Brown Rice Burgers

1 large onion, chopped
1 cup chopped celery
1/2 cup minced parsley
3 cloves garlic, minced
2 tablespoons vegetable oil
4 cups cooked brown rice
2 cups grated carrots
2 eggs, beaten
1/2 cup whole wheat flour
Salt and pepper to taste
Oil for frying
6 slices sharp Cheddar cheese

In a large skillet, saute onion, celery, parsley and garlic in oil until tender. Mix in rice, carrots, eggs, flour and season to taste with salt and pepper. Shape into eight to 12 patties according to your preference. Fry in oil over medium heat until browned on one side. Turn, top with slice of cheese and continue frying until second side is brown and cheese is melted. Serves four to six.

Easy Raisin Bars

1 cup raisins
1 cup boiling water
3/4 cup sugar
1/2 cup vegetable oil
1 egg, beaten
1¾ cups flour
1 teaspoon salt
1 teaspoon baking soda
1 teaspoon cloves
1 teaspoon cinnamon
1/2 cup chopped nuts (optional)
Lemon Glaze (see directions)

In a medium bowl, combine raisins, boiling water, sugar and oil. Mix well and cool to lukewarm. Stir in remaining ingredients, blending well. Pour into a greased 13x9-inch pan. Bake at 350° for about 20 minutes, or until surface springs back when touched lightly with fingertips. Frost with Lemon Glaze while still warm. Cut into bars. Makes about 3 dozen bars.
  Lemon Glaze: Beat together 1¾ cups powdered sugar, 1/4 cup melted butter or margarine, 1/4 teaspoon lemon extract and enough milk to reach desired consistency.

Contributors	Recipes

Albert King

Old Fashioned Fudge

*Residency: College Park,
  Maryland*
Age: 19
Height: 6'6"
Weight: 197
School: University of Maryland
Training hours per week: 20

2 cups sugar
3/4 cup milk
1 1-ounce square unsweetened
  chocolate, shaved
1/4 cup peanut butter
1 teaspoon vanilla
1/4 cup chopped nuts (optional)

Butter a 13x9-inch baking pan. In a medium pan, combine sugar and milk. Heat and add chocolate. Cook to soft-ball stage. Remove from heat and immediately blend in peanut butter, vanilla and nuts. Pour into buttered pan. Refrigerate until firm. Makes about eight dozen small pieces.

Nancy Lieberman

Southern Fruit Pie

Residency: Norfolk, Virginia
Age: 20
Height: 5'10"
Weight: 150
*School: Old Dominion
  University*

2 eggs
1 cup sugar
1/2 cup melted butter
1 teaspoon vinegar
1/2 cup raisins
1 teaspoon vanilla
1/2 cup pecans, whole or
  broken
1/2 cup flaked coconut
1 9-inch unbaked pie shell

In a large bowl, beat eggs until foamy. Beat in sugar, butter and vinegar. Stir in remaining ingredients until well blended. Pour into pie shell. Bake at 300° for 50 minutes. Cool completely before cutting. Serves eight.

Clifford Trent Robinson

Chicken Surprise

*Residency: Los Angeles,
  California*
Age: 18
Height: 6'10"
Weight: 220
School: USC
Training hours per week: 15

2 2½ to 3-pound broiler-fryer
  chickens, cut up
1 10-ounce jar apricot
  preserves
1 1⅞-ounce packet dry onion
  soup mix
1 16-ounce bottle red Russian
  salad dressing

Arrange chicken skin-side-up in a large baking pan or pans. Combine remaining ingredients. Pour over chicken. Bake at 350° for 1½ hours. Serves six to eight.

Darnell Valentine

Oatmeal Chocolate Chip Cookies

Residency: Lawrence, Kansas
Age: 20
Height: 6'2"
Weight: 180
School: Kansas University
Training hours per week: 21

1 cup vegetable shortening
1 cup white sugar
1 cup brown sugar
2 eggs
1½ cups flour
1 teaspoon salt
1 teaspoon baking soda
2 teaspoons vanilla
3 cups quick or old-fashioned
  rolled oats
1 cup chocolate chips, or nuts,
  coconut, raisins

Cream shortening with sugars. Beat in eggs. Stir in remaining ingredients until well blended. Drop from a teaspoon onto a lightly greased cookie sheet. Bake at 350° for 10 minutes. Makes four to five dozen.

Ernest "Kiki" Vandeweghe

Residency: Los Angeles, California
Age: 20
Height: 6'8"
Weight: 225
School: UCLA
Training hours per week: 20

Pineapple Coffee Bread

2 cups sugar
1 cup vegetable shortening
1 15-ounce can crushed pineapple, drained
3 bananas, sliced
4 eggs
2½ cups cake flour
1 teaspoon salt
2 teaspoons baking soda

In a large bowl, cream sugar and shortening. Beat in drained pineapple and bananas. Beat in eggs, one at a time. Combine remaining dry ingredients and blend into batter. Turn into a greased and floured 10-inch bundt or tube pan. Bake at 350° for 45 to 50 minutes. Cool in pan for 15 minutes before removing. Serves 12.

Elephant Ears

1 cup butter
2 cups flour
1/2 cup sour cream
1 egg yolk
Sugar

Cut butter into 1/2-inch cubes. In a medium bowl, using a pastry blender or two knives, cut butter into flour until mixture forms particles the size of peas. Combine sour cream with egg yolk. Stir into flour mixture with fork until well blended. Form dough into two balls. Wrap in plastic and chill four hours to four days. Lightly sprinkle board with sugar. Roll each pastry ball into an 8x16-inch rectangle. Sprinkle sugar over top; press gently with rolling pin. Fold narrow ends in towards the middle until they meet. Fold in half (like closing a book) to make an eight-layer log. Cover with plastic and chill 30 minutes. With sharp knife, cut logs into slices about 1/4-inch thick. Place slightly apart on brown paper-covered baking sheets. Chill for 10 minutes. Bake at 400° for eight to 10 minutes, turning once. Makes about two dozen.

Cream Cheese Foldovers

2 cups sifted flour
1/4 teaspoon salt
1 cup butter, softened
1 8-ounce package cream cheese, softened
Powdered sugar
Jelly or jam

Combine flour and salt. In a medium bowl, cream butter and cheese until light and fluffy. Blend in flour mixture. Wrap in plastic and chill for several hours, or until firm enough to roll. On a board sprinkled with powdered sugar, roll to 1/8-inch thick. Cut into squares. Spread with jelly or jam. Fold over into triangles and seal edges. Bake on ungreased cookie sheets at 375° for 15 minutes. Do not brown. Sprinkle with powdered sugar. Store in a tightly covered container in a cool, dry place. Makes about two dozen.

Recipes

Holly Warlick

Residency: Knoxville, Tennessee

Age: 20

Height: 5'7"

Weight: 128

School: University of Tennessee

Training hours per week: 24

Dumplings

2 cups flour

1 teaspoon salt

1 heaping teaspoon baking powder

1 teaspoon butter or margarine

Milk

Combine dry ingredients in a medium bowl. With fingers, rub in butter. Add enough sweet milk to make a soft dough that can be dropped from a spoon. Have a pot of tender chicken, well covered with broth, simmering. Drop dough into broth by the spoonful. Cover pot tightly and simmer for 15 minutes. Serve at once. Serves four to six.

4
Boxing

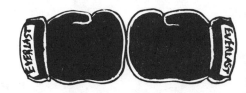

Event Days:

Sunday, July 20, 1980	Friday, July 25, 1980	Wednesday, July 30, 1980
Monday, July 21, 1980	Saturday, July 26, 1980	Thursday, July 31, 1980
Tuesday, July 22, 1980	Sunday, July 27, 1980	Saturday, August 2, 1980
Wednesday, July 23, 1980	Monday, July 28, 1980	
Thursday, July 24, 1980	Tuesday, July 29, 1980	

Contributors:

Israel Acosta
Johnny Bumphus
Jerome Coffee
Clinton Jackson
Alex Ramos

Boxing made its debut on the Olympic program in 1904 at St. Louis where the Games were a part of the Centennial of the Louisiana Territory Purchase from France.

In 1952 and 1976 the USA won five boxing titles, a record unsurpassed by any other nation. Since 1952, Eastern Europe and Cuba have been cutting into the medal awards formerly shared by the USA, South America and Western Europe.

Currently *numero uno* among the amateur boxers is Teofila Stevenson, Cuba, winner of the heavyweight title in both 1972 and 1976, after having the referee stop his contests with Duane Bobick, USA, at Munich and John Tate, USA, at Montreal in 1976.

At Montreal the following USA boxers were crowned Olympic Champions: Leo Randolph, flyweight; Howard Davis, lightweight; Sugar Ray Leonard, light welterweight; Michael Spinks, middleweight; and Leon Spinks, light heavyweight.

The following USA Olympic Champions, in order, have acceded to the professional world heavyweight title: Floyd Patterson, 1952 middleweight champion; Cassius Clay, 1960 light heavyweight champion; Joe Frazier, 1964 heavyweight champion; George Foreman, 1968 heavyweight champion; and Leon Spinks, 1976 light heavyweight champion.

The greatest of all Olympic boxers is Laszlo Papp, Hungary, a southpaw, who won the middleweight title in 1948 and the light middleweight title in 1952 and 1956.

Contributors	Recipes

Israel Acosta

Residency: Milwaukee, Wisconsin

Age: 23

Height: 5'3"

Weight: 106

School: South Division High School

Training hours per week: 20

Cheese Ball

1 pound pasteurized process cheese food

1 8-ounce package cream cheese, softened

1 4-ounce package dried beef, chopped

1/8 teaspoon garlic powder (optional)

Dash of chili powder

Dash of salt

1 cup finely chopped nuts

With hands, blend cheese, beef, garlic powder, chili powder and salt until thoroughly combined. Shape into a ball or log. Roll in nuts. Wrap in plastic and refrigerate until firm. Makes one cheese ball, about six inches in diameter.

Braided Orange Bread

5 cups flour

2 packets dry yeast

1/2 teaspoon ground cardamon

1 cup milk

1/2 cup sugar

1/2 cup butter or margarine

1 teaspoon salt

1/3 cup fresh orange juice

2 tablespoons grated orange rind

2 eggs

1 tablespoon milk

1 egg yolk

In a large bowl, combine 2 cups flour with yeast and cardamon. In a saucepan, heat milk, sugar, butter and salt until butter melts. Add to dry mixture along with orange juice and rind. Beat for one minute at low speed, adding eggs one at a time. Beat for three minutes at high speed, scraping sides of bowl. Add enough remaining flour by hand to form a soft dough. Turn out onto a floured surface and knead until smooth and elastic, working in as much additional flour as necessary. Place in a greased bowl, cover and let rise in a warm place until doubled, about one hour. Punch down and divide dough in half. Let rest for 10 minutes. Divide each half into thirds, shaping into 16-inch ropes. On greased baking sheets, braid ropes together, pinching ends and tucking under, to form two loaves. Cover and let rise until double, about 30 minutes. In a small bowl with a fork, beat egg yolk with milk. Brush over braids. Bake at 350° for 25 to 30 minutes or until golden brown. If loaves brown too quickly, cover loosely with foil during last 10 to 15 minutes. Makes two large loaves.

Johnny Bumphus

Residency: Nashville, Tennessee

Age: 18

Height: 5'11"

Weight: 139

School: Pearl High School Graduate

Training hours per week: 10

Peanut Butter Cookies

1/2 cup butter or margarine

1/2 cup peanut butter

1/2 cup sugar

1/2 cup brown sugar

1 egg

1/2 teaspoon vanilla

1 1/4 cups flour

3/4 teaspoon baking soda

1/4 teaspoon salt

Blanched, salted Virginia peanuts (optional)

In a medium bowl, cream butter, peanut butter, sugar and brown sugar. Beat in egg and vanilla. Combine remaining dry ingredients and blend into creamed mixture. With hands, roll into one-inch balls and roll in additional granulated sugar. Place two inches apart on a greased cookie sheet. Press five peanut halves into the top of each cookie to form a flower shape. Or, flatten with a fork, making a criss-cross pattern. Bake at 375° for 10 to 12 minutes. Makes about four dozen.

Contributors	Recipes

Johnny Bumphus

Taco Salad

1 pound ground beef

1 1⅞-ounce packet dry onion soup mix

3/4 cup water

1 medium head lettuce, torn into small pieces

2 large tomatoes, cut in wedges

1 small onion, thinly sliced and separated into rings

1/4 cup chopped green pepper

1/2 cup sliced ripe olives

2 cups (8 ounces) shredded sharp Cheddar cheese

1 7½-ounce bag corn chips

In a large skillet, brown beef. Sprinkle with soup mix and stir in water. Simmer, uncovered, for 10 minutes. Meanwhile, combine all remaining ingredients except corn chips in a large salad bowl and toss well. Arrange lettuce mixture on individual salad plates. Top with meat mixture and corn chips. Serves four to six.

Oven Pot Roast

1 3 to 4-pound beef chuck or arm roast

1 1⅞-ounce packet dry onion soup mix

1 10¾-ounce can cream of mushroom soup

Place roast on a large piece of heavy-duty aluminum foil. Sprinkle all sides of meat with dry soup mix. Spoon mushroom soup over meat. Seal in foil. Place in a baking pan and bake at 350° for 2½ to 3 hours. Remove meat to heated platter. Skim fat from juices. Serve juices as is or thicken for gravy if desired. Serves six to eight.

Jerome Coffee

Residency: Nashville, Tennessee

Age: 20

Height: 5'7"

Weight: 112

School: Pearl High School

Training hours per week: 10

Homemade Vegetable Soup

1 soup bone

1 pound beef stew meat, cut in small pieces

2 16-ounce cans whole tomatoes

2 16-ounce cans mixed vegetables

3 large potatoes, peeled and diced

1/2 head cabbage, chopped

1 cup chopped celery

1 cup chopped carrots

2 tablespoons sugar

Salt and pepper

Water

In a large kettle, combine all ingredients. Add water to cover. Bring to a boil and simmer, covered, for three to four hours. Remove soup bone, pick off any meat, and return meat to soup. Serves six to eight.

Contributors	Recipes

Jerome Coffee

Homemade Chili

1 large onion, chopped

1 green pepper, chopped

1 pound ground beef

1/2 cup butter or margarine

3 10¾-ounce cans tomato soup

2 cups water

1/2 cup chili powder

2 tablespoons sugar

2 16-ounce cans kidney beans

Salt and pepper

4 ounce uncooked spaghetti

In a large pot, brown onion, pepper and beef in butter. Add soup, water, chili powder, sugar, beans, salt and pepper. Bring to a boil and simmer for 30 minutes. Cook spaghetti according to package directions, drain and add to chili. Serves six.

Clinton Jackson

Residency: Nashville, Tennessee

Age: 24

Height: 5'11½"

Weight: 160

Training hours per week: 14

Meat Loaf With Cheesey Tomato Sauce

2 pounds ground beef

1 medium onion, chopped

1 egg

1 cup flavored stuffing mix

1/2 cup water

1 tsp. salt

1/2 teaspoon pepper

1 8-ounce can tomato sauce

1 10¾-ounce can condensed Cheddar cheese soup

In a large bowl, combine all ingredients except tomato sauce and soup. Mix well with hands and form into a loaf. Place in a crock pot. Mix sauce and soup until smooth. Pour over meat loaf. Cover. Turn heat control to low and cook for eight to 10 hours. Serves six to eight.

Alex Ramos

Residency: Bronx, New York

Age: 18

Height: 5'10"

Weight: 165

School: Herbert H. Lehman High School, Bronx, New York

Training hours per week: 20

Garden Chicken

2 pounds broiler-fryer chicken breasts

2 tablespoons olive oil

2 teaspoons honey

4 tablespoons soy sauce

1 cup water

1/2 head medium cabbage, shredded

4 large carrots, sliced

1 yellow plantain, sliced

4 stalks celery, sliced

1 green pepper, cut in strips

Skin and bone chicken breasts. Cut into 1-inch chunks. In a large electric frying pan set at 350° or a large heavy skillet over medium heat, stir-fry chicken in olive oil until it is white and firm. Lower heat. Stir in honey and soy sauce. Add water. Add vegetables. Bring to a boil, reduce heat and simmer for 30 to 40 minutes until chicken is tender and vegetables are tender-crisp. Serves four.

5
Canoe and Kayak

Event Days:

Wednesday,
July 30, 1980

Thursday,
July 31, 1980

Friday,
August 1, 1980

Saturday,
August 2, 1980

Contributors:

Bruce Barton
Greg Barton
Kurt Doberstein
Linda Murray Dragan
Ann Turner

Canoeing and kayaking for men made their debut at Berlin in 1926 and kayaking for women in 1948. Eastern Europe has taken over domination of the men's and women's events in recent years.

Currently the men's program consists of canoeing singles and doubles for men over the 500 and 1,000 meters courses. The men also have kayak races in singles and doubles for 500 and 1,000 meters and kayak fours over 1,000 meters. The women singles and doubles kayakists race over the 500-meter course.

In the 1936 Olympic Games, Ernest Riedel placed third in the then 10,000 singles kayak race. Then in the first of the post-World War II Games, Stephen Lysak and Stephan Macknowski were gold medalists in the 10,000 meters Canadian canoe doubles

competition, and silver medalists in the 1,000 meters Canadian doubles.

The USA women enjoyed their greatest success in 1964 at Tokyo. Francine Fox and Glorianne Perrier placed second in the kayak doubles and Marcia Jones was the bronze medalist in the kayak singles competition. Marcia Jones, later Marcia Jones Smoke, also was a member of the 1968 and 1972 teams. [After the birth of a daughter and son, Marcia participated in the inaugural USOC-sponsored National Sports Festival in 1978 at Colorado Springs.]

Bruce Barton

Residency: Homer, Michigan
Age: 21
Height: 5'11"
Weight: 160
*School: Michigan State
   University*
Training hours per week: 15

Sweet and Sour Pork

1½ pounds lean pork, cut into
   1-inch cubes

2 tablespoons lard

1 cup water

1 chicken bouillon cube or 1
   teaspoon instant bouillon

1/4 teaspoon salt

1 green pepper, cut into strips

1/4 cup sliced onion (optional)

1 20-ounce can pineapple
   chunks, drained

1 11-ounce jar sweet and sour
   sauce

Hot cooked rice

In a heavy skillet or Dutch oven, brown pork in lard.
Add water, bouillon and salt. Cover and simmer until
tender, about one hour. Drain. Add green pepper and
onion to pork and cook, stirring frequently, until
tender-crisp. Add drained pineapple and sweet and
sour sauce. Heat through. Serve over hot cooked rice.
Serves four.

Pumpkin Bars

4 eggs

1 cup vegetable oil

1⅔ cups sugar

1 16-ounce can pumpkin

2 cups flour

2 teaspoons cinnamon

1 teaspoon baking soda

2 teaspoons baking powder

1 teaspoon salt

Cream Cheese Icing (see
   directions)

In medium mixing bowl, beat together eggs, oil,
sugar and pumpkin until light and fluffy. Combine
remaining dry ingredients. Add to pumpkin mixture
and stir well. Spread batter in ungreased
15x10x1-inch baking pan or jelly roll pan. Bake at
350° for 25 to 30 minutes. Cool. Frost with Cream
Cheese Icing. Cut into bars. Makes about 3 1/2
dozen bars.
   Cream Cheese Icing: Cream together 1 3-ounce
package softened cream cheese and 1/2 cup
softened butter or margarine. Stir in 1 teaspoon
vanilla. Gradually add 2 cups powdered sugar,
beating well, until mixture is smooth. Makes enough
to frost one 15x10-inch cake or pan of bars.

Greg Barton

Residency: Homer, Michigan
Age: 19
Height: 5'9"
Weight: 160
School: University of Michigan
Training hours per week: 15

Glazed Strawberry Pie

1 9-inch baked pie shell

1 cup sugar

Dash of salt

2 tablespoons cornstarch

1 tablespoon lemon juice

1 cup water

Red food coloring

1 envelope unflavored gelatin

1 quart fresh strawberries

In a medium saucepan, combine sugar, salt and
cornstarch. Stir in lemon juice. Stir in water slowly.
Cook over medium heat, stirring constantly, until
thick. Add coloring for desired shape of red. Soften
gelatin in 2 to 3 tablespoons water. Stir into glaze
until dissolved. Cool to room temperature. Fill baked
pie shell with sliced or halved strawberries. Pour
glaze over berries. Chill. If desired, garnish with
sweetened whipped cream. Serves six to eight.

Baked Pork Chops

6 pork chops

1/4 cup milk

1 teaspoon seasoned salt

Place pork chops in a 13x9-inch baking pan. Pour
milk over chops and sprinkle with salt. Bake at 375°
for 45 minutes.

Contributors	Recipes

Kurt Doberstein

Residency: Lombard, Illinois
Age: 23
Height: 6'2"
Weight: 180
School: College of Du Page
Training hours per week: 35

Toasted Aromatic Pecans

4 cups pecan halves, about 1¼ pounds

1/4 cup butter

1 teaspoon or more Angostura bitters

Seasoned salt

Arrange pecans in a 13x9-inch pan. Toast in oven at 300° for 20 minutes. In a small saucepan, melt butter and stir in bitters and 1 teaspoon seasoned salt. Pour over pecans and toast for 15 more minutes, stirring occasionally. If desired, sprinkle with more seasoned salt. Spread on paper towels to dry and cool. Store in a covered container in a cool, dry place, or freeze. Makes one quart.

Canadian Cheese Soup

2 quarts chicken broth

1/2 cup diced celery

1/2 cup diced carrots

1/2 cup diced onion

1/3 pound bacon

1 pound American or Cheddar cheese, shredded

Dash of Tabasco sauce

1 tablespoon lemon juice

1 tablespoon minced parsley

1 teaspoon baking soda

1 quart milk

In a large saucepan, combine broth, celery, carrots and onion. Boil for 30 minutes, or until vegetables are very soft. Meanwhile, dice bacon and fry until crisp. Stir in cheese, Tabasco, lemon juice, parsley and bacon. Stir in baking soda. Add milk and heat through, stirring constantly until cheese melts and soup is smooth. Adjust seasoning to taste with salt and pepper. Serves eight.

Spinach Salad

1/2 pound raw spinach

2 oranges

1 medium red or sweet onion, sliced

Vinegar

1 medium avocado (optional)

Wash spinach and remove stems. Tear into bite-size pieces. Peel and section oranges over spinach so juice won't be wasted. Peel and dice avocado. Combine all ingredients with vinegar to taste. Toss well. Serves six.

Linda Murray Dragan

Residency: Washington, D.C.
Age: 26
Height: 5'6"
Weight: 140
School: University of Maryland Graduate School
Training hours per week: 18

Grandma's Jello

1 6-ounce package lemon jello

1 cup sliced bananas

1 cup pineapple chunks, drained

1/2 cup chopped walnuts

Prepare jello according to package directions and let stand in refrigerator for 15 minutes. Stir in remaining ingredients. Chill for two hours or until set. Serve with whipped cream, if desired. Serves six.

Contributors	Recipes

Linda Murray Dragan

Chocolate Nut Waffles With Ice Cream Topping

2 cups flour

4 teaspoons baking powder

1/2 cup sugar

1 teaspoon salt

2 eggs, separated

1½ cups milk

1/2 cup vegetable shortening

2 1-ounce squares unsweetened chocolate or 3 tablespoons cocoa

1/2 cup chopped nuts

1 teaspoon vanilla

Vanilla ice cream

Maple syrup

Combine flour, baking powder, sugar and salt in a large bowl. Beat egg yolks with milk and stir into flour mixture. In a small pan, melt shortening and chocolate together. Cool and stir into batter, along with nuts and vanilla. In a medium bowl, with clean beaters, beat egg whites until stiff. Fold into batter. If batter seems too stiff, stir in a little milk. Bake on waffle iron. Serve with two scoops vanilla ice cream and drizzle with maple syrup. Serves four.

Ann Turner

Residency: Wasco, Illinois
Age: 22
Height: 175 cm (5'9")
Weight: 64 kg
School: University of Montana
Training hours per week: 18

Grape Krem

2 cups grape juice

3 tablespoons sugar

2 tablespoons cornstarch

3 tablespoons water

1 teaspoon lemon juice

Whipped cream (optional)

In a medium pan, heat juice to boiling. Add sugar. Make a smooth paste of cornstarch and water. Slowly stir into boiling juice. Lower heat and simmer, stirring constantly, until thick and clear. Cool in covered container to prevent skin from forming. When chilled and ready to serve, pudding will be thick but not solid. Serve garnished with whipped cream, if desired. Serves four.

Heavenly Cake Brownies

2 cups sugar

2 cups flour

1 cup water

1 cup margarine

1/4 cup cocoa

2 eggs, beaten

1 teaspoon soda

1/2 cup buttermilk

Chocolate Nut Frosting (see directions)

In a large bowl, combine flour and sugar. In a medium saucepan, combine water, margarine and cocoa. Bring to a boil, stirring constantly, until well blended. Pour hot cocoa mixture over flour. Beat smooth. Beat in eggs. Dissolve soda in buttermilk and stir into batter. Batter will be thin. Pour into a greased 15x10-inch pan. Bake at 400° for 20 minutes. Frost while still warm with Chocolate Nut Frosting. Cut into bars. Makes about four dozen bars.
Chocolate Nut Frosting: In a medium pan, combine 1/2 cup margarine, 1/4 cup cocoa and 5 tablespoons milk. Bring to a boil, stirring constantly. Add enough sifted powdered sugar for spreading consistency. Stir in 1 cup chopped pecans. Spread on warm brownies. Makes enough to frost one 15x10-inch cake or pan of bars.

6

Cycling—

Road-
Track

Event Days:

Sunday,
July 20, 1980

Saturday,
July 26, 1980

Tuesday,
July 22, 1980

Monday,
July 28, 1980

Wednesday,
July 23, 1980

Thursday,
July 24, 1980

Friday,
July 25, 1980

Contributors:

Jeff Bradley
Gregory J. Demgen
Bruce M. Donaghy
Mark Brian Gorski
David M. Grylls
George Lewis Mount
Thomas A. Prehn
Wayne Stetina

Cycling is one of six sports on the program for the Games of the 1st Olympiad (Athens, 1896), which has been on the program at every Olympic Games. The others are athletics, rowing, fencing, gymnastics, and swimming.

The USA has never had a gold medalist in the events (for men only) on the current Olympic program: 1,000-meter match sprints, 1,000-meter time trial, 4,000-meter team pursuit, and 4,000-meter time trial pursuit among the track events ridden in a velodrome. The "road" events are an individual road race and a team road race, both of which attract up to a million spectators when held in foreign countries.

Each nation is permitted to enter a maximum of 15 cyclists, all of whom may act as substitutes in any race for which they have been specifically entered.

Among the 1976 Olympic champions were:
Anton Tkac, Czechoslovakia, in the match sprints.
Klaus-Jurgen Grunke, German Democratic Republic, 1000-meter time trial.
Gregor Braun, German Federal Republic, 4000-meter individual pursuit.
The German Federal Republic team in the 4,000-meter team pursuit.
Bernt Johanson, Sweden, individual road race. George Mount, USA, was sixth.
The USSR won the team road race over a 100-kilometer route as the USA foursome placed 19th out of 27 finishers, ten minutes behind the winning Soviet riders.

Jeff Bradley

Residency: Davenport, Iowa
Age: 17
Height: 6'
Weight: 160
School: Davenport West High School
Training hours per week: 18

Wheat Germ Bread

1 packet dry yeast
2 tablespoons warm water
2 tablespoons sugar
1 tablespoon vegetable oil
2 teaspoons salt
2 cups warm water
1 cup wheat germ
5 cups unbleached white flour

Soften yeast in warm water. In large bowl, combine yeast with sugar, oil, salt and warm water. Beat in wheat germ and one cup flour until smooth. Gradually mix in enough remaining flour to form a stiff dough. Turn out onto floured surface and knead until smooth and elastic, working in more flour if necessary. Place in a greased bowl, cover and let rise until doubled. Punch down, let rise again. Punch down, shape into two loaves and place in two medium greased bread pans. Cover and let rise until doubled. Bake at 400° for 40 to 45 minutes. Brush tops with butter or margarine while still warm. Makes two medium loaves.

Quick Homemade Pizza

Crust:
2 cups flour
3 teaspoons baking powder
1 teaspoon salt
1/4 cup vegetable shortening
3/4 cup milk
Filling:
1 8-ounce can tomato sauce
1/4 teaspoon onion powder
1/2 teaspoon Italian seasoning
1/2 pound ground beef
1/2 pound grated Mozzarella cheese
Grated Parmesan cheese

Combine dry ingredients in a medium bowl. Cut in shortening with a pastry blender or two knives. Stir in milk with a fork. With hands, pat dough out to cover a greased 17x11x1-inch jelly roll pan or cookie sheet. Spread with tomato sauce. Sprinkle with onion powder and Italian seasoning. Brown ground beef in a small skillet until crumbly. Sprinkle beef over pizza. Top with Mozzarella and a generous amount of Parmesan cheese. Bake at 425° for 10 minutes or until crust is lightly browned. Cut into squares and serve hot. Serves four.

Gregory J. Demgen

Residency: LaCrosse, Wisconsin
Age: 18
Height: 5'10"
Weight: 155
School: Graduate Central H.S., LaCrosse Wisconsin
Training hours per week: 30

Cracked Wheat Bread

4 cups cracked wheat
4 cups boiling water
2 tablespoons salt
2/3 cup brown sugar
1/4 cup butter or margarine
1/2 cup bran
1/2 cup wheat germ
3 packets dry yeast
1/2 cup warm water
9 to 10 cups white flour

In a large bowl, combine cracked wheat, boiling water, salt, brown sugar, butter, bran and wheat germ. Mix well and cool to lukewarm. Dissolve yeast in warm water. Stir into cracked wheat mixture. Stir in white flour to form a stiff dough. Turn out onto a floured surface and knead until smooth and elastic, adding flour as necessary. Place in a greased bowl, cover and let rise in a warm, draft-free place until doubled in bulk, about 50 minutes. Punch down and divide into four pieces. Shape into loaves and place in four large greased loaf pans. Let rise. Bake at 375° for 30 minutes. Makes four large loaves.

Contributors	Recipes

Gregory J. Demgen

Wild Rice Pilaf

1/2 cup butter or margarine

1/2 cup chopped onion

1 cup wild rice

1 10¾-ounce can chicken broth

1 cup water

Salt and pepper

In a large skillet, saute onions in 1/4 cup butter for two to three minutes. Add rice and saute, stirring constantly, for one minute. Add broth, water, salt and pepper to taste. Bring to boil, reduce heat, cover and simmer for 45 to 60 minutes or until rice is done. Stir in remaining 1/4 cup butter before serving. Serves six.

Pro Burgers

1 pound lean ground beef

1/2 cup wheat germ

1 2½- to 3-ounce can chopped mushrooms, drained

1/2 cup grated sharp Cheddar cheese

1/2 cup tomato juice

1 teaspoon salt

1/8 teaspoon pepper

6 hamburger buns

In a medium bowl, combine all ingredients, except buns. Mix well. Shape into six patties. Broil three to four inches from heat, turning once, until done as desired. Serve on buns. Makes six burgers.

Bruce M. Donaghy

Residency: Emmaus, Pennsylvania

Age: 19

Height: 5'11"

Weight: 173

School: Lehigh County Community College

Training hours per week: 23

Cranberry Gelatin Mold

1 3-ounce package raspberry jello

1 cup diced, peeled orange sections or canned Mandarin oranges

1/4 cup chopped walnuts

1/2 cup drained pineapple tidbits

1 16-ounce can whole cranberry sauce

Prepare jello according to package directions. Chill until slightly thickened. Fold in remaining ingredients. Pour into a one-quart mold. Chill until set. Unmold to serve. Serves six.

Pumpkin Bread

3 cups brown sugar

3½ cups whole wheat flour

1½ teaspoons salt

1½ teaspoons nutmeg

1½ teaspoons cinnamon

2 teaspoons baking soda

1 cup vegetable oil

2/3 cup water

4 eggs

1 16-ounce can pumpkin or 2 cups cooked, mashed pumpkin

1 cup chopped nuts

Combine dry ingredients in a large mixing bowl. Make a well in the center and add oil, water, eggs and pumpkin. Beat until smooth. Stir in nuts. Pour into three medium greased loaf pans. Bake at 350° for one hour. Cool in pans for 10 minutes before removing. Makes three medium loaves.

Mark Brian Gorski

Residency: Itasca, Illinois
Age: 19
Height: 6'2"
Weight: 175
School: University of Michigan, Ann Arbor
Training hours per week: 35

Dutch Rye Bread

2 cakes compressed yeast
3 cups lukewarm milk
2 tablespoons butter or margarine
2 tablespoons honey
1½ cups whole wheat flour
1 cup wheat germ
4 cups rye flour

In a large bowl, dissolve yeast in one cup milk. Scald remaining milk with butter and honey. Cool to lukewarm. Add to yeast mixture. Stir in remaining ingredients. Turn out onto a floured surface and knead until smooth and elastic, adding more whole wheat or rye flour as necessary. Place in a greased bowl, cover and let rise in a warm place until doubled. Punch down, shape into two loaves and place in two medium greased loaf pans. Let rise again. Bake at 400° for 20 minutes. Reduce heat to 350° and bake for 30 to 40 minutes more. Makes two medium loaves.

David M. Grylls

Residency: Grosse Pointe, Michigan
Age: 21
Height: 6'1/2"
Weight: 175
School: Michigan State University
Training hours per week: 40

Greg's Hot Fudge Sauce

4 1-ounce squares unsweetened chocolate
1/2 cup margarine
3 cups sifted powdered sugar
1 8-ounce can evaporated milk
1¼ teaspoon vanilla

In a medium saucepan, melt chocolate and margarine, stirring constantly. Remove from heat. Add sugar and milk, alternately, blending well after each addition. Return to heat and boil eight minutes, stirring constantly. Stir in vanilla. Store in refrigerator. Serve heated over ice cream. Makes about three cups sauce.

Quiche Taste Treat

1 9-inch unbaked pie shell
8 slices bacon, cooked and crumbled, or hot sausage, ham, mushrooms, onions, etc.
1/2 pound grated cheese (Swiss, Gruyere, sharp Cheddar, etc., or a mixture)
1 tablespoon flour
3 eggs
1 cup milk
1/2 teaspoon salt
1/2 teaspoon pepper

Prick pie shell all over. Bake at 425° for seven minutes. Remove shell. Reduce oven to 325°. Place bacon or whatever in bottom of pie shell. Toss grated cheese with flour; place in pie shell. Beat remaining ingredients together and pour over cheese. Bake at 325° for 45 minutes or until set and lightly browned on top. Let cool for 10 minutes before cutting into wedges. Serves four to six.

Polly's Cream

2 packets unflavored gelatin
1/2 cup sugar
1 cup cream
1 cup milk
1 cup cream, whipped
1 teaspoon vanilla

Mix gelatin with sugar. In a medium saucepan, mix sugar with cream and milk, heating just enough to dissolve sugar and gelatin. Chill until mixture begins to solidify. Fold in whipped cream. Flavor with vanilla. Chill until set. Spoon into dessert dishes. Delicious served with fresh raspberries or strawberries. Half and half may be substituted for the milk-cream mixture. Serves six.

George Lewis Mount

Residency: Berkeley, California

Age: 23

Height: 5'10"

Weight: 140

School: Acalanes High School, Lafayette, California

Training hours per week: 28

Philadelphia Cheese Cake

1 10-ounce box butter cookies, crushed finely

2 tablespoons sugar

3 tablespoons melted butter

3 eggs, beaten

1 cup sugar

2 8-ounce packages cream cheese

1/4 teaspoon salt

2 teaspoons vanilla extract

3 cups sour cream

Mix crumbs with sugar and melted butter. Reserve one tablespoon for topping. Press remainder into bottom and sides of an 8-inch springform pan. In a large bowl, beat together eggs, sugar, cheese, salt and vanilla until smooth. Blend in sour cream. Pour into crust. Sprinkle with reserved crumb mixture. Bake at 375° for one hour or until set. Cool. Chill at least four hours before serving. Serves 12.

George's Peanut Butter Cookies

1/2 cup pure peanut butter

1/2 cup brown sugar

1/2 cup honey

1/2 cup butter

1 teaspoon vanilla extract

1 egg

1½ cups whole wheat pastry flour

2 teaspoons baking powder

1/2 teaspoon salt

Dashes of cinnamon, ginger and nutmeg

Cream peanut butter, brown sugar, honey and butter. Beat in egg and vanilla. Combine remaining dry ingredients and mix into creamed mixture until well blended. Roll into one-inch balls. Place on an ungreased cookie sheet. Flatten with a fork dipped in flour or sugar, making a criss-cross pattern. Bake at 350° for 12 minutes or until lightly browned. Makes about three dozen.

Vegetarian Tostados

12 corn tortillas

Peanut oil

3 16-ounce cans beans in chili sauce, mashed

1 pound shredded Cheddar or Monterey Jack cheese

1 head romaine, finely chopped

1 to 4 avocados, peeled, seeded and diced

4 to 8 ounces alfalfa sprouts

2 to 3 tomatoes, chopped

2 cups sour cream

2 cups plain yogurt

2 cups hot sauce

Optional additional ingredients: pitted black olives, diced green pepper, diced onions, shredded carrots

Fry tortillas in oil until crisp. Have remaining ingredients ready, arranged on a buffet or table in bowls or plates. Combine yogurt with sour cream and place on table. Mound ingredients in order of preference on a hot tortilla. Top with sour cream mixture and hot sauce. Serves six.

Contributors	Recipes

Thomas A. Prehn

Residency: Annapolis, Maryland

Age: 21

Height: 5'8½"

Weight: 140

School: W. T. Woodson High School, Fairfax, Virginia

Training hours per week: 33

Spinach Lasagna

1 pound lasagna noodles, cooked and drained

1 medium onion, chopped

1 clove garlic, minced

1½ tablespoons olive oil

2 cups cooked, chopped spinach

2 pounds Ricotta cheese

1/4 pound grated Parmesan cheese

3 eggs, beaten

Salt, pepper and chopped parsley to taste

6 cups of your own homemade tomato sauce or 3 15-ounce cans purchased tomato sauce

1/2 pound shredded Mozzarella cheese

In a large skillet, saute onion and garlic in olive oil until tender. Remove from heat. Stir in spinach, Ricotta, Parmesan, eggs, salt, pepper and parsley. Place a layer of noodles in the bottom of a buttered 13x9-inch pan. Cover with a layer of spinach mixture. Sprinkle with Mozzarella. Smooth over with tomato sauce. Repeat layers, ending with tomato sauce and Mozzarella. Bake at 350° for 45 minutes. Cool for 15 minutes before cutting into squares. Serves six to eight.

Fruit Smoothie

1 peeled banana, frozen

1 cup plain yogurt

1 cup apple juice

Honey to taste

Pecans to taste (optional)

Combine all ingredients in electric blender and blend until thick and smooth. If not cold or thick enough, add a few ice cubes. Good with any fruit. Serves one.

Honey Popcorn Crunch

1/2 cup melted butter

1/2 cup honey

3 quarts freshly popped corn

Combine butter with honey and heat to boiling in a medium saucepan. Pour over popcorn in a large roasting pan. Stir well to coat. Bake at 350° for 10 to 15 minutes, stirring once or twice. Cool. Store in a tightly covered container in a cool, dry place. Makes three quarts.

Wayne Stetina

Residency: Indianapolis, Indiana

Age: 25

Height: 6'

Weight: 165

Training hours per week: 33

Banana Bread

2 cups whole wheat flour

2 teaspoons baking powder

1/2 teaspoon salt

1 teaspoon cinnamon

1 cup raisins (optional)

1/2 cup sunflower seeds or walnuts (optional)

1/2 cup melted butter

1/2 cup honey

2 eggs, beaten

1/2 cup plain yogurt

1½ cups mashed bananas

In a medium bowl, combine dry ingredients, including raisins and seeds. Combine remaining wet ingredients and thoroughly mix into dry ingredients. Turn into a large greased loaf pan. Bake at 350° for one hour. Cool in pan for 10 minutes before removing. Makes one large loaf.

7

Diving

Event Days:

Sunday, July 20, 1980	Saturday, July 26, 1980
Monday, July 21, 1980	Sunday, July 27, 1980
Tuesday, July 22, 1980	Monday, July 28, 1980
Wednesday, July 23, 1980	
Friday, July 25, 1980	

Contributors:

Philip G. Boggs   Kent Vosler
Melissa Briley   Barb Weinstein
Brian P. Bungum
Robert Cragg
Greg Alan Garlich
James Edward Kennedy
Gregory E. Louganis
Cynthia Ann Potter
Mark Virts

Platform diving for men first appeared on the program in 1900 at Paris, with men's springboard diving coming aboard in 1904 at St. Louis. Stockholm was the scene of the first women's platform or high board diving competition, with the 1920 Olympic Games at Antwerp the inaugural meet for women's springboard.

Diving is one of two sports on the program for the Olympic Games in which subjective scoring is used in determining the order of finish; the other one is gymnastics. Both sports have been plagued with disputes over the judges' scoring.

The USA is the premier nation in diving and has captured at least one title in each Olympic Games in the men's or women's competition since 1920.

In the men's springboard competition, won by Capt. Phil Boggs, USAF in 1976, the USA has now won 13 of the last 14 in platform diving (including back-to-back titles for Dr. Sammy Lee, 1948, 1952, and Robert Webster, 1960, 1964).

Marjorie Gestring, by winning the 1936 Springboard at Berlin at the age of 13 years and 4 months, became the nation's youngest-ever gold medalist. At Montreal, Jennifer Chandler, 17, won the women's springboard competition, the 11th for the USA in 14 Olympic Games since 1920.

Our greatest diver in history was Patricia McCormick Mead who in 1952 and 1956 won both the springboard and platform events, the most amazing "double-double" in Olympic history.

Contributors	Recipes

Philip G. Boggs

Residency: Ann Arbor, Michigan
Age: 29
Height: 5'5"
Weight: 129
School: University of Michigan Law School
Training hours per week: 20

Sour Cream Pound Cake

1 cup butter, softened
3 cups sugar
6 eggs, separated
1/2 teaspoon almond extract
3 cups flour
1/4 teaspoon soda
1 cup sour cream

In a large bowl, cream butter and sugar. Beat in egg yolks, one at a time. Stir in almond extract. Combine flour and soda and add to creamed mixture alternately with sour cream, mixing well after each addition. In a separate bowl with clean beaters, beat egg whites until stiff. Fold into batter. Turn into a greased and floured 10-inch tube pan. Bake at 300° for 1½ to 2 hours. Let stand in pan for 15 minutes before removing. Serves 12.

Melissa Briley

Residency: Miami, Florida
Age: 22
Height: 5'3"
Weight: 110
School: University of Miami
Training hours per week: 20

Chile Quiche

2 4-ounce cans whole green chile peppers
12 ounces Monterey Jack cheese, shredded
4 eggs
1 teaspoon Worcestershire sauce

Drain chilies, cut in half and remove seeds. Line a 9-inch pie pan with chilies. Place shredded cheese over chilies. Beat eggs with Worcestershire sauce. Pour over cheese. Bake at 275° for 45 minutes or until set. Serves four to six.

Brian P. Bungum

Residency: Bloomington, Minnesota
Age: 23
Height: 5'8½"
Weight: 148
School: Indiana University
Training hours per week: 18

The Basic Quiche, With Variations

1 unbaked 9-inch pie crust
3 eggs, beaten
1½ cups half and half
3/4 cup seasoned filling (see variations at right)
1/2 to 1 cup shredded Swiss cheese
Parmesan cheese
Paprika

Line unbaked pie shell with foil. Cover foil with dry beans or raw rice, to prevent crust from puffing. Bake at 375° for 15 minutes or until slightly brown. Remove beans and foil. Combine filling ingredients and pour into shell. Sprinkle with Parmesan cheese and paprika. Bake at 375° for 35 to 40 minutes or until puffed and set. Let set for 10 minutes before cutting. Serves four to six.

Spinach Filling: Thaw and drain 1 10-ounce package frozen chopped spinach. In a large skillet, saute 2 to 3 chopped green onions in 3 tablespoons butter. Stir in 1 teaspoon instant chicken bouillon until dissolved. Stir in spinach, nutmeg and pepper to taste. Combine with basic egg mixture.

Bacon: Fry 8 to 10 strips bacon until crisp. Crumble and place in bottom of crust. Add salt, pepper and nutmeg to taste to egg mixture.

Mushroom: Saute 1 pound sliced fresh mushrooms in 2 to 3 tablespoons butter. Season with 1 tablespoon lemon juice, 1 tablespoon dry white wine, salt, and dried parsley flakes. Cook until liquid evaporates. Combine with egg mixture.

Seafood: Saute 2 to 3 chopped green onions in 2 tablespoons butter. Stir in 1 tablespoon lemon juice and 3/4 cup cooked shrimp or crab. Add salt, pepper and 1 tablespoon tomato paste to egg mixture. Combine seafood mixture with eggs.

Contributors	Recipes

Brian P. Bungum

The Basic Souffle With Variations

3 tablespoons butter

3 tablespoons flour

1 cup milk

Salt and pepper to taste

3/4 cup seasoned filling (see directions)

1/2 cup grated Swiss cheese

5 egg whites

Parmesan cheese

Butter a 1½-quart souffle dish. Coat inside of dish with a mixture of fine dry bread crumbs and Parmesan cheese. In a medium pan, melt butter. Blend in flour and cook over low heat for one or two minutes. Gradually stir in milk and cook, stirring constantly, until thick. Combine sauce, seasoned filling and grated cheese. Beat egg whites until stiff. Gently fold sauce mixture into whites. Pour into souffle dish, sprinkle with Parmesan and bake at 375° for 30 minutes until puffy and brown. Serves four to six.

Spinach: Thaw and drain 3/4 cup frozen chopped spinach. Saute 2 to 3 chopped green onins in 2 tablespoons butter. Add spinach and 1 tablespoon instant chicken bouillon and cook, stirring, until liquid is absorbed. Stir into sauce mixture.

Ham and Cheese: Increase cheese to one cup and add 1/2 cup minced cooked ham to sauce mixture.

Seafood: Saute 2 to 3 chopped green onions in 2 tablespoons butter. Stir in 1 tablespoon lemon juice, 1 tablespoon white wine, 1/8 teaspoon dill and 3/4 cup minced cooked crab or shrimp. Stir into sauce mixture.

Monkey Bread

2 packets dry yeast

1/4 cup warm water

1 teaspoon salt

1 cup sugar

2 cups scalded milk

1 cup melted butter or margarine

4 eggs, beaten

6 cups flour

1 cup melted butter or margarine

In large bowl, dissolve yeast in warm water. Stir in salt, sugar and warm milk. Beat in melted butter and eggs. Beat in flour, three cups at a time, to form a stiff dough. Cover and let rise in a warm place until doubled. Punch down and divide into two parts. (Dough will be sticky.) Roll out each part on a floured surface to one-inch thickness. Cut into rounds with biscuit cutter. Dip rounds in melted butter and layer in two buttered 10-inch tube or bundt pans. Cover and let rise until doubled. Bake at 375° for 30 minutes or until golden brown. Makes two large loaves.

Robert Cragg

Residency: Ann Arbor, Michigan

Age: 25

Height: 6'1"

Weight: 180

School: University of Pennsylvania

Training hours per week: 20 (summer)

Goulash A La Sarah Jones

1½ pounds ground beef

1 large onion, chopped

1 16-ounce can stewed tomatoes

Salt and pepper to taste

8 ounces noodles, cooked

In a large skillet, brown meat with onion. Drain off excess fat. Stir in tomatoes, salt, pepper and noodles. Heat through and serve. Or, turn into a buttered casserole and bake at 350° for 20 minutes or until heated through. Serves six.

Contributors	Recipes

Robert Cragg

Sour Cream Coffee Cake

1/2 cup butter
1 cup sugar
2 eggs
2 cups flour
1 teaspoon baking soda
1/2 teaspoon salt
1 teaspoon baking powder
1 cup sour cream
1/4 cup sugar
2 teaspoons cinnamon
1/2 cup chopped nuts (optional)

In a large bowl, cream butter with sugar. Beat in eggs. Combine flour, soda, salt and baking powder. Add to creamed mixture alternately with sour cream, beating well after each addition. Combine sugar, cinnamon and nuts. Pour half of batter into a greased 9-inch tube pan. Sprinkle with half of nut mixture. Top with remaining batter. Sprinkle with remaining nut mixture. Bake at 350° for 40 minutes. Cool in pan for 15 minutes before removing. Serves 12.

Greg Alan Garlich

Residency: Kirkwood, Missouri
Age: 23
Height: 5'9"
Weight: 155
School: University of Miami Graduate Business School
Training hours per week: 28

Broiled Stuffed Mushroom Caps

12 jumbo fresh mushrooms
1 8-ounce can or package crab meat
2 tablespoons minced onion
2 tablespoons minced chives or green onion tops
1 tablespoon mayonnaise
1 teaspoon English mustard
1/4 cup cheese sauce or pasteurized process cheese spread
Dash of Worcestershire sauce
Dash of Tabasco sauce
Salt and pepper
Pinch of garlic powder
Fine dry bread crumbs
Melted butter
Bernaise sauce (see directions)

Remove stems from mushrooms by twisting and pulling gently. (Save stems for another use.) Drain and flake crab meat. Combine crab with onion, chives, mayonnaise, mustard, cheese sauce. Season with Worcestershire, Tabasco, salt, pepper and garlic to taste. Mix with enough bread crumbs to form a stiff paste. Brush mushroom caps inside and out with melted butter. Fill caps with crab mixture, using a small ice cream scoop or mounding mixture up. Brush or drizzle with melted butter. Bake at 375° for 10 minutes, or broil until lightly browned. Garnish with Bernaise sauce. Serves four to six.
  Bernaise sauce: In a bowl over hot water, heat 4 egg yolks with 1 tablespoon tarragon vinegar until they reach the consistency of custard. Gradually add 1 cup clarified butter in a thin stream, beating constantly. Season with 1/4 teaspoon tarragon, 1/8 teaspoon garlic powder, 1/4 teaspoon onion powder, salt and white pepper.

James Edward Kennedy

Residency: Knoxville, Tennessee
Age: 25
Height: 5'5½"
Weight: 138
School: University of Tennessee
Training hours per week: 11

Peanut Butter Omelet

3 eggs
2 tablespoons milk
salt
pepper
3 tablespoons peanut butter

Spray omelet pan with non-stick coating. Beat eggs with milk, salt and pepper. Pour into heated pan. Cook over medium heat until partially cooked. Add peanut butter to one side. Flip other side over and continue cooking until desired degree of doneness is reached. Serves one to two.

Contributors	Recipes

James Edward Kennedy

Pastitsio

1/2 cup chopped onion

3 tablespoons olive oil

2 pounds ground beef

2 tablespoons tomato puree

1 teaspoon cinnamon

1 teaspoon salt

1/2 teaspoon pepper

1 7-ounce package elbow macaroni, cooked and drained

1 egg, beaten

1/2 cup grated Parmesan cheese

White Sauce:

3 tablespoons butter

1/3 cup flour

2 cups milk

2 eggs, beaten

1/4 teaspoon salt

In a large skillet, brown onions and beef in oil. Add tomato puree, cinnamon, salt and pepper. Reduce heat and simmer uncovered, stirring occasionally, for 10 minutes. Combine macaroni, egg and Parmesan cheese. Spoon half of macaroni mixture into a lightly greased 13x9-inch baking pan. Cover with all of meat mixture. Top with remaining macaroni mixture. In a medium pan, melt butter. Blend in flour. Cook, stirring constantly, for two minutes. Gradually stir in milk and cook, stirring constantly, until thick. Beat eggs in small bowl with salt. Gradually stir 1/2 cup hot sauce into eggs. Stir egg mixture into remaining sauce. Pour over macaroni. Bake at 350° for 45 to 60 minutes or until edges are golden brown. Let set 10 minutes. Cut into squares. Serves eight or more.

Gregory E. Louganis

Residency: El Cajon, California
Age: 19
Height: 5'9"
Weight: 145
School: University of Miami
Training hours per week: 20

Moussaka

1 large eggplant, peeled and sliced 1/2-inch thick

3 tablespoons olive oil

1½ pounds ground beef or lamb

3/4 cup chopped onions

1 clove garlic, minced

1 12-ounce can whole tomatoes

1/2 teaspoon basil

1/4 teaspoon cinnamon

1 teaspoon salt

1/8 teaspoon pepper

1/4 cup butter

3 tablespoons flour

Salt and white pepper

2 cups hot milk

1 cup Ricotta cheese

Dash of nutmeg

1 egg, beaten

1 cup grated Parmesan cheese

In a large skillet, fry eggplant slices in hot oil until golden. Drain and set aside. In remaining oil, cook beef, stirring to break up, until all redness is gone. Add onions, garlic, tomatoes with juice, basil, cinnamon, salt and pepper. Simmer for 25 minutes. Meanwhile, prepare the white sauce: In a medium pan, melt butter. Stir in flour, salt and pepper. Lower heat and gradually add hot milk, cooking and stirring constantly until thick. Stir in the Ricotta cheese, nutmeg and egg until well blended. Line a greased 13x9-inch baking pan with eggplant. Top with meat sauce. Sprinkle with Parmesan cheese. Top with white sauce. Bake at 350° for one hour. Let set for 15 minutes before cutting into squares. Serves eight to 10.

Gregory E. Louganis

Artichoke Nibbles

2 6-ounce jars marinated
   artichoke hearts
1 small onion, minced
1 clove garlic, minced
4 eggs, beaten
1/4 cup fine dry bread crumbs
1/4 teaspoon salt
1/8 teaspoon pepper
1/8 teaspoon oregano
1/8 teaspoon Tabasco sauce
1/2 pound shredded sharp
   Cheddar cheese
2 tablespoons minced parsley

Drain marinade from one jar artichokes into medium skillet. Drain second jar, but save marinade for another purpose. Chop artichokes and set aside. Over medium heat, saute onion and garlic in marinade until soft. In a medium bowl, combine eggs, crumbs, salt, pepper, oregano and Tabasco. Mix well. Stir in cheese, parsley, artichokes and onion mixture. Turn into a greased 11x7-inch baking pan and bake at 325° for 30 minutes or until set. Cool slightly and cut into one-inch squares. Serve warm, at room temperature, or chilled. Serves about 25.

Spanakopeta (Spinach Pie)

3 pounds fresh spinach
2 bunches green onions,
   chopped
1/4 cup olive oil
1/2 cup minced parsley
1/2 teaspoon dill
1 pound Feta cheese, crumbled
8 eggs, beaten
Salt to taste
1/2 pound filo pastry sheets
1 cup melted butter
1/2 cup olive oil

Wash and stem spinach, drain well and chop. In a medium skillet, saute onions in olive oil until tender. In a large bowl, combine onions with spinach, parsley, dill, cheese and eggs and season with salt. Mix well. Line a 13x9-inch baking pan with half of the filo sheets, brushing each sheet with a mixture of melted butter and olive oil. Spread with spinach mixture. Top with remaining filo sheets, again brushing each with butter and oil mixture. Bake at 350° for 45 minutes. Let set for 15 minutes and cut into squares. Serve hot or cold, as an appetizer, side dish or main dish. As a main dish, it serves 10.

Cynthia Ann Potter

Residency: Dallas, Texas
Age: 28
Height: 5'1½"
Weight: 98
*School: Indiana University,
   Bloomington, Indiana—B.S.
   in secondary education*
Training hours per week: 25

Zucchini Quiche

1 unbaked 9-inch pie shell
1½ pounds zucchini
8 slices bacon, cooked crisp
   and crumbled
1/2 pound shredded Swiss
   cheese
4 eggs
1½ cups light cream
1/8 teaspoon nutmeg
Salt and pepper to taste

Slice zucchini 1/4-inch thick. Drop into a large pan of boiling water and boil three minutes. Drain well. Place bacon in bottom of pie crust. Sprinkle cheese over bacon. Layer half the zucchini over the cheese. Beat together eggs, cream, nutmeg, salt and pepper. Pour over zucchini. Top with remaining zucchini. Bake at 375° for 40 minutes or until set. Let set 10 minutes before slicing. Serves four to six.

Mark Virts

Residency: Austin, Texas
Age: 24
Height: 5'7"
Weight: 140
School: Purdue University
Training hours per week: 18

Nachos Con Guacamole

12 corn tortillas

Oil for frying

1 16-ounce can refried beans

Shredded Cheddar or Colby cheese

1 4-ounce can jalapeno peppers, sliced

Guacamole (see directions)

Cut tortillas into quarters and fry in oil until crisp. Drain. Spread each tortilla chip with refried beans, pepper slices and shredded cheese. Broil for about four minutes or until cheese melts. Remove from oven, top with a blob of guacamole and return to broiler for one more minute. Makes 48 nachos.

Guacamole: Combine the following ingredients and mix well: 2 large ripe avocadoes, peeled, seeded, diced and mashed; 2 tablespoons lemon or lime juice; 1 4-ounce can chopped green chilies, drained; 1 teaspoon minced garlic; 1 teaspoon salt; 1/2 teaspoon coriander; 2 tablespoons grated onion; 1/4 teaspoon pepper; 1 large tomato, peeled and finely chopped. Store in refrigerator. Serve as a dip or spread. Makes about 2½ cups.

Omelet

3 eggs

1 tablespoon water

Cheddar, Colby and/or Monterey Jack cheese

Diced onion

Diced green pepper

Alfalfa sprouts

Sliced avocado

Worcestershire sauce

Piquant or hot sauce

Beat eggs with water and pour into a hot, well-greased omelet pan or skillet. Cook over medium heat until eggs begin to set. Sprinkle half of omelet with cheese, onion, pepper, sprouts. Add a few avocado slices and a dash of Worcestershire. When egg mixture is almost set, fold omelet in half. Serve with piquant sauce. Serves one or two.

Layered Vegetable Cheese Bake

1 tablespoon vegetable oil

1 large onion, chopped

1 large green pepper, cut in chunks

1 small eggplant, peeled and cubed

1/2 pound fresh mushrooms, sliced

1 large tomato, peeled and chopped

1 teaspoon salt

1/8 teaspoon pepper

3/4 teaspoon thyme

1 cup packaged herbed stuffing mix

2 cups shredded Swiss cheese

In a large skillet, saute onion and green pepper in oil for three minutes. Add eggplant and mushrooms and saute three more minutes. Add tomato and seasonings and cook one more minute. Spread stuffing mix in the bottom of a two-quart casserole or baking dish. Layer vegetable mixture with cheese, ending with cheese. Bake at 350° for 30 minutes. If desired, sprinkle with additional cheese and return to oven until melted. Serves four to six.

Contributors	Recipes

Kent Vosler

Residency: Columbus, Ohio
Age: 23
Height: 5'5"
Weight: 138
School: The Ohio State University
Training hours per week: 28

Vegetable Sukiyaki

1 onion, sliced
1 carrot, sliced
1 bunch broccoli, chopped
1 head cauliflower, cut into flowerettes
1 stalk celery, diced
1 green pepper, chopped
1/4 pound fresh mushrooms, sliced
1 teaspoon salt
1/2 teaspoon pepper
1 teaspoon curry powder
1 teaspoon turmeric or saffron
1 cup water
4 cups creamy garlic dressing
Hot cooked rice

Layer vegetables and spices in a large, oiled baking pan. Add water, cover and steam in oven at 375° for 45 minutes or until vegetables are tender. Pour garlic dressing over vegetables. Serve over hot rice. Serves four to six.

Barb Weinstein

Residency: Cincinnati, Ohio
Age: 20
Height: 5'3"
Weight: 104
School: University of Michigan
Training hours per week: 19

Cheese Cake

1½ cups graham cracker crumbs
1/4 cup sugar
1/4 cup melted butter or margarine
5 8-ounce packages cream cheese, softened
1½ cups sugar
2 tablespoons flour
1/8 teaspoon salt
5 eggs, plus 2 egg yolks
1/2 cup cream
1 teaspoon vanilla

Combine crumbs with sugar and butter. Press into the bottom of a 9-inch springform pan. In a large bowl, beat cheese until soft and creamy. Beat in sugar, flour and salt. Beat in five eggs, one at a time. In a small bowl, beat egg yolks with cream and vanilla. Beat into cheese mixture. Pour slowly into pan. Bake at 475° for 10 minutes. Reduce heat to 225°. Bake for one hour and 10 minutes. Turn off oven. Leave cheesecake in oven with door open for 10 minutes. Cool on a rack to room temperature. Remove from pan. Chill in refrigerator before serving. Serves 12 or more.

Spinach Salad With Hot Bacon Dressing

1 pound fresh spinach, washed, dried and chilled
4 slices bacon, diced
2 teaspoons brown sugar
1/4 cup sliced green onions
1/4 teaspoon salt
1½ tablespoons vinegar
1/8 teaspoon dry mustard
Dash of paprika

With scissors, snip spinach coarsely into salad bowl. In a medium skillet, fry bacon until crisp. Reduce heat to medium. Stir in remaining ingredients. Bring to a boil. Remove from heat. Just before serving, pour hot dressing over spinach and toss to coat leaves. Serves four.

8

Equestrian

Event Days:

Thursday, July 24, 1980	Wednesday, July 30, 1980
Friday, July 25, 1980	Thursday, July 31, 1980
Saturday, July 26, 1980	Friday, August 1, 1980
Sunday, July 27, 1980	Sunday, August 3, 1980
Tuesday, July 29, 1980	

Contributors:

Derek di Grazia
Hilda Gurney
Alexsandra P. Howard
Mike Huber
Michael Matz
Gwen Stockebrand
James C. Wofford
Linda L. Zang

The equestrian sports are one of three on the Olympic program catering to both sexes on the same team. Shooting and yachting are the other two.

There are three disciplines included among the equestrian sports—dressage (a series of magnificent maneuvers requiring perfect coordination between horse and rider), show jumping, and "eventing" (a grueling three-day event which combines exercises in dressage, a cross-country ride testing the endurance of the horse and the equestrian skills of the rider, and on the final day show jumping).

This is one of the sports on the Olympic program which has both individual awards and synthetic team awards. The place finishes in the "team" competitions are determined by combining the individual scores of the top three (of four) horses and riders.

At Montreal, the USA Tad Coffin, 21, and J. Michael Plumb, 36, finished one, two in the individual competition and were joined by Bruce Davidson and Mary Anne Tauskey in the gold-medal team performance.

Age is no limiting factor in the equestrian sports. The only USA individual show jumping gold medalist is William Steinkraus who celebrated his 43rd birthday at Mexico City before he went on to capture the prized Olympic title.

Derek di Grazia

Residency: S. Hamilton, Massachusetts

Age: 23

Height: 6'

Weight: 150

School: Georgetown University 1977

Training hours per week: 38

Grandmother's English Pound Cake

1 pound butter, softened

1 pound sugar (2 cups)

10 eggs, separated

1 teaspoon vanilla

Juice of 1 lemon

1 pound sifted cake flour (4½ cups)

1 teaspoon baking powder

In a large mixing bowl, cream butter and sugar. Beat in egg yolks, along with vanilla and lemon juice. Add flour and baking powder and mix well. In another bowl, with clean beaters, beat egg whites until stiff. Fold whites into batter until well combined. Pour into a greased 10-inch tube pan. Bake at 350° for 1 to 1½ hours or until toothpick inserted in center comes out clean. Cool in pan for 15 minutes. Remove from pan and finish cooling on rack. Serves 12 or more.

Hilda Gurney

Residency: Woodland Hills, California

Age: 35

Height: 5'6"

Weight: 138

Training hours per week: 42

Apple Cake

6 apples

1/2 cup sugar

1 teaspoon cinnamon

1 cup water

6 tablespoons butter or margarine

1/2 cup brown sugar

1 cup flour

1 teaspoon baking powder

1/2 teaspoon salt

Peel and core apples and cut into eighths. In a medium saucepan, cook apples with sugar, cinnamon and water until tender. Place in an 8x8-inch baking pan. In a medium bowl, using a pastry blender or two knives, cut butter into remaining ingredients. Spread over top of apple mixture. Bake at 350° for about 45 minutes. Serves eight.

Mexicali Casserole

1¼ pounds lean ground beef

1/2 cup chopped onion

1½ teaspoons salt

2 7¼-ounce packages macaroni and cheese

1 12-ounce can Mexicali-style corn, drained

1 2¼ ounce can sliced ripe olives, drained

2 15-ounce cans tomato sauce

1/2 teaspoon chili powder

In a large skillet, brown meat with onion and 1/2 teaspoon salt. Break up meat into small chunks. Drain off fat. Cook macaroni according to directions on packages, but cook only five minutes. Drain. (Do not add cheese mixture.) Pour macaroni into a four-quart buttered casserole or 13x9-inch baking dish. Stir in corn and olives. Sprinkle on 1½ packages of cheese from macaroni mix. Mix. Add meat. In a medium saucepan, simmer tomato sauce, remaining salt and chili powder for five minutes. Add to casserole and mix all ingredients well. Top with remaining cheese. (If desired, add chopped green pepper to casserole, and top with additional freshly grated cheese and a dash of paprika.) Chill in refrigerator overnight, then bake at 350° for about 30 minutes or until bubbly and heated through. Or, freeze until ready to use, then bake, frozen, at 350° for 45 minutes or until heated through. Serves 12.

Alexsandra P. Howard

*Residency: El Granada,
    California*

Age: 37

Height: 5'5½"

Weight: 124

*School: San Jose State
    University*

Training hours per week: 30

Split Pea Rarebit

1/4 cup vegetable oil

1 small onion, chopped

1/4 cup whole wheat flour

1½ cups water

1/2 tsp. salt

1 tablespoon tomato paste

1/4 teaspoon dry mustard

1/2 teaspoon Worcestershire
    sauce

Pinch of dried chili peppers

1½ cups grated sharp
    Cheddar cheese

1/2 cup cooked split peas

1/2 cup beer

1½ cups raw brown rice,
    cooked

In a medium saucepan, saute onion in oil until
tender. Blend in flour and cook for two to three
minutes. Gradually stir in water and cook over low
heat, stirring constantly, until thick. Stir in salt, tomato
paste, mustard, Worcestershire and chili. Gradually
add cheese, stirring constantly until melted. Add split
peas and beer and stir well. Serve over cooked
brown rice. Serves four.

Honey Wheat Bread

2 cups milk

1/4 cup butter or margarine

1 tablespoon salt

1/2 cup honey

1/3 cup warm water

2 packages dry yeast

8 cups "fortified" whole wheat
    flour (see directions)

To fortify flour, before measuring each cup, to the
bottom of the cup add 1 tablespoon soy flour, 1
tablespoon skim milk powder and 1 teaspoon wheat
germ. Then fill cup with flour. In a medium saucepan,
scald milk with butter, salt and honey. Cook to
lukewarm. Dissolve yeast in warm water. In a large
mixing bowl, combine milk mixture with dissolved
yeast. Stir in four cups flour and beat 300 strokes.
Stir in enough remaining flour to form a soft dough.
Turn out onto a floured surface and knead in as
much remaining flour as necessary to form a smooth,
elastic dough. Place in a buttered bowl, cover, and
let rise in a warm, draft-free place until almost
double, about one hour. Punch down. Divide dough
into two or three pieces. Shape loaves. Place in two
large or three medium buttered loaf pans. Set to rise
again until almost double, about 45 minutes. Bake at
350° for 45 to 50 minutes. Makes two large or three
medium loaves.

Butter-Rum Bananas

4 firm bananas, split in half
    lengthwise

1/3 cup butter

1/3 cup brown sugar

1½ tablespoons cinnamon

1/3 cup dark rum

In a large skillet, saute bananas in butter until brown,
turning once. Sprinkle with sugar and cinnamon and
turn to coat. Add rum and turn to coat again. Serve
hot, plain or with ice cream. Serves four to eight.

Contributors	Recipes

Mike Huber

Residency: S. Hamilton, Massachusetts
Age: 18
Height: 6'
Weight: 140
School: Oklahoma University
Training hours per week: 48

Cinnamon Cake

4 eggs
1 box yellow cake mix (two-layer size)
1 cup sour cream
1/2 cup vegetable oil
1/2 cup sugar
2 teaspoons cinnamon

In a large bowl, beat together eggs, cake mix, sour cream and oil. Pour half of batter into a greased and floured bundt pan or 10-inch tube pan. Combine sugar with cinnamon. Sprinkle half the sugar mixture over batter in pan. Top with remaining batter. Sprinkle with remaining sugar mixture. Bake at 350° for 45 minutes. Cool in pan for 15 minutes before removing. Serves 12.

Hawaiian Rice

1 pound mild pork sausage
1/2 pound ground beef (optional)
1 cup diced celery
1/2 cup chopped onion
1 small green pepper, diced
2 1⅞-ounce envelopes instant chicken noodle soup
1 cup raw rice
5 cups hot water
1 8-ounce can sliced pineapple, drained (optional)

In a large skillet, brown sausage with ground beef. Drain off excess fat and add celery, onion and green pepper. Continue to cook, stirring frequently, until onion is soft. Stir in rice, dry soup mix and hot water. (Pineapple juice from can may be used in place of some of the water.) Turn into a 13x9-inch pan and bake, covered, at 325° for 45 minutes or until liquid is absorbed and rice is done. Uncover, lay pineapple slices on top and return to oven for five more minutes. Serves six to eight.

Michael Matz

Residency: Plymouth Meeting, Pennsylvania
Age: 28
Height 5'10"
Weight: 150
School: Governor Miflin High School
Training hours per week: 38

Stuffed Green Peppers

1 small onion, chopped
1 tablespoon butter or margarine
1/4 cup raw rice
1½ cups water
1 pound ground beef
1 teaspoon salt
1/4 teaspoon pepper
6 medium green peppers
1/4 cup butter or margarine
2 tablespoons flour
1 16-ounce can tomato sauce
Shredded cheese

In a large skillet, saute onion in butter until soft. Add rice and cook, stirring constantly, for about one minute. Stir in 1/2 cup water. Cover and simmer until rice is tender, about 10 minutes. Remove from heat and thoroughly mix in meat, salt and pepper. Cut tops off green peppers. Chop usable portion of tops and add to meat mixture. Remove membranes and seeds from peppers. Stuff loosely with rice-meat mixture. In a Dutch oven, melt butter and stir in flour. Slowly stir in tomato sauce and remaining 1 cup water. Simmer, stirring constantly, until thick. Stand peppers upright in sauce. Cover and simmer over low heat or bake at 350° until tender, about one hour. Top with grated cheese. Serves six.

Contributors	Recipes

Michael Matz

Sweet and Sour Chicken

2 pounds boned chicken meat, cut in chunks

1 cup sliced celery

2 green peppers, cut in chunks

1 sweet red pepper, cut in chunks

1 large onion, sliced

1 pound fresh mushrooms, sliced

Other optional Chinese vegetables, such as bamboo shoots, water chestnuts, bean sprouts, Chinese cabbage or bok choy

1 8-ounce can or jar sweet and sour sauce

Combine all ingredients in a large casserole or baking dish. Mix to combine. Cover and bake at 375° for one hour or until chicken is done and vegetables are tender-crisp. Serve with hot cooked rice or fried rice. Serves four to six.

Braised Fish

1 pound fish fillets

3 carrots, thinly sliced

2 stalks celery, sliced

3 onions, sliced

1 green pepper, chopped

3 tablespoons butter

3 tablespoons lemon juice

1 clove garlic, minced

Salt and pepper to taste

White vermouth

In a large skillet, saute carrots, celery, onions and green pepper in butter for five minutes. Lay fish fillets over bed of vegetables. Sprinkle with lemon juice, garlic and salt and pepper. Add enough vermouth to come halfway up the side of the fish. Bring to a boil and continue to cook on top of the stove or in a 350° oven, basting frequently and allowing 10 minutes cooking time for each inch of thickness at the fillet's thickest point. Serves two.

Gwen Stockebrand

Residency: Santa Rosa, California

Age: 24

Height: 5'5½"

Weight: 125

School: University High, Los Angeles, California

Training hours per week: 35

Best-Ever Chocolate Mousse

5 eggs, separated

1/2 lb. dark, sweet or semi-sweet chocolate

5 tablespoons cold water

2 teaspoons rum

Break chocolate into small pieces and place in a medium-sized heavy pan or double boiler. Add cold water. Stir over low heat until chocolate dissolves. Remove from heat. Stir in egg yolks and rum until well blended. Set aside. With a clean bowl and beaters, beat egg whites until stiff. Carefully fold in chocolate mixture. Spoon into individual dessert dishes or one serving bowl. Chill at least four hours. Serves eight.

Contributors	Recipes

Gwen Stockebrand

Onion Bread

1 packet dry yeast

1/4 cup warm water

1 cup sour cream

2 tablespoons butter or margarine

1 cup warm water

1 1⅞-ounce packet dry onion soup mix

2 tablespoons sugar

1 teaspoon salt

1/4 teaspoon baking soda

2 eggs, beaten

6½ or more cups flour

Sesame seeds

Dissolve yeast in warm water. In a small pan, warm sour cream over low heat. Stir in margarine until melted. Combine sour cream and yeast in large bowl. Stir in warm water, soup mix, sugar, salt and soda. Reserve 2 tablespoons beaten egg. Add remaining egg to yeast mixture. Stir in enough flour to make a soft dough. Turn out onto a floured surface and knead until smooth and elastic, about 10 minutes, working in more flour as necessary. Place in a greased bowl and let rise in a warm place until doubled. Punch down. Divide dough in half. Roll dough into a rectangle. Cut into three long strips and braid. Place on a greased cookie sheet. Repeat with other half of dough. Brush with beaten egg. Let rise until doubled. Brush again with egg. Sprinkle with sesame seeds. Bake at 350° for 35 to 40 minutes. Makes two large loaves.

James C. Wofford

Residency: Upperville, Virginia

Age: 34

Height: 5'8"

Weight: 150

School: University of Colorado

Training hours per week: 14

Coach Stop Chili

3 pounds ground beef

1 cup chopped onion

4 16-ounce cans kidney beans

4 16-ounce cans tomatoes, undrained and slightly mashed

Salt and pepper to taste

6 tablespoons chili powder

In a heavy four-quart kettle, brown ground beef with onions. Add remaining ingredients. Bring to a boil and simmer for one hour, stirring occasionally. Serves 10.

Peach Cobbler

3 cups sliced fresh or canned peaches, drained

1 tablespoon lemon juice

1 cup self-rising flour

1 cup sugar

1 egg, beaten

6 tablespoons melted butter or margarine

Arrange peaches in the bottom of an 8x8-inch baking pan. Sprinkle with lemon juice. In a medium bowl, combine flour with sugar. Stir egg in with a fork until mixture is the consistency of coarse meal. Spread over peaches. Drizzle with melted butter. Bake at 375° for 30 to 35 minutes. Serve warm with cream, milk or vanilla ice cream. Serves six to eight.

Linda L. Zang

Residency: Davidsonville, Maryland

Age: 31

Height: 5'6"

Weight: 130

School: Anne Arundel Community College and Baltimore Institute

Training hours per week: 18

Pecan Pie

Pastry for 1 9-in. pie crust

3 eggs

2/3 cup sugar

1/3 teaspoon salt

1/3 cup melted butter

1 cup dark corn syrup

1 cup pecan halves

In a medium bowl, beat together all ingredients except pecans. Mix in pecans. Pour into pastry-lined pie pan. Bake at 375° for 40 to 50 minutes, until filling is set and pastry browned. Cool before serving. Serves eight.

9

Fencing

Event Days:

Tuesday, July 22, 1980	Sunday, July 27, 1980
Wednesday, July 23, 1980	Monday, July 28, 1980
Thursday, July 24, 1980	Tuesday, July 29, 1980
Friday, July 25, 1980	Wednesday, July 30, 1980
Saturday, July 26, 1980	Thursday, July 31, 1980

Contributors:

Gay K. D'Asaro
Stanley V. Lekach
John Nonna

The individual sabre competition, bringing to the Olympic Games all the dash and *éclat* of a warrior or Middle Ages' hero of the past, has been a fixture on the program for the Olympic Games since the inaugural Games in Athens, 1896. The men's foil competition has been on every program except 1908 in London. Men's épée was added in 1900 and has been on every program since that time, while the women's foil competition was introduced in 1924 at Paris.

For the first 60 years the sport was dominated by the Italians, French, as well as Hungary's sabre fencers. The swing has been to Eastern Europe in the last 16 years, with an emphasis on the splendid fencers from the Soviet Union.

The team competition in fencing is spirited competition as the squads move through preliminary pools, semi-finals and finals.

The United States has had no Olympic champions in the individual and team events on the program today. The last USA medalist in the Olympic Games was bronze medalist Albert Axelrod in the men's foil at Italy in 1960. The men's sabre team also won a bronze in London, 1948.

At Montreal, the individual winners included Idiko Schwarczenberger, Hungary, women's foil; Fabio dal Zotto, Italy, men's foil; Viktor Krovopouskov, USSR, sabre and Alexander Pusch, German Federal Republic, épée.

Gay K. D'Asaro

Residency: San Jose, California

Age: 24

Height: 5'9"

Weight: 135

School: San Jose State University

Training hours per week: 10

Loo Son Ngow Yuk (Asparagus and Beef)

1 pound flank steak

1 teaspoon salt

1 teaspoon cornstarch

2 teaspoons soy sauce

1 2-pound bunch asparagus (or green beans, broccoli, zucchini)

2 medium onions

6 cloves garlic

7 tablespoons vegetable oil

1 teaspoon salt

1/2 teaspoon sugar

1 tablespoon soy sauce

Optional ingredients: water chestnuts, bean sprouts, mushrooms or tofu (bean curd)

Hot cooked rice

Slice steak across grain into very thin 2½-inch-long strips. Place in a medium bowl with salt, cornstarch and soy sauce. Let stand while preparing vegetables. Slice asparagus or other vegetables into diagonal slices about 1/4-inch thick and 2-inches long. Set aside. Cut onions in half lengthwise; lay cut sides down; slice crosswise. Set aside. Smash garlic cloves with side of knife and remove skin. Place a large wok or heavy skillet over a high flame. Add 4 tablespoons oil. Add garlic and cook until brown. Remove and discard garlic. Add meat and stir-fry until almost brown. Remove meat and set aside. Add remaining 3 tablespoons oil. Add onion and stir-fry until translucent. Add asparagus and sprinkle with salt, sugar and soy sauce. Reduce heat, cover and cook, stirring frequently, until asparagus has turned from white to light yellow-brown on the inside. Place meat on top. Heat through and serve over hot rice. Serves six.

Pork Chops and Rice Casserole

8 pork chops

Salt and pepper to taste

3 cups raw rice

1 10¾-ounce can beef consomme

3 cups hot water

1 chicken bouillon cube or 1 teaspoon instant chicken bouillon

2 pinches rosemary

Brown chops in a large heavy skillet, salting and peppering to taste. In a 13x9-inch baking pan or a large casserole, spread raw rice. Place chops on top of rice. Add consomme, water and bouillon cube to pan used for browning chops. Bring to a boil, scraping pan to loosen all brown bits. Pour over chops and rice. Sprinkle with rosemary. Cover and bake at 350° for 25 minutes or until rice is tender and liquid is absorbed. Remove cover and return to oven for five to 10 minutes to brown chops. Serves six to eight.

Frittata

1 10-ounce box frozen chopped spinach

3 large eggs

3 tablespoons grated Romano or Parmesan cheese

Salt and pepper

2 tablespoons vegetable oil (preferably olive oil)

Cook spinach according to package directions, drain well. Beat eggs with cheese and salt and pepper. Add spinach to eggs and mix well. Heat oil in a heavy 9-inch skillet over a high flame. When oil is hot, add spinach mixture. Cook over high heat until bottom is firm and browned. Reduce heat to low; turn frittata to cook top. Variations: For spinach, substitute any cooked vegetable that has been chopped or shredded. Serves four to six.

Stanley V. Lekach

Residency: Upton, New York
Age: 32
Height: 5'10"
Weight: 155
School: University of California at Berkeley
Training hours per week: 15

Pirozhki (Small Meat-Filled Pastries)

4 cups flour

1/2 teaspoon salt

1 cup unsalted butter, cut into 1/4-inch bits and chilled

1/2 cup lard cut into 1/4-inch bits and chilled

8 to 12 tablespoons ice water

Filling:

4 tablespoons butter

3 cups finely chopped onions

1½ pounds lean ground beef

3 hard-boiled eggs, finely chopped

6 tablespoons minced fresh dill, or 3 teaspoons dried dill

2 teaspoons salt

1/4 teaspoon freshly ground black pepper

To make pastry: In a large bowl, combine flour, salt, butter and lard. With your fingers, rub flour and fat together until mixture resembles flakes of coarse meal. Add 8 tablespoons ice water all at once and gather dough into a ball. If mixture is too dry, add up to 4 more tablespoons water, 1 tablespoon at a time. Wrap dough in plastic and chill one hour. On a lightly floured surface, shape pastry into a rough triangle 1-inch thick. Roll into a strip about 21x6 inches. Fold into thirds to make three-layered packet about 7x6 inches. Repeat rolling and folding process three more times, ending with the folded packet. Wrap and chill for one hour.

To make filling: Melt butter over high heat in a large heavy skillet. Reduce heat to medium and saute onions until transparent. Stir in beef, breaking up lumps with a fork. Cook briskly until no traces of pink remain. Grind meat-onion mixture through fine blade of meat grinder or chop as fine as possible with a knife. In a large bowl, combine meat mixture with remaining filling ingredients. Mix well and taste for seasoning.

To make pastries: On a lightly floured surface, roll dough into a circle about 1/8 inch thick. With a 3- to 3½-inch round cookie or biscuit cutter, cut as many circles as possible. Gather scraps and roll again, cutting additional circles. Repeat process until dough is used up. Drop 2 tablespoons filling into center of each round and flatten slightly. Fold one side of dough over filling, almost covering it. Fold in two ends about 1/2 inch. Fold over remaining side of dough. Place pastries on a buttered baking sheet, seam sides down. Bake at 400° for 30 minutes or until golden brown. Serve hot or cold, as an appetizer or as a first course, alone or with a clear soup. Makes about 40 pastries.

Rice Cooked in Chicken Stock

2 tablespoons butter

1/2 cup chopped onion

1 cup raw rice

2 cups hot chicken stock or bouillon

In a medium saucepan, melt butter. Saute onion until golden brown. Add rice and stir until grains are coated with butter. Stir in hot stock. Cover and simmer for 20 minutes until liquid is absorbed. Or, transfer to a covered casserole and bake at 375° for about 30 minutes until liquid is absorbed. Toss with fork before serving. Serves four.

Stanley V. Lekach

Sliced Marinated Chicken Breasts Sauteed

2 to 3 whole broiler-fryer chicken breasts, split in half

Juice and grated rind of 1 lemon

1 teaspoon salt

1/8 teaspoon pepper

1/2 teaspoon rosemary or thyme

1 to 2 cloves garlic, minced

1/4 cup olive oil

Fresh bread crumbs

Grated Parmesan cheese

Olive oil

Skin and bone chicken breast halves. In a large bowl, combine lemon, salt, pepper, rosemary, garlic and olive oil. Marinate chicken in oil mixture for at least 30 minutes. Scrape marinade off meat and pat meat dry with paper towels. Slice meat into strips. Coat strips with a mixture of crumbs and Parmesan cheese. In a large skillet of medium-high heat, saute breaded meat strips in olive oil until they turn white, only a couple minutes. Serves two to four.

John Nonna

Residency: Pleasantville, New York

Age: 30

Height: 5'11"

Weight: 170

School: N.Y.U. Law School

Training hours per week: 10

Carottes Marinees (Marinated Carrots)

6 carrots

3/4 cup dry vermouth

1 cup water

Salt and pepper

2 tablespoons sugar

2 tablespoons lemon juice

1 clove garlic, crushed

1/3 cup olive oil

Bouquet garni or mixture of 1 bay leaf, 1 tablespoon minced parsley, 1/4 teaspoon thyme, 1/4 teaspoon tarragon, 1/4 teaspoon chervil

Peel or scrape carrots and cut lengthwise into quarters. In a saucepan, combine remaining ingredients. Bring to a boil and simmer for 10 minutes. Add carrots and boil until just tender. Cool in marinade. Chill. Drain and serve as vegetable or appetizer. As a vegetable, serves four to six.

10
Field Hockey

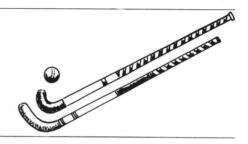

Event Days:

Sunday,
July 20, 1980

Monday,
July 21, 1980

Wednesday,
July 23, 1980

Thursday,
July 24, 1980

Friday,
July 25, 1980

Saturday,
July 26, 1980

Sunday,
July 27, 1980

Monday,
July 28, 1980

Tuesday,
July 29, 1980

Wednesday,
July 30, 1980

Thursday,
July 31, 1980

Friday,
August 1, 1980

Contributors:

Gwen W. Cheeseman
Barbara Doran
R. Scott Gregg
Manzur M. Iqbal
Hewlett V. Johnson
John Kovach
Anita C. Miller
Bikriamjit Singh Randhawa
Nancy Pitkin White

The ancient and honorable sport of field hockey was introduced on the program at London in 1908 where the host country won the gold, Ireland placed second, and Scotland and Wales (both now a part of the Great Britain sports forces) tied for third place. Men's competition has been held at every Olympic Games since, except for 1912 and 1924.

Women's field hockey, long a standard sport in USA schools and colleges, will be on the program for the Olympic Games at Moscow for the first time. This will be a six-team tournament, including the host team from the USSR, the world championship team, and four others to be decided by qualifying tournaments.

The only medal earned by the USA men's team was a bronze at Los Angeles in 1932, with such outstanding players as Henry Greer, Jimmy Gentle, Dave McMullan, Charles Shaeffer, and Horace Disston.

Since 1924 India has won a lion's share of the honors, placing first seven times, second once and third twice. A seventh place finish at Montreal is the only time India has finished out of the money.

The USSR will be making its debut in field hockey at Moscow, challenging the three medal winners at Montreal, in order, New Zealand, Australia, and Pakistan. At Munich in 1972, West Germany won its only gold medal, followed by Pakistan and India, in that order.

Contributors	Recipes

Gwen W. Cheeseman

*Residency: West Chester,
Pennsylvania*

Age: 27

Height: 5'2"

Weight: 121

*School: West Chester State
College*

Training hours per week: 20

Cheeseman's Stir-Fried Chicken

2 large, whole broiler-fryer
chicken breasts, skinned,
halved, boned and sliced
diagonally into 1/4-inch thick
strips

2 tablespoons peanut oil

1 cup thinly sliced celery

1 medium green pepper, cut
into thin strips

1 small onion, sliced

1/4 teaspoon ginger

1 pound fresh bean sprouts

1 5-ounce can water chestnuts,
drained and sliced

1/2 pound fresh mushrooms,
sliced

1/3 cup raw cashews, halved

1 chicken bouillon cube, or 1
teaspoon instant chicken
bouillon

1/2 cup water

2 teaspoons cornstarch

1/4 cup soy sauce

3 cups hot cooked rice

In a wok over high heat, heat peanut oil. Stir-fry celery, pepper, onion and ginger in oil until tender-crisp, about three minutes. With slotted spoon, slide vegetables up onto side of wok to keep warm. To remaining oil, add chicken and stir-fry until meat turns white, about three to five minutes. Slide vegetables back down and add bean sprouts, water chestnuts, mushrooms, cashews, bouillon and water. Blend cornstarch with soy sauce; gradually stir into wok and cook, stirring constantly, until mixture is heated through and thickened. Serve over hot rice. Serves four.

Barbara Doran

*Residency: New York, New
York*

Age: 25

Height: 5'5"

Weight: 125

School: Penn State University

Training hours per week: 9

Aunt Ruth's Fudge Cookies

4 cups sugar

3/4 cup cocoa

1 cup butter

1 cup milk

2 teaspoons vanilla

1½ cups peanut butter

6 cups quick-cooking rolled
oats

1 cup raisins

1 cup flaked coconut

1 cup chopped walnuts

In a large pan, combine sugar, cocoa, butter and milk. Heat, stirring constantly; bring to a boil and boil two minutes. Remove from heat and quickly beat in vanilla and peanut butter. Gradually stir in remaining ingredients. Drop from a teaspoon onto waxed paper. Cool. Store in a tightly covered container in the refrigerator. Makes about six to eight dozen cookies.

Barbara Doran

Quiche Lorraine

1 unbaked 9-inch pie shell

1/4 pound bacon, cooked and crumbled

1/4 pound fresh mushrooms, sliced (optional)

1/2 cup chopped onions

1/2 pound shredded Swiss or Gruyere cheese

1 tablespoon flour

3 eggs, beaten

2 cups milk or cream

1/2 teaspoon salt

Dash of cayenne pepper

Dash of nutmeg

Bake pricked pie shell at 450° for five minutes. Sprinkle bacon over bottom of crust. Saute mushrooms and onions in bacon fat or butter until soft. Remove with a slotted spoon and scatter over bacon. Toss cheese with flour and sprinkle over mushrooms. Combine remaining ingredients and pour over cheese. Bake at 450° for 10 minutes. Reduce heat to 325° and bake for 20 more minutes or until set. Cool for 10 minutes before slicing. Serves four to six.

R. Scott Gregg

Residency: Whitehall, Pennsylvania

Age: 24

Height: 6'2"

Weight: 165

School: Leigh County Community College

Training hours per week: 15

Venison Stew

3 pounds venison, cut into 1½-inch cubes

1/2 cup flour

1/3 cup vegetable shortening

2 onions, chopped

6 potatoes, peeled and cubed

4 carrots, sliced

1 10-ounce package frozen peas

1 10-ounce package frozen green beans

Salt and pepper to taste

Dredge meat in flour. In a large heavy kettle, brown onions and meat in melted shortening. Fill kettle half full of water. Add potatoes and carrots. Bring to a boil, cover and simmer for one hour, stirring occassionally. Add peas and beans and simmer one more hour. Season with salt and pepper. If desired, thicken gravy with cornstarch. Serves eight.

Vegetable Soup

6 quarts beef stock

1/2 head of cabbage, chopped or shredded

4 carrots, sliced

5 potatoes, cubed

3 stalks celery, sliced

3 onions, chopped

1 medium zucchini, sliced

5 fresh tomatoes, peeled and chopped

1 10¾-ounce can condensed tomato soup

1/2 teaspoon thyme

Salt, pepper and chopped parsley to taste

In a large kettle, combine all ingredients. Bring to a boil and simmer several hours. Refrigerate overnight to blend flavors. Reheat the next day and serve. Serves 12 or more.

Manzar M. Iqbal

Residency: Livermore, California
Age: 20
Height: 5'9"
Weight: 143
School: UC Berkeley
Training hours per week: 20

Pea and Mushroom Curry

2 onions, thinly sliced
1 clove garlic, minced
1 tomato, peeled and chopped
2 tablespoons vegetable oil
1 pound fresh mushrooms, sliced
1 10-ounce package frozen peas
1 teaspoon turmeric
1/2 teaspoon coriander
1/2 teaspoon cumin
Dash of cinnamon
Dash of cloves
1/2 teaspoon chili powder
Salt to taste
Hot cooked rice or pasta

In a large skillet, saute onions and garlic in oil until golden. Add tomatoes and simmer for five minutes. Add remaining ingredients, stir well and simmer for 15 to 20 minutes. If desired, add a little water. Serve over hot rice or noodles. Serves four.

Kristiana Kringel

2 cups flour
1 cup butter
1 cup plus 2 tablespoons water
3 eggs
1/4 teaspoon salt
1/2 teaspoon almond extract
Powdered Sugar Frosting (see directions)

In a medium bowl, cut 1/2 cup butter into 1 cup flour as for pie crust. Mix in 2 tablespoons water with a fork. Shape dough into two balls. On an ungreased cookie sheet, using the heel of your hand, press the two balls of dough into two 3-inch-wide strips as long as the sheet. In a medium pan, bring water and remaining butter to a boil. Remove from heat and stir in remaining flour until smooth. Beat in eggs, one at a time. Add salt and almond extract. Spread over top of first mixture. Bake at 375° for 45 minutes. Frost. Serves 12.

Powdered Sugar Frosting: Beat together until smooth: 1½ to 2 cups powdered sugar, 2 tablespoons melted butter and 1/2 teaspoon almond extract.

Turkey or Chicken Rice Salad

3 cups cooked rice
3 cups cooked diced turkey or chicken
1 teaspoon grated onion
1½ cups mayonnaise
2 teaspoons curry powder
1/4 cup soy sauce
2 tablespoons vinegar

Combine all ingredients and refrigerate for two hours or more. Serve on salad greens, garnished with toasted sliced almonds, if desired. Serves six to eight.

Contributors	Recipes

Hewlett V. Johnson

Residency: Yonkers, New York
Age: 29
Height: 6'
Weight: 165
School: Minerva College
Training hours per week: 23

Fish Broth

1 medium redfish (ocean perch)

1 small onion, chopped

1 medium tomato, chopped

1 clove garlic, minced

2 tablespoons butter or margarine

1 tablespoon vinegar

4 cups water

1 bay leaf

1 sprig thyme, or 1/2 teaspoon dry thyme

2 tablespoons Angostura orange bitters

Salt and pepper to taste

1 lime, thinly sliced

Clean, filet and skin fish. Cut into bite-size pieces. Set aside. In a large kettle, saute onion, tomato and garlic in butter until soft. Add remaining ingredients, except lime, and season to taste. Bring to a boil and simmer 30 to 40 minutes until fish is done and flakes easily with a fork. Garnish with thin slices of lime. Serves four to six.

Vegetable Meat Savoury

4 ounces vermicelli or spaghettini

1/4 cup chopped onion

1/4 cup vegetable shortening or oil

1 pound ground beef

2 cups peas

1 16-ounce can tomatoes

2 teaspoons salt

1/2 cup bread crumbs

Cook pasta as package directs. Meanwhile, brown onion and meat in oil. Drain pasta and add to meat. Place meat-pasta mixture in a layer in the bottom of a 13x9-inch baking dish or a large casserole. Top with a layer of peas and then a layer of tomatoes. Season with salt. Top with bread crumbs. Bake at 350° for 20 to 30 minutes. Serves six.

John Kovach

Residency: Chevy Chase, Maryland
Age: 22
Height: 6'0"
Weight: 180
School: University of Maryland
Training hours per week: 17

Old Fashioned Pumpkin Pie

2 eggs, beaten

1½ cups cooked, mashed pumpkin or canned pumpkin

3/4 cup sugar

1/2 teaspoon salt

2 heaping teaspoons cinnamon

1/4 teaspoon ginger

1/8 teaspoon cloves

1⅔ cups light cream

1 9-inch unbaked pie shell with a high edge

In a medium bowl, mix eggs and pumpkin. Stir in sugar, salt, cinnamon, ginger and cloves. Mix in cream. Pour into pie shell. Bake at 425° for 15 minutes. Reduce heat to 350° and continue baking for 45 minutes more or until knife inserted into center comes out clean. Serves six to eight.

Contributors	Recipes

John Kovach

Green Bean and Mushroom Casserole

1 pound fresh mushrooms, sliced

1 medium onion, sliced

1/2 cup butter or margarine

1/2 cup flour

2 cups milk

1 cup light cream

3/4 pound sharp Cheddar cheese, shredded

1/8 teaspoon Tabasco sauce

1 teaspoon salt

1/2 teaspoon pepper

2 teaspoons soy sauce

1 5-ounce can water chestnuts, drained and sliced

3 10-ounce packages frozen French-cut green beans

1/2 cup toasted slivered almonds

In medium pan, saute mushrooms with onion in butter. Add flour and stir until smooth. Stir in milk and cream. Over low heat, stirring constantly, cook until thick. Remove from heat. Stir in cheese, Tabasco, salt, pepper and soy sauce until cheese melts. Stir in water chestnuts. Cook beans according to package directions and drain. In a two-quart casserole or large baking dish, combine beans with sauce. Bake at 375° for 20 minutes or until heated through. Top with almonds. Serves eight.

Italian Style Fried Chicken

1 2½- to 3-pound broiler-fryer chicken, cut up

1/4 cup flour

2 tablespoons lemon juice

1/4 cup vegetable oil

1/2 teaspoon salt

1/4 teaspoon pepper

1 bay leaf

Grated Parmesan cheese

4 tablespoons butter

Coat chicken pieces lightly with flour and place on a large plate or shallow pan. Combine lemon juice, oil, salt, pepper and bay leaf. Beat well. Pour over chicken. Let stand one hour. Drain. Coat chicken with Parmesan cheese. In a large skillet, fry chicken in butter over medium heat until fork-tender, about 30 minutes. Serves four.

Anita C. Miller

Residency: Irvine California

Age: 27

Height: 5'8"

Weight: 130

School: Instructor Phys. Ed & Coach of field hockey at California State University, Long Beach

Training hours per week: 10

Rascal Salad

1/2 cup sugar

1/2 cup plus 1 tablespoon vinegar

1/3 cup vegetable oil

3 tablespoons water

1 tablespoon salt

1 small head cabbage, shredded

2 cucumbers, thinly sliced

1 carrot, sliced

1 green pepper, diced

1 onion, chopped

In a medium bowl, combine sugar, vinegar, oil, water and salt and mix well. Add vegetables, toss well, and marinate in refrigerator for 48 hours before serving. Serves six.

Contributors	Recipes

Anita C. Miller

Crabmeat Casserole Dip

1 8-ounce package cream cheese, softened

1 tablespoon milk

2 tablespoons finely chopped onion

1/2 teaspoon prepared horseradish

1/4 teaspoon salt

1 7-ounce package frozen crab meat, thawed, drained and flaked

Slivered or sliced almonds

In a medium bowl, blend all ingredients with electric mixer. Turn into a small (1 quart) casserole. Sprinkle with almonds. Bake at 375° for 15 minutes or unitl heated through. Serve with crackers. Serves 12.

Bikramjit Singh Randhawa

Residency: Hercules, California
Age: 26
Height: 5'11½"
Weight: 165
School: London
Training hours per week: 10

Double Fudge Pecan Brownies

1/2 cup butter

2 1-ounce squares unsweetened chocolate

1 cup sugar

½ cup flour

1 teaspoon baking powder

1 teaspoon vanilla

1 cup chopped pecans

2 eggs

Double Fudge Frosting (see directions)

In a medium pan, melt butter and chocolate together, stirring constantly, over low heat. Remove from heat. Stir in remaining ingredients, except eggs, and mix well. Add eggs and mix well. Turn into a greased 8x8-inch pan. Bake at 350° for 30 to 45 minutes or until a toothpick inserted in the center comes out clean. Cool slightly and frost with Double Fudge Frosting. Makes 16.

Double Fudge Frosting: In a medium pan over low heat, melt 2 1-ounce squares unsweetened chocolate with 3 tablespoons margarine and 1/3 cup milk, stirring constantly until well blended. Beat in 2 cups powdered sugar, 1/4 teaspoon salt and 1 teaspoon vanilla. Makes enough to frost a 8x8-inch cake or pan of brownies.

Homemade Noodles

1½ cup unbleached white flour

1/2 teaspoon salt

2 eggs

Combine flour with salt and dump in a mound on a wooden or marble surface. Make a well in the center. Break eggs into well. With a fork, gently beat eggs, stirring in flour at the same time. Mix and knead with hands, working in more flour if necessary, to form a stiff dough. Flour the working surface, or use a pastry cloth. With a well-floured rolling pin, roll dough out very thin. Turn dough often, rolling first one side, then the other. Keep pin and surface well-floured. Roll dough up into a tight, long roll. With a very sharp knife, cut into slightly diagonal slices about 1/4-inch thick. Separate and unroll slices. Place in a 200° oven for 30 minutes to one hour to dry. Cool and store in a tightly covered container in a cool, dry place. To cook, cook in boiling salted water for 20 to 25 minutes or until tender. May be cooked in soup. Makes about 8 ounces of noodles.

Nancy Pitkin White

Residency: McLean, Virginia
Age: 20
Height: 5'10"
Weight: 145
School: Stanford University
Training hours per week: 14

Hawaiian Broil Flank Steak

1 flank steak, about 1 pound
Freshly ground black pepper
1 cup pineapple juice
1/4 cup water
1/4 cup soy sauce
1 tablespoon brown sugar
1½ teaspoons ginger

Pierce meat all over with a fork. Sprinkle liberally with pepper and rub in. Place in a glass pan. Combine remaining ingredients and pour over steak. Cover and marinate for four hours or longer in refrigerator. Drain. Broil three inches from the heat, for four minutes on each side or until desired degree of doneness is reached. Slice in thin strips across the grain. Serves two.

Black Walnut Carrot Cake

2 cups sugar
1½ cups vegetable oil
4 eggs
1 tablespoon walnut extract
3 cups shredded carrots
2 cups self-rising flour
1½ teaspoons cinnamon
1 cup chopped black walnuts
Cream Cheese Frosting (see directions)

In a large bowl, cream sugar with oil. Beat in eggs and walnut extract. Beat in carrots. Beat in flour and cinnamon. Stir in nuts. Turn into a greased 10-inch tube pan. Bake at 350° for 1½ hours. Cool in pan for 15 minutes before removing. Frost with Cream Cheese Frosting when cool. Serves 12.

Cream Cheese Frosting: In a medium bowl beat 1 8-ounce package softened cream cheese with 1/4 cup softened butter or margarine and 2 teaspoons vanilla. Beat in 2 to 3 cups powdered sugar until desired consistency is reached. Makes enough to frost a 10-inch tube cake.

11

Gymnastics

Contributors:

Heidi A. Anderson
Christa Canary
Jackie Cassello
Bart Conner
James N. Hartung
Linda Kardos
Leslie Pyfer
Rhonda Schwandt
Kurt B. Thomas
Peter Vidmar

Jayne Jennifer Weinstein
Michael Gower Wilson
Tory Wilson

Although men's individual gymnastics appeared in the Olympic program in 1904, the popularity of the sport actually dates from TV coverage of the Rome Olympics in 1960. In the last five Games, the Japanese men have outscored the USSR every time; the USSR women have captured every team title since first entering the Games in Helsinki in 1952.

The USA has not won a gold medal in individual work since 1932 at Los Angeles when George Gulack won on the rings and Dallas Bixler took the horizontal bar exercise. In 1976 Peter Kormann was a bronze medalist in the floor exercises. For the 1980 Olympics, a new international rule prohibits judges from scoring events if there is a member of their own team competing.

The greatest woman gymnast in Olympic history is Laris Latynina, USSR with nine gold medals spread over three sets of Games—1956, 1960 and 1964. Winners of the combined exercises who have thrilled TV audiences include Czechoslovakia's Vera Caslavska in 1964 and 1968; Ludmilla Tourisheva, USSR 1972, and most recently at Montreal, Nadia Comaneci, who strung together several "perfect tens."

Japan's Sawao Kato was the men's combined exercises individual winner in 1968 and 1972. Kato was also runner up to Nikalai Andrianov, USSR for top honors in Montreal.

Contributors	Recipes

Heidi A. Anderson

Residency: Furlong,
Pennsylvania

Age: 16

Height: 4'11"

Weight: 86

School: Central Bucks East
High School

Training hours per week: 35

Green Bean Casserole

2 10-ounce packages frozen
French-cut green beans, or 2
16-ounce cans French-cut
green beans, drained

1/4 cup milk

1 10¾-ounce can cream of
mushroom soup

1/4 teaspoon pepper

1 3-ounce can French fried
onions

Cook frozen beans and drain. In a 1½-quart casserole, combine beans, milk, soup, pepper and half of onions. Bake at 350° for 30 minutes or until heated through. Garnish with remaining onions and bake five more minutes. Serves six.

Potato Chip Tuna
Noodle Casserole

1 pound noodles, cooked and
drained

1 12½-ounce can tuna, drained

2 10¾-ounce cans cream of
mushroom or chicken soup

2 soup cans milk

Potato chips

In a four-quart casserole or large baking dish, place a layer of noodles, followed by layers of tuna, crushed potato chips and soup mixed with milk. Repeat, until ingredients are used up, ending with a layer of potato chips. Bake at 325° for one hour. Serves six to eight.

Three Minute
Yogurt Pie

1 9-inch graham cracker crust

2 8-ounce cups lemon yogurt

1 9-ounce container frozen
nondairy whipped topping

1 tablespoon grated lemon rind

Fold yogurt and lemon rind into whipped topping. Pour into pie shell. Freeze about four hours or until firm. Remove from freezer 30 minutes before serving. Cut into wedges. Serves eight.

Christa Canary

Residency: Northbrook, Illinois

Age: 16

Height: 5'1"

Weight: 90

School: Glenbrook North High
School

Training hours per week: 30

Jello Salad

2 3-ounce packages lemon jello

3 bananas, sliced

8 marshmallows, cut up

1 15½-ounce can crushed
pineapple

1 tablespoon flour

1 egg

1/2 cup sugar

1 cup cream, whipped

Prepare jello as package directs. Stir in bananas, marshmallows and drained pineapple. (Reserve juice.) Pour into a 13x9-inch pan and chill. Meanwhile, measure pineapple juice and add water if necessary to make 1 cup. In a medium saucepan, combine juice, flour, egg and sugar. Bring to a boil and beat constantly until thick. Cool. Fold in whipped cream. Spread over chilled jello. Chill. Cut into squares. Serves 18.

Contributors	Recipes

Christa Canary

Chicken and Broccoli Casserole

4 chicken breasts, split in half

2 10-ounce packages frozen broccoli spears

2 10¾-ounce cans cream of chicken soup

1 cup mayonnaise

1 teaspoon lemon juice

1/2 teaspoon curry powder

1/2 cup shredded sharp Cheddar cheese

Cook chicken breasts in boiling water until meat turns white. Skin and bone breasts. Cook broccoli according to package directions, but only until thawed enough to separate spears. In a large casserole or 13x9-inch baking pan, place broccoli. Lay chicken over broccoli. Combine soup, mayonnaise, lemon juice and curry. Pour over chicken. Sprinkle with cheese. Bake at 350° for 25 minutes or until hot and bubbly. Serves four to six.

Jackie Cassello

Residency: Silver Spring, Maryland

Age: 13

Height: 4'7"

Weight: 70

School: Farquhar Middle School

Training hours per week: 30

Zucchini Bread

3 eggs

1 cup vegetable oil

2¼ cups sugar

2 cups grated zucchini

2 teaspoons vanilla

3 cups flour

1 teaspoon salt

1 teaspoon baking soda

1/4 teaspoon baking powder

2 teaspoons cinnamon

1 cup chopped nuts

In a large bowl beat eggs with oil and sugar. Beat in zucchini and vanilla. Stir in remaining dry ingredients. Stir in nuts. Pour into a greased 9x5-inch loaf pan. Bake at 325° for one hour. Bakes one large loaf.

Pineapple-Orange Jello

1 3-ounce package orange jello

1 cup boiling water

1 15½-ounce can crushed pineapple

1 raw carrot, grated

In a medium bowl, dissolve jello in boiling water. Stir in juice drained from can of pineapple. Chill until the consistency of unbeaten egg whites. Stir in pineapple and carrot. Chill until set. Serves four.

Nutritious Milkshake

8 ice cubes

1 cup water

1 cup skim milk powder

1/4 teaspoon vanilla

Combine all ingredients in electric blender and blend until the consistency of a milkshake. For variations, add honey, wheat germ, fresh or canned fruit or other flavorings. Serves one.

Contributors	Recipes

Bart Conner

Residency: Norman, Oklahoma
Age: 20
Height: 5'5"
Weight: 120
School: University of Oklahoma
Training hours per week: 21

Cheese and Bacon Puff

1 1/2 cups milk
3 eggs
1 cup flour
1 teaspoon bacon drippings
1 teaspoon Worcestershire sauce
1 teaspoon salt
1/2 teaspoon dry mustard
1/4 teaspoon cayenne pepper
1 cup shredded Cheddar cheese
6 slices bacon, cooked and crumbled
1/4 pound sliced mushrooms
1 cup chopped green pepper

Beat together eggs, flour, drippings, Worchestershire, salt, mustard and cayenne. Stir in cheese, bacon, mushrooms and green pepper. Pour into a greased 9-inch pie pan. Bake at 325° for 45 minutes. Serves four to six.

Special Salad

1/4 cup sugar
1 teaspoon salt
1 teaspoon dry mustard
1 tablespoon onion juice
1/3 cup wine vinegar
1 cup vegetable oil
1 tablespoon poppy seeds
1/2 pound fresh mushrooms, sliced
Fresh spinach
Red leaf lettuce
1½ cups small curd cottage cheese
1/2 cup bacon bits

In a pint jar, combine sugar, salt, mustard, onion juice, vinegar, oil and poppy seeds. Shake well to blend. In a large salad bowl, place mushrooms and salad greens, torn into bite-size pieces. Combine with dressing and let set to blend flavors. Add cottage cheese and bacon bits and toss. Serves four to six.

James N. Hartung

Residency: Omaha, Nebraska
Age: 18
Height: 5'5"
Weight: 135
School: Nebraska University
Training hours per week: 24

Sesame Citrus Dressing

2 tablespoons toasted sesame seeds
2 tablespoons honey
1 teaspoon grated orange rind
1 teaspoon grated lemon rind
1/8 teaspoon salt
1 cup plain yogurt

Combine all ingredients in a small bowl or jar. Stir until well blended. Cover and refrigerate. Serve over fruit salads. Makes about one cup.

Contributors	Recipes

James N. Hartung

Beef Sprout Patties

1 pound ground beef

1 cup chopped bean sprouts

1 clove garlic, minced

1/4 cup minced onion

1/4 cup tomato juice, sauce or ketchup

2 tablespoons soy sauce

1 teaspoon basil

Combine all ingredients, mixing by hand until soft, moist and well blended. Shape into patties. Broil or fry as desired. Serves four.

Linda Kardos

Residency: Bethel Park, Pennsylvania

Age: 16

Height: 4'11"

Weight: 80

School: Bethel Park High School

Training hours per week: 6

Baked Stuffed Chicken Breasts

3 whole broiler-fryer chicken breasts, split in half

6 thin slices cooked ham

6 thin slices Swiss cheese

1 package seasoned coating mix for chicken

Skin and bone chicken breasts. With a rolling pin, pound meat between layers of waxed paper until very thin. Top each piece of chicken with a slice of ham and a slice of cheese. Roll up and secure with a toothpick. Dredge in coating mix. Bake on an ungreased baking sheet at 400° for 20 minutes or until fork-tender. Serves four to six.

Hot Tuna-Filled Finger Rolls

1/4 pound American cheese, cut into 1/4-inch cubes

3 hard-boiled eggs, chopped

1 7-ounce can tuna

2 tablespoons chopped green pepper

2 tablespoons chopped onion

2 tablespoons sliced stuffed green olives (optional)

2 tablespoons chopped sweet pickles or pickle relish

1/2 cup mayonnaise

8 hot dog buns

Combine all ingredients except buns. Mix well and fill buns. Wrap in foil and bake at 325° for 25 minutes. Makes eight sandwiches.

Pallidos (Anise Sticks)

2 cups flour

1 teaspoon baking powder

1/4 teaspoon salt

3/4 cup sugar

1/4 cup vegetable shortening

2 eggs, beaten

2 drops anise oil or extract

Melted margarine or butter

Combine dry ingredients in medium bowl. With a pastry blender or two knives, cut in shortening until mixture is the size of peas. Stir in eggs and anise. Mix well with hands. Roll out on a floured surface 1/4-inch thick. Cut into sticks 4x1/2-inch. Place on an ungreased baking sheet about 1/2-inch apart. Brush with melted margarine or butter. Bake at 375° for 10 to 12 minutes. Makes three to four dozen.

Leslie Pyfer

Residency: Eugene, Oregon

Age: 16

Height: 5'2"

Weight: 90

*School: South Eugene
High School*

Training hours per week: 7

Hamburger Soup

2 pounds ground beef

2 tablespoons olive oil or
vegetable oil

1/2 teaspoon salt

1/4 teaspoon pepper

1/4 teaspoon oregano

1/4 teaspoon basil

1/8 teaspoon seasoned salt

1 1⅞-ounce packet dried
onion soup mix

6 cups boiling water

1 8-ounce can tomato sauce

1 tablespoon soy sauce

1 cup chopped celery leaves

1 cup sliced carrots

1/3 cup dried split peas

1 cup elbow macaroni

Grated Parmesan cheese

In a large kettle with a tight lid, brown meat in oil. Add salt, pepper, oregano, basil, seasoned salt and soup mix. Stir in water, tomato sauce and soy sauce. Cover and simmer for 15 minutes. Add celery leaves, carrots, split peas and macaroni. Cover and simmer for 30 minutes, adding more water if necessary. Serve topped with grated cheese. Serves eight or more.

Orange Julius

1 12-ounce can frozen orange
juice concentrate

1 to 2 cups milk

1 teaspoon vanilla

5 to 6 ice cubes

Combine all ingredients in electric blender and blend until thick and foamy. For variations, add yogurt, fresh fruit or other kinds of fruit juices. Serves two.

Green Beans Deluxe

1 10-ounce package frozen
French-cut green beans, or 1
16-ounce can French-cut
green beans

1 tablespoon butter or
margarine

1/2 cup diced cooked ham

1 clove garlic, minced

1/2 teaspoon salt

Dash of pepper

1 medium tomato, cut in
wedges

Cook frozen green beans according to package directions. Or, heat canned beans and drain. Melt butter in medium saucepan. Add ham and garlic and cook until garlic is soft. Stir in beans, salt and pepper. Top with tomato wedges. Cover and heat through. Serves four.

Contributors	Recipes

Rhonda Schwandt

Residency: Los Alamitos,
California

Age: 15

Height: 4'11½"

Weight: 110

School: Los Alamitos High
School

Training hours per week: 25

Peanut Butter Fudge

2 cups sugar

1 cup milk

2 teaspoons light corn syrup

1 teaspoon butter

1 cup marshmallow creme

1 cup chunky peanut butter

Combine sugar, milk and corn syrup in a medium saucepan. Cook over medium heat, stirring frequently, to soft ball stage. Remove from heat. Stir in remaining ingredients until well blended. Pour into a buttered 8 x 11-inch glass pan. Cool in refrigerator. Cut into squares. Makes about three dozen pieces.

Power Shake

1 cup pineapple juice

1/2 cup frozen unsweetened strawberries

1/3 cup skim milk powder

1 cup cracked ice

Combine all ingredients in electric blender and blend until thick and foamy. Other fruit may be substituted for strawberries. Serves two.

Kurt B. Thomas

Residency: Terre Haute,
Indiana

Age: 22

Height: 5'5"

Weight: 127

School: Indiana State
University

Training hours per week: 42

Stuffed Celery

1 3-ounce package cream cheese, softened

1 4-ounce can deviled ham

1/2 cup finely chopped walnuts

Celery stalks

Combine cheese, ham and nuts until well blended. Stuff celery stalks. Makes about 1 cup stuffing mixture.

Sugar Cream Pie

1 9-inch baked pie shell

1 cup sugar

1/4 cup cornstarch

2¼ cups half and half or mixture of milk and cream

1/4 cup butter or margarine

1 teaspoon vanilla

Cinnamon or nutmeg

Combine sugar and cornstarch in a medium pan. Stir in half and half. Over low heat, stirring constantly, cook until thick. Stir in butter until melted. Stir in vanilla. Pour into pie shell. Sprinkle with cinnamon or nutmeg. Chill. Serves six to eight.

Contributors	Recipes

Kurt B. Thomas

Broccoli Casserole

1 medium onion, chopped

1/4 cup butter or margarine

1/2 cup pasturized process cheese spread

1/2 cup milk

1/4 cup water

1 10¾-ounce can cream of chicken soup

1 cup quick-cooking rice

1 10-ounce package frozen chopped broccoli

In a large saucepan, saute onion in butter until tender. Remove from heat and stir in cheese, milk, water and soup. If necessary, heat slightly, stirring constantly, to thoroughly blend mixture. Stir in rice and broccoli. Turn into a greased two-quart casserole and bake at 350° for 30 minutes. Stir with a fork halfway through cooking time to fluff rice and distribute broccoli. Serves four to six.

Peter Vidmar

Residency: Los Angeles, California

Age: 17

Height: 5'5"

Weight: 127

School: Brentwood School

Training hours per week: 30

Italian Style Stuffed Chicken Breasts

3 whole boiler-fryer chicken breasts, split in half

Sharp Cheddar cheese

1 egg

2 tablespoons milk

Flour

Italian seasoned bread crumbs

Skin and bone chicken breasts. Place each breast half between two sheets of waxed paper. With a rolling pin, pound until quite thin. Place wedge of cheese in center of meat. Roll up and secure with toothpicks. In a small bowl, beat together milk and egg. Coat chicken rolls with flour, then milk mixture and finally bread crumbs. Place in a greased small casserole or 8x8-inch baking pan. Bake at 350° for 45 minutes or until tender and lightly browned. Serves four.

Sugar Cookies

1 cup butter

2 teaspoons vanilla

1½ cups sugar

2 eggs, beaten

4 cups flour

1/4 teaspoon nutmeg

1 teaspoon soda

Pinch of salt

In medium mixing bowl, cream together butter, vanilla and sugar. Beat in eggs. Combine remaining dry ingredients and stir into egg mixture. Work in last of flour mixture with hands, if necessary, using only enough flour to keep dough from being too soft. Chill dough for several hours for easier handling. Roll dough out on floured surface and cut into desired shapes. Sprinkle with sugar, place on ungreased cookie sheets and bake at 350° for 12 minutes. Makes about four dozen cookies.

Jayne Jennifer Weinstein

Residency: Eugene, Oregon

Age: 15

Height: 5'

Weight: 85

School: Sheldon High School

Training hours per week: 42

Strawberry Supreme

1 3-ounce package strawberry jello

1/4 cup sugar

1½ cups boiling water

1 1-pound package frozen strawberries (unsweetened)

1 cup whipping cream, whipped

In large bowl, dissolve jello and sugar in boiling water. Add strawberries and stir until berries separate. Refrigerate until slightly thick. Fold in whipped cream. Spoon into individual sherbet glasses. Chill. Serves six to eight.

Contributors	Recipes

Jayne Jennifer Weinstein

Bagel Sandwiches

6 egg bagels

1/2 pound sliced hard salami

1 8-ounce package cream cheese

1 avocado, sliced

2 tomatoes, sliced

1 cucumber, sliced

Lettuce

Mayonnaise

Slice bagels in half and spread with mayonnaise. On one half, place cream cheese and salami. On other half place tomato, cucumber and lettuce. Put halves together. Serves four to six.

Michael Gower Wilson

Residency: Moore, Oklahoma
Age: 22
Height: 5'5"
Weight: 125
School: University of Oklahoma
Training hours per week: 19

Oriental Green Casserole

1½ pounds ground beef

1/2 cup chopped celery

1/2 cup chopped onion

1/2 cup chopped green pepper

1½ cups water

1/4 cup cornstarch

1 tablespoon sugar

3/4 teaspoon ginger

1/3 cup soy sauce

1/4 cup water

1 6-ounce can bamboo shoots, drained

1 6-ounce package frozen pea pods, thawed

1 10-ounce package frozen peas

1 3-ounce can chow mein noodles

In a large skillet, brown meat with celery, onion and green pepper. Drain off excess fat. Add water and bring to a boil. In a small bowl, mix cornstarch, sugar, ginger, soy sauce and water until smooth. Stir into meat mixture and cook, stirring frequently, until thickened. Stir in bamboo shoots, pea pods and peas. Turn into a three-quart casserole. Top with noodles. Bake at 375° for 40 minutes. Serves 10 to 12.

Tory Wilson

Residency: Lawton, Oklahoma
Age: 15
Height: 5'
Weight: 94
School: Eisenhower Senior High School
Training hours per week: 26

Mexican Casserole

2 pounds ground beef

1 medium onion, chopped

1 10-ounce package frozen or refrigerated tortillas, quartered (about 12)

½ pound grated Cheddar cheese

1 10¾-ounce can cream of mushroom soup

1 10¾-ounce can cream of chicken soup

1 8-ounce can evaporated milk

1 8-ounce can or bottle taco sauce

1 4-ounce can green chilies

In a large skillet, brown meat with onions. Line a shallow, greased two-quart casserole with quartered tortillas. Layer meat, cheese and tortillas. Repeat, ending with tortillas. Combine remaining ingredients. Pour over top. Bake at 350° for 35 to 40 minutes. Serves eight.

Tory Wilson

Shrimp Tempura

2 eggs, beaten

2 teaspoons soy sauce

3/4 cup water

1 cup flour

1/4 teaspoon salt

6 large shrimp, peeled and deveined

Assortment of fresh vegetables, sliced 1/2-inch thick, such as broccoli flowerets, sweet potatoes, green onions and eggplant

Oil for frying

In a small bowl, combine eggs, soy sauce and water. Gradually add flour and salt and beat until smooth. Dip shrimp and vegetables into batter and fry in at least three inches of oil at 350° to 375° in a deep fryer or a Dutch oven until golden. Drain and serve. Serves two.

Stuffed Cabbage Rolls

8 large cabbage leaves

1 pound ground beef

1 cup cooked rice

1/4 cup chopped onion

1 egg, beaten

1 teaspoon salt

1/4 teaspoon pepper

1 10¾-ounce can condensed tomato soup

In a large pan, cook cabbage leaves in boiling salted water until soft. Drain. Combine beef, rice, onion, egg, salt, pepper and 2 tablespoons soup. Divide meat mixture among cabbage leaves. Roll and secure with toothpicks. Place rolls in an 8x8-inch baking dish. Pour remaining soup over rolls. Cover. Bake at 350° for about 40 minutes. Serves four.

B & M Beans

2 20-ounce cans pork and beans

4 to 5 tablespoons molasses

4 to 5 tablespoons catsup

4 to 5 tablespoons barbecue sauce

3 to 4 strips bacon

In a three-quart casserole or baking dish, combine beans with molasses, catsup and barbecue sauce. Lay strips of raw bacon over top of beans. Bake at 375° for one hour. Serves six to eight.

12

Judo

Event Days:

Sunday, July 27, 1980	Friday, August 1, 1980
Monday, July 28, 1980	Saturday, August 2, 1980
Tuesday, July 29, 1980	
Wednesday, July 30, 1980	
Thursday, July 31, 1980	

Contributors:

Brett Dewey Barron
Charles L. Hooks
Teimoc Jonston-Ono
Thomas Gerard Martin
Paul K. Maruyama
Keith Nakasone
John Saylor
Michael L. Swain

Although Judo did not make its debut in the games until 1964 this comparatively young Olympic sport has its roots in the much older wrestling school of jujitsu. This appears to have gotten its start during Japan's feudal age when class distinctions forbade commoners from wearing swords. Thus jujitsu was born out of necessity for self defense.

The father of Judo was Jigoro Kano who introduced it at a Judo Institute in Tokyo in 1882. Since it is theoretically possible for a skilled *judoka* to win over an opponent twice his weight, Kano used competitive classes based on skills rather than weight. These are the recognized belt ratings.

Kano in 1909 became the first Japanese appointed to the prestigious International Olympic Committee. Judo was introduced in the USA in 1902 when Professor Yamishita came to this country at the invitation of President Theodore Roosevelt.

When judo was contested at Tokyo there were four weight classes and James Bregman USA, won a bronze medal in the middleweight class. At Montreal there were six classes and Allen Coage won a bronze medal in the heavyweight class.

Japan and the Netherlands had been dominant countries in the early years. However at Montreal, Japan won three gold, one silver and one bronze, followed by the Soviet Union with two gold and two silver medals.

Brett Dewey Barron

Residency: San Mateo,
*   California*

Age: 19

Height: 5'10"

Weight: 172

Training hours per week: 25

Quick Beef Stroganoff

8 ounces uncooked noodles

1 beef bouillon cube, or 1
   teaspoon instant beef
   bouillon

1 clove garlic, minced

1/3 cup chopped onion

2 tablespoons vegetable oil

1 pound ground beef

2 tablespoons flour

2 teaspoons salt

1/2 teaspoon paprika

2 3-ounce cans sliced or whole
   mushrooms

1 10¾-ounce can cream of
   chicken soup

1 cup sour cream

Chopped parsley for garnish

Begin cooking noodles in bouillon and water, according to package directions. In a large skillet, brown garlic, onion and ground beef in oil. Sprinkle with flour, salt, paprika and mushrooms and stir. Cook over medium low heat for about five minutes. Stir in soup and simmer for 10 minutes. Stir in sour cream and heat through over low heat; do not boil. Pile drained noodles on a platter, top with stroganoff and sprinkle with parsley. Serves four.

Spaghetti Sauce

2 tablespoons olive oil

1 clove garlic, minced

1/4 cup chopped onion

1 cup chopped fresh
   mushrooms

1 pound ground beef

1 8-ounce tomato sauce

1 16-ounce can whole
   tomatoes

1 6-ounce can tomato paste

1/2 teaspoon basil

1/2 teaspoon oregano

1/2 teaspoon thyme

2 tablespoons sugar

1/2 teaspoon salt

Dash of pepper

In a large saucepan, brown garlic, onion, mushrooms and beef in olive oil. Add remaining ingredients; mix well. Cover and simmer for 1½ hours, stirring occasionally. Serve over cooked spaghetti. Makes 5½ cups sauce, enough to serve four to six.

Contributors	Recipes

Brett Dewey Barron

Peanut Blossoms

1/2 cup sugar

1/2 cup brown sugar

1/2 cup vegetable shortening

1/2 cup creamy peanut butter

1 egg

2 tablespoons milk

1 teaspoon vanilla extract

1¾ cups flour

1 teaspoon baking soda

1/2 teaspoon salt

48 milk chocolate kisses, unwrapped

In a large bowl, cream sugars with shortening and peanut butter. Beat in egg, milk and vanilla. Combine remaining dry ingredients and mix in until well combined. Chill dough for 30 minutes. Roll dough into one-inch balls. Place on ungreased cookie sheets. Bake at 375° for 12 minutes or until lightly browned. Remove from oven. Immediately press a chocolate kiss in the center of each. (Cookie will crack around edges.) Remove from cookie sheets and cool. Makes four dozen cookies, about 70 calories each.

Charles L. Hooks

Residency: Granger, Indiana
Age: 40
Height: 6'2"
Weight: 238
School: Kent State University
Training hours per week: 12

Italian Salad

1 small head fresh cauliflower, separated into flowerettes

1/2 cup pitted ripe olives

1 green pepper, cut into strips

1 large carrot, sliced

1/2 pound fresh mushrooms, sliced

1½ cups regular or wine vinegar

1/4 cup sugar

1/2 teaspoon pepper

1 cup vegetable oil

1½ teaspoons salt

2 teaspoons oregano

Combine all vegetables in a large bowl. In a medium pan, combine remaining ingredients and heat, stirring, until sugar is dissolved. Cool dressing. Pour over salad, toss to coat well and refrigerate for 24 hours before serving, stirring occasionally. Serves six to eight.

Granola

4 cups quick-cooking rolled oats

1½ cups unsweetened flaked coconut

1 cup almonds or cashews

1 cup sunflower seeds

1 cup sesame seeds

1 cup wheat germ

1/2 cup flax seed (optional)

1/2 cup toasted soy beans (optional)

1 cup bran

1 teaspoon salt

1/2 cup vegetable oil

3/4 cup honey

1 teaspoon vanilla

Combine all dry ingredients in a large roasting pan. In a small pan, bring oil, honey and vanilla to a boil. Pour over dry ingredients. Mix well. Bake at 325° for 15 minutes, stirring several times. Cool and store in a tightly covered container in a cool, dry place. Makes about three quarts.

Contributors	Recipes

Charles L. Hooks

Company Wild Rice

1 6¼-ounce box fast-cooking long grain and wild rice

1 small onion, chopped

2 stalks celery, chopped

1/4 cup chopped green pepper

2 to 3 cups chopped cooked meat, such as chicken, turkey, beef

1 10¾-ounce can cream of mushroom soup

1 10¾-ounce can Cheddar cheese soup

1 4-ounce can button mushrooms (optional)

Dash of soy sauce

1/2 teaspoon salt

1/4 teaspoon pepper

Milk

Cook rice according to package directions. In a two-quart casserole, combine rice with all ingredients except milk and mix well. Add enough milk to cover rice mixture. Cover and bake at 350° for 45 to 55 minutes. Serves four.

Teimoc Jonston-Ono

Residency: New York City, New York

Age: 23

Height: 6'

Weight: 174

School: Christie's Fine Arts Course

Training hours per week: 18

Blender Bender

1½ cups raw milk or fresh orange juice

1 egg, shell and all

1/4 cup high-protein powder

2 tablespoons brewer's yeast

1 very ripe banana

2 tablespoons raw honey

2 tablespoons lecithin

1 tablespoon wheat germ oil

4 cubes or 2/3 cup ice

Combine all ingredients in electric blender. Blend until smooth and drink slowly. Serves one.

Thomas Gerard Martin

Residency: Stockton, California

Age: 22

Height: 5'11"

School: Delta College

Training hours per week: 6

Mushroom Savory T-Bone Steak

T-bone steak (amount depends on servings desired)

1 tablespoon vegetable oil

1 small onion, chopped

1 clove garlic, minced

1 1⅞-ounce packet dry mushroom soup mix

2 cups water

1/4 cup dry red wine

In a large skillet, brown steak on both sides in oil. Remove steak and set aside. Saute onion and garlic until golden. Stir in soup mix and water, scraping pan to loosen brown bits. Cook, stirring constantly, until slightly thick. Stir in wine. Place steak in gravy. Cover and simmer for 30 to 45 minutes. Number of servings depends on size and amount of steak. Round steak or chuck steak may also be used.

Contributors	Recipes

Thomas Gerard Martin

Fish Chowder

2 ounces salt pork, diced

1 medium onion, chopped

2 stalks celery, chopped

1 bay leaf

1/2 teaspoon thyme

1 tablespoon chopped parsley

2 cups water

1 cup clam juice

1 cup dry white wine

1/2 teaspoon salt

1/2 teaspoon pepper

1/2 pound fish fillets, cut in pieces

1 pound shelled raw shrimp, fresh or frozen

1 pound mussels in their shells, cleaned

1 10-ounce package frozen corn

Fry salt pork in a skillet until brown. Add to crockpot with all ingredients except fish, shrimp, mussels and corn. Cover and cook on low for six to eight hours. Add remaining ingredients and cook on high, covered, for 30 minutes. Serves six.

Shrimp Quiche

1 10-inch baked pie shell

2 tablespoons butter

1/2 teaspoon salt

1/8 teaspoon nutmeg

1 teaspoon oregano

1/8 teaspoon pepper

1½ cups cooked shrimp, whole or broken

1/2 cup dry white wine

1/2 cup shredded Gruyere cheese

5 eggs

2 cups milk

1 tablespoon tomato paste

2 dashes Tabasco sauce

Melt butter in a large skillet. Add salt, nutmeg, oregano, pepper and shrimp. Saute about two minutes. Add wine and boil until most of liquid has evaporated. Spread shrimp mixture over bottom of pie shell. Sprinkle with cheese. Beat together remaining ingredients and pour over cheese. Bake at 375° for 35 to 45 minutes or until set. Serves four to six.

Contributors	Recipes

Paul K. Maruyama

Residency: Monument, Colorado

Age: 37

Height: 5'6"

Weight: 154

School: BS–San Jose State University, MBA–University of Hawaii

Training hours per week: 20

Crab Hot Dish

1 medium onion, diced

1/2 medium green pepper, diced

1/4 cup butter or margarine

2 cups cooked rice

2 tablespoons diced pimiento

1 cup grated American cheese

1 6 to 7-ounce can crab meat

1⅓ cups half and half

Celery salt, salt and pepper

In a medium skillet, saute onion and green pepper in butter until tender. Combine with remaining ingredients. Season to taste. Turn into a 1½-quart casserole and bake uncovered at 350° for 40 minutes. Serves four.

Fried Shrimp Toast

1 pound shrimp, cleaned and minced

1/2 pound ground pork, minced

1 teaspoon ginger juice

1 tablespoon rice wine or dry white wine

1 teaspoon salt

1 egg white

1 tablespoon cornstarch

1/2 teaspoon pepper

2 tablespoons chopped ham

2 tablespoons chopped parsley

8 slices day-old bread, crusts removed, cut into small squares

Oil for deep frying

Thoroughly combine shrimp, pork, ginger, wine, salt, egg white, cornstarch and pepper. Shape small mounds of shrimp mixture on each square of bread. Sprinkle with ham and parsley. Press down lightly. Heat oil in deep fryer or deep heavy pan to 375°. Deep fry, shrimp side down, then bread side down, until golden brown. Drain and serve hot. Makes 32 appetizers.

Keith Nakasone

Residency: San José, California

Age: 23

Height: 5'6"

Weight: 143

School: San José State University

Training hours per week: 10

Broccoli Chicken Casserole

1 10-ounce package frozen chopped broccoli

2 6-ounce cans boned chicken, or 1½ cups chopped, cooked chicken or turkey

1 10¾-ounce can cream of mushroom soup

1/2 cup mayonnaise

1/4 teaspoon curry powder

1/2 cup bread crumbs

1/2 cup melted butter or margarine

Cook broccoli according to package directions; drain well and place in the bottom of a buttered 1½-quart casserole or baking dish. Arrange chicken over broccoli. Mix together soup, mayonnaise, and curry; pour over chicken. Sprinkle with bread crumbs. Drizzle with butter. Bake at 350° for 30 to 40 minutes. Serves four.

Contributors	Recipes

Keith Nakasone

Joe's Special

1 10-ounce package frozen chopped spinach

3 tablespoons olive oil

1 pound ground beef

1 small onion, chopped

1/4 to 1/2 pound fresh mushrooms, sliced

6 eggs, beaten

Salt and pepper to taste

Cook spinach according to package directions. Drain well and set aside. In a large skillet, brown beef, onion and mushrooms in olive oil. Stir in spinach. Pour in beaten eggs and cook, stirring, until eggs are firm. Season to taste with salt and pepper. Serves four to six.

John Saylor

Residency: Lucas, Ohio

Age: 25

Height: 6'1"

Weight: 228

School: Ohio State University,

Training hours per week: 23

Granola

10 cups rolled oats, quick or old-fashioned or a mixture

1 cup skim milk powder

1 cup raw wheat germ

1 cup bran

1 cup nuts and/or seeds (such as sunflower, sesame or almonds)

1/2 cup raisins

1/2 cup unsweetened flaked coconut

2 eggs, beaten

1 cup vegetable oil

1 cup honey

1½ teaspoons vanilla

Combine all dry ingredients in a large roasting pan. Beat eggs until foamy. Beat in oil, honey and vanilla. Pour over dry ingredients. Stir until well mixed. Bake at 225° for one hour, stirring occasionally. Makes about three quarts.

Michael L. Swain

Residency: Bridgewater, New Jersey

Age: 18

Height: 5'10"

Weight: 143

School: Bridgewater-Raritan High School

Training hours per week: 8

Pineapple Casserole

1/2 cup butter or margarine

1 cup sugar

4 eggs

1 16-ounce can crushed pineapple

5 slices white bread, crusts removed, cubed

In a medium bowl, cream butter and sugar. Beat in eggs one at a time. Stir in pineapple with juice. Fold in bread cubes. Turn into a greased 1½-quart casserole. Bake uncovered at 350° for 45 minutes or until lightly browned. Serves six to eight.

Cheese Bake Judy

12 slices white bread, crusts removed

1/2 pound shredded Cheddar cheese

2 cups cooked, crumbled bacon

6 eggs, beaten

3 cups milk

Salt, pepper and paprika

Place six slices of bread in a buttered 13x9-inch pan. Sprinkle with cheese and bacon. Top with remaining bread slices. In a medium bowl, beat eggs, milk, salt and pepper. Pour over bread. Refrigerate three hours or overnight. Bring to room temperature. Sprinkle with paprika. Bake at 350° for 45 minutes or until set and golden brown. Serves six to eight.

13

Modern Pentathlon

Event Days:

Sunday,
July 20, 1980

Monday,
July 21, 1980

Tuesday,
July 22, 1980

Wednesday,
July 23, 1980

Thursday,
July 24, 1980

Contributors

Michael E. Burley
John D. Fitzgerald
Neil Glenesk
R. Gregory Losey

The modern pentathlon was introduced in the 1912 Olympic Games at Stockholm where the USA competitor was a young Army lieutenant, George S. Patton, Jr., who placed fifth.

The modern pentathlon consists of five different sports over a five-day period. The first event is the show jumping, followed by a round robin épée fencing tournament followed by pistol shooting. The final two events are a 300-meter freestyle swim against the clock and then the grueling 4,000 meter cross-country run over hill and dale (against the clock). The Olympic champion should be recognized as the No. 1 versatile athlete of the Games.

There is an individual competition and synthetic team competition in the Olympic Games. In the first nine individual competitions, Swedish pentathletes won eight times, including victories by Lars Hall in 1952 and 1956.

In the last five Olympic Games Sweden has had only a single winner, Hungary has had two, the USSR and Poland one each. The synthetic team competition dates from 1952 and Hungary has won four times, the USSR twice and Great Britain in 1976.

The competition in Montreal was almost earth shattering. The individual victor was Janusz Pyciak-Peciak of Poland while Great Britain nailed down its first team diadem by a superior performance in the cross-country run. But along with the thrilling competition the saddest note was the disqualification of USSR's many-time medalist, Boris Onishenko, for "altering" his épée.

Contributors	Recipes

Michael E. Burley

Residency: Austin, Texas
Age: 26
Height: 6'
Weight: 145
*School: University of
  Texas/Austin*
Training hours per week: 25

Bar-B-Q Sauce

1/4 cup butter
1 medium onion, finely
  chopped
1/4 cup lemon juice
1/2 cup catsup or 1 6-ounce
  can tomato paste
1½ teaspoons salt
2 tablespoons brown sugar
1/2 cup chicken broth or
  bouillon
1 tablespoon prepared mustard
1 clove garlic, minced
1/4 teaspoon Tabasco sauce
1/2 teaspoon freshly ground
  black pepper
1 teaspoon Worcestershire
  sauce

In a medium pan, saute onion in butter until tender. Add remaining ingredients and simmer, uncovered, stirring occasionally, for about 30 minutes. Store in refrigerator. Makes about two cups sauce.

John D. Fitzgerald

Residency: San Antonio, Texas
Age: 30
Height: 6'1"
Weight: 170
School: Villanova University
Training hours per week: 32

Parkie's French Dressing

1 10-ounce bottle catsup
1½ cups vegetable oil
1 cup vinegar
1 tablespoon salt
1/2 cup sugar
1 tablespoon Worcestershire
  sauce
1 cube ice

Combine all ingredients in electric blender and blend until creamy. (Dressing can also be made in a quart jar; it won't look as creamy, but will have the same taste and texture.) Makes about one quart dressing.

Fitz's Lemon Icebox Cake

1 cup sugar
1/2 cup butter
2 egg yolks
Juice and grated rind of 1
  lemon
2 egg whites, beaten stiff
1½ dozen lady fingers
Whipped cream

In a medium bowl, cream butter and sugar. Beat in egg yolks and lemon juice and rind. Carefully fold in egg whites. In a loaf pan lined with waxed paper, alternate mixture with layers of lady fingers. Refrigerate for 24 hours. Serve with whipped cream. Serves eight.

Contributors	Recipes

Neil Glenesk

Residency: San Antonio, Texas
Age: 26
Height: 5'6"
Weight: 135
School: Trinity University
Training hours per week: 40

Crab Quiche

1 9-inch unbaked pie shell
1/2 cup mayonnaise
1/2 cup milk
2 tablespoons flour
2 eggs, beaten
1 8-ounce can or package
  crab, drained and flaked
1/2 pound grated Swiss cheese
1/2 cup sliced green onions

Beat together mayonnaise, milk, flour and eggs, stir in crab, cheese and onions. Pour into pie shell. Bake at 350° for 40 to 45 minutes. Serves four.

R. Gregory Losey

Residency: San Antonio, Texas
Age: 29
Height: 6'2"
Weight: 180
*School: U.S. Military
  Academy–West Point*
Training hours per week: 40

Banana Thirst Quencher

2 cups pineapple juice
2 peeled ripe bananas
1 tray ice cubes

Combine all ingredients in electric blender and blend until frothy and ice is crushed. Serves two.

Whole Wheat Gingerbread

2 cups molasses
3/4 cup butter or margarine
1/2 teaspoon baking soda
1 teaspoon ginger
1 teaspoon nutmeg
1 teaspoon cinnamon
3 cups whole wheat flour
1 teaspoon baking powder
1 cup milk
1 tablespoon lemon juice
1 egg, beaten
1 cup heavy cream, whipped

In a large pan, bring molasses and butter to a boil, stirring constantly. Remove from heat. Stir in soda and spices. Combine flour and baking powder. Combine milk and lemon juice. Add flour and milk alternately in thirds, mixing well after each addition. Mix in egg. Pour into a greased 13x9-inch pan. Bake at 350° for 45 minutes. Cool, cut into squares and serve with whipped cream. Serves 12.

Salad Sandwich Surprise

2 slices whole wheat bread
Alfalfa sprouts
1/2 avocado, sliced
Sliced cheese
Sliced cucumber
Mayonnaise
Pepper

Spread bread with mayonnaise. Arrange other ingredients on bread for either an open-face or closed sandwich. Sprinkle with pepper. Serves one.

14
Rowing

Event Days:

Sunday, July 20, 1980	Friday, July 25, 1980
Monday, July 21, 1980	Saturday, July 26, 1980
Tuesday, July 22, 1980	Sunday, July 27, 1980
Wednesday, July 23, 1980	
Thursday, July 24, 1980	

Contributors:

Carol P. Brown
Richard M. Cashin, Jr.
Cosema E. Crawford
Anita L. DeFrantz
Hollis Straley Hatton
Elizabeth Hills
Joan Lind
William D. Purdy
Kurt F. Somerville
Gregg Stone

Nancy Storrs
Tom Woodman

Rowing for men has been a part of the Olympic program since the 1900 Games in Paris; the women rowed for the first time in Montreal in 1976.

The USA has enjoyed great success in the sport with 128 men sharing in the total output of 137 gold medals. Greatest success has come in the eights with coxswain with ten Olympic titles; eight in a row between 1920 and 1956 using college crews—three for the U. of California at Berkely, two for the U.S. Naval Academy and Yale and one for Washington. The Vesper Boat Club of Philadelphia won the inaugural eights at Paris in 1900 and also notched the last USA triumph in 1964 in Japan, with the most mature eight entered by the USA up to that time.

John B. Kelly, Sr., stroked the winning double sculls in 1920 and 1924 and rowed to victory in a single in 1920. Paul V. Costello was a gold medalist in 1920, 1924 and 1928 in the double sculls event, pairing with Charles McIlvaine in 1928 and with Mr. Kelly in the other two races.

In the last three Olympics, East Germany has accounted for two gold medals in 1968, three in 1972, and five in 1976 for men, three for women. For the USA women in Montreal, Joan Lind finished second in the single sculls and the women's eight placed third behind East Germany and the USSR. Only medals won by men were in the pairs without coxswain, Calvin Coffey and Michael Staines, earning the silver.

Carol P. Brown

*Residency: Seattle,
Washington*

Age: 25

Height: 5'7½"

Weight: 148

*School: Princeton University,
Graduate School–University
of Washington*

Training hours per week: 35

Zucchini Supreme

2 medium zucchini, sliced

Parmesan cheese

Salt and pepper

1 15-ounce can whole
tomatoes, drained

1 medium onion, chopped

1/4 pound fresh mushrooms,
sliced, or 1 4-ounce jar sliced
mushrooms

2 cups grated Cheddar cheese

In a two-quart casserole or baking dish, place a layer of zucchini. Sprinkle with Parmesan cheese and salt and pepper. Then add layers of tomatoes, onions, mushrooms and Cheddar cheese. Repeat layers. Bake at 350° for one hour. Serves four.

Orange Whip Dessert

1 3-ounce package orange jello

1 9 ounce container frozen
nondairy whipped topping

1 pound cottage cheese

1 11-ounce can mandarin
oranges, drained

In a medium bowl, stir unprepared jello and whipped topping together until blended. Stir in cottage cheese and drained oranges. Refrigerate until serving time. (Other flavors of jello and fruit may be used.) Serves six.

Broccoli Casserole

2 10-ounce packages frozen
chopped broccoli, or 1 large
bunch fresh broccoli,
chopped

1 10¾-ounce can cream of
mushroom soup

1/2 cup mayonnaise

2 eggs, beaten

1 1/2 cups shredded sharp
Cheddar cheese

2 tablespoons minced onion

1/2 teaspoon salt

1/4 teaspoon pepper

1 cup finely crushed
cheese-flavored crackers

Butter

Cook broccoli according to package directions. Drain. Mix well with all remaining ingredients except cracker crumbs and butter. Turn into a two-quart casserole or baking dish. Top with crumbs and dot with butter. Bake at 350° for 40 minutes. Serves four.

Margie's Beans

1/2 pound bacon

1 cup chopped onion

1/2 cup vinegar

1 cup brown sugar

2 cups catsup

1 16 ounce can green beans

1 16 ounce can wax beans

1 16 ounce can kidney beans

1 16 ounce can pork and
beans

In a heavy skillet, fry bacon until crisp. Drain and set aside. Brown onion in bacon drippings. Add sugar, vinegar and catsup. Simmer 20 minutes, stirring occasionally. In a three-quart casserole or baking dish, combine sauce with beans and crumbled bacon. Bake at 350° for 1½ hours. Remove from oven, cover and let stand for 30 minutes before serving. Serves eight.

Contributors	Recipes

Richard Marshall Cashin, Jr.

Residency: Boston, Massachusetts

Age: 25

Height: 6'5"

Weight: 205

School: Harvard College

Training hours per week: 12

Jane's Cinnamon Carrot Cake

2 cups sugar

1½ cups vegetable oil

4 eggs

2 cups flour

2 tablespoons cinnamon

1 teaspoon salt

2 teaspoons baking soda

2 cups finely grated carrots

In a medium bowl, cream sugar and oil. Beat in eggs. Combine dry ingredients and mix into creamed mixture. Stir in carrots. Pour into a greased 13x9-inch cake pan. Bake at 300° for 1½ hours. Serves 12.

Anne's Date Nut Loaf

1 cup pitted, diced dates

3/4 cup raisins

1/4 cup golden raisins

1 teaspoon baking soda

1 cup boiling water

1/2 cup sugar

1/2 cup butter or margarine

1 teaspoon vanilla

1 egg

1 ⅓ cups flour

3/4 cup broken walnuts

Grease a 9½x5½-inch loaf pan. Line bottom with waxed paper. Grease and flour paper. Place dates and raisins in a medium bowl. Dissolve soda in hot water and pour over date mixture. In another bowl, cream sugar and butter. Beat in vanilla and egg. Add flour and mix well. Mix in nuts and date mixture, with liquid. (Batter will be thin.) Pour into prepared pan and smooth over top. Bake at 350° for one hour or until top is dark brown and knife inserted in center comes out clean. Cool for five minutes. Remove from pan and finish cooling on rack. Peel off paper. Makes one large loaf.

Cosema E. Crawford

Residency: Westgate, Washington, D.C.

Age: 23

Height: 6'½"

Weight: 163

School: Princeton University Graduate School

Training hours per week: 15

Inspiration Cake

1 cup finely chopped pecans

2 1-ounce squares semi-sweet chocolate, grated

2½ cups flour

4 teaspoons baking powder

1 teaspoon salt

1½ cups sugar

2/3 cup vegetable shortening

1½ cups milk

1 teaspoon vanilla

4 egg whites

Chocolate Frosting (see directions)

Sprinkle pecans evenly over bottoms of two greased and floured 9-inch round layer cake pans. Grate chocolate and set aside. In a large bowl, combine dry ingredients. Beat in shortening, milk and vanilla for 1½ minutes at medium speed. Beat in egg whites for 1½ minutes. Spoon 1/4 of batter into each pan. Sprinkle grated chocolate evenly over batter. Carefully spoon remaining batter over chocolate. Bake at 350° for 35 to 40 minutes. Cool in pans for 10 to 15 minutes before removing. Cool completely. Assemble layers, nut-sides-up, by frosting between layers and on sides, but only 1/2 inch around top edge. (Allow nuts on top to show.) Decorate around top edge with white frosting. Serves 12.

Chocolate Frosting: In a small pan over low heat, melt 2 1-ounce squares unsweetened chocolate with 1/2 cup sugar and 1/4 cup water. Stir constantly until smooth and thick. Remove from heat and beat in 4 egg yolks. Cool, and set aside. Cream 1/2 cup vegetable shortening with 1 teaspoon vanilla. Gradually beat in 2 cups powdered sugar. Reserve 1/3 cup for top of cake. Add chocolate mixture to remaining white frosting and beat until smooth. Makes enough to frost a two-layer cake.

Contributors	Recipes

Anita L. DeFrantz

Residency: Philadelphia, Pennsylvania

Age: 26

Height: 5'11"

Weight: 155

School: University of Pennsylvania Law School JD, Pennsylvania Graduate School

Training hours per week: 36

Mexican Popcorn Seasoning

1/4 cup popcorn salt

2 teaspoons chili powder

1 teaspoon paprika

1 teaspoon imitation butter-flavored salt

1/8 teaspoon onion powder

Combine all ingredients in a small bowl until well blended. Store in a shaker. Sprinkle as desired over freshly popped popcorn. Makes 1/3 cup.

Hollis Straley Hatton

Residency: Philadelphia, Pennsylvania

Age: 30

Height: 5'5"

Weight: 105

School: Moore College of Art

Training hours per week: 16

Pheasant Run Mocha

1 tablespoon hot chocolate mix

1 tablespoon sugar

1 tablespoon instant coffee

1 tablespoon malt powder

1 tablespoon nondairy coffee creamer

Boiling water

Whole milk

Vanilla ice cream (optional)

Irish whiskey (optional)

Combine dry ingredients in a large mug. Stirring constantly, fill mug about 5/8 full with boiling water. Top off with whole milk and a scoop of ice cream. If desired, add a shot of Irish whiskey. Serves one.

Lemon Bread

6 tablespoons butter or margarine

1 cup sugar

2 eggs

1 tablespoon grated lemon rind

1/2 cup milk

1½ cups flour

1 teaspoon baking powder

1/2 teaspoon salt

1 cup chopped walnuts

Lemon Glaze (see directions)

In a medium bowl, cream butter with sugar. Beat in eggs, rind and milk. Combine remaining dry ingredients and mix into batter. Stir in nuts. Turn into a greased medium loaf pan. Bake at 350° for one hour. Cool loaf on rack for about 15 minutes. Place a plate under rack. With a pastry brush, coat top and sides of loaf with glaze, applying two or more layers. Makes one medium loaf.

Lemon Glaze: In a small pan, bring 1/2 cup sugar and 3 tablespoons lemon juice to a boil, stirring, until sugar dissolves.

Contributors	Recipes

Hollis Straley Hatton

Snickerdoodle Cookies

1 cup vegetable shortening, softened

1½ cups sugar

2 eggs

2¾ cups flour

1 teaspoon baking soda

2 teaspoons cream of tartar

1/2 teaspoon salt

Cinnamon-sugar mixture (see directions)

In a medium bowl, cream shortening with sugar. Beat in eggs. Combine remaining dry ingredients and mix into creamed mixture to form a soft dough. Chill dough for about 30 minutes. Roll into balls the size of small walnuts. Roll in cinnamon-sugar mixture, place on greased cookie sheets and bake at 400° for eight to 10 minutes. Makes about four dozen cookies.

Cinnamon-sugar mixture: In a small bowl, combine 4 tablespoons sugar with 4 teaspoons cinnamon and mix well.

Elizabeth Hills

Residency: Hingham, Massachusetts

Age: 24

Height: 5'10"

Weight: 155

School: University of New Hampshire

Training hours per week: 20

Curried Turkey Casserole

3 cups cooked wild rice

2 cups sliced, cooked turkey or chicken

1 10¾-ounce can cream of chicken soup

1/2 cup mayonnaise

Juice of 1 lemon

3/4 teaspoon curry powder

Place rice in a shallow two-quart casserole or baking dish. Cover with turkey. Combine remaining ingredients and pour over turkey. Bake at 350° for 25 minutes. Serves four.

Apple Cake

3 cups Macintosh apples, peeled and sliced

1 cup pecans or walnuts

1 cup flour

2 eggs

2 cups sugar

1½ cups vegetable oil

1 teaspoon vanilla

2 cups flour

1 teaspoon baking soda

1/2 teaspoon salt

1 teaspoon cinnamon

1 teaspoon nutmeg

Dredge apples and nuts with 1 cup flour and set aside. In large mixing bowl, beat eggs and sugar. Beat in oil and vanilla. Mix in remaining flour, soda, salt, cinnamon and nutmeg. Stir in apple mixture. Batter will be thick. Turn into a buttered bundt pan or 10-inch tube pan. Bake at 375° for one hour. Cool in pan for 15 minutes. Remove from pan and dust with powdered sugar while still warm. Serves 12 or more.

Joan Lind

*Residency: Long Beach,
  California*

Age: 26

Height: 5'9"

Weight: 144

*School: California State
  University, Long Beach*

Training hours per week: 23

Spinach Noodle Casserole

2 10-ounce packages frozen chopped spinach

1 16-ounce carton sour cream

Salt and pepper to taste

4 ounces noodles, your choice

1/4 cup butter or margarine

3 to 4 tablespoons instant minced onion

10 ounces Monterey Jack cheese, shredded

Cook spinach according to package directions and drain well. Combine spinach with half the sour cream; salt and pepper to taste. Cook noodles according to package directions. Drain, butter and mix with spinach. Moisten onion with a little water and stir into spinach. In a two-quart casserole or baking dish, layer spinach-noodle mixture with grated cheese, ending with cheese. Dot with additional butter, if desired. Top with remaining sour cream. Bake at 350° for 30 minutes. Serve hot or cold. Serves six.

Zucchini Rice Casserole

1 small onion, sliced thinly

1/4 cup olive oil

5 to 6 medium zucchini, sliced thinly

3 cloves garlic, minced or pressed

1/4 cup chopped parsley

1 teaspoon oregano

Salt and pepper to taste

4 cups cooked brown rice

2 large fresh tomatoes, sliced

2 teaspoon basil

1 cup grated Monterey Jack cheese, or any soft white cheese

In a large skillet, saute onion in oil until soft. Add zucchini and saute until slightly soft. Mix in garlic, parsley, oregano, salt, pepper and brown rice. Spread in a greased 13x9-inch baking dish or large shallow casserole. Cover with sliced tomatoes. Sprinkle with basil and cheese. Cover and bake at 350° for 20 minutes until just heated through. (Do not overcook.) Serves six.

Cranberry Coffee Ring

1/2 cup butter or margarine

1 cup sugar

2 eggs

1 teaspoon almond extract

2 cups flour

1 teaspoon baking powder

1 teaspoon baking soda

Pinch of salt

1 16-ounce container sour cream

1 16-ounce can whole cranberry sauce

1/2 to 1 cup chopped walnuts

Almond Glaze (see directions)

In a large bowl, cream butter with sugar. Beat in eggs and almond extract. Combine flour, baking powder, soda and salt. Beat into creamed mixture alternately with sour cream. Beat well. In a greased and floured 10-inch tube pan, spread a third of the batter. Add a thin layer of cranberry sauce, about a third. Repeat two more times, ending with a layer of sauce. Sprinkle with nuts. Bake at 375° for 45 to 50 minutes. Cool in pan until warm. Carefully remove from pan. Drizzle with almond glaze. Serves 12.

Almond Glaze: Beat together 1 cup powdered sugar, 1 teaspoon hot water and 1 teaspoon almond extract. Makes enough to glaze one 10-inch tube or bundt cake.

William D. Purdy

Residency: Liverpool, New York
Age: 21
Height: 6'5"
Weight: 200
School: Syracuse University
Training hours per week: 15

Cashew Chili

1 cup dry kidney beans
1 quart water
2 to 3 tablespoons vegetable oil
4 onions, chopped
2 green peppers, chopped
2 stalks celery, chopped
3 cloves garlic, minced
1 tablespoon basil
1 tablespoon chili powder
1 tablespoon cumin
1 bay leaf
1 tablespoon chili powder
1/2 teaspoon pepper
1 cup or more raw cashews
4 cups tomato puree or tomato juice
Dry red wine to taste
Grated cheese

In a medium pan, soak beans overnight in water; bring to a boil and simmer, covered, about one hour or until tender. (Or, for a quick soak, bring beans and water to a boil, cover, remove from heat and soak one hour. Then proceed with cooking as above.) In a heavy kettle or Dutch oven, saute onions, peppers, celery and garlic in oil. Stir in seasonings, cashews, tomato puree and red wine to taste. Cover and simmer for about 30 minutes. Add beans and cooking water and simmer for 30 minutes. Serve topped with grated cheese and additional cashews, if desired. Serves four to six.

Spaghetti Pie

6 ounces uncooked spaghetti
2 tablespoons butter or margarine
1/3 cup grated Parmesan cheese
2 eggs, well beaten
1 pound ground beef or bulk Italian sausage
1/2 cup chopped onion
1/4 cup chopped green pepper
1 8-ounce can tomatoes, chopped
1 6-ounce can tomato paste
1 teaspoon sugar
1 teaspoon oregano
1/4 teaspoon salt
1/4 teaspoon garlic salt
1 cup cottage cheese, drained
1/2 cup shredded Mozzarella cheese

Cook spaghetti according to package directions. Drain well and stir in butter, cheese and eggs. Line a buttered 10-inch pie pan with spaghetti to form a crust. In a large skillet, brown meat, onion and green pepper. Drain off excess fat. Stir in tomatoes, tomato paste and seasonings. Spread cottage cheese over bottom of spaghetti crust. Top with tomato mixture. Cover and chill two to 24 hours. Bake, covered, at 350° for one hour. Uncover, sprinkle with cheese and return to oven for five minutes. (Uncooked pie may also be frozen. Bake frozen pie at 350° for two hours.) Serves six.

Contributors	Recipes

William D. Purdy

Baklava

1 pound frozen phyllo sheets (21 16x12-inch sheets)

1 cup melted butter

2 cups finely chopped or ground walnuts

1 cup finely chopped or ground blanched almonds

3 tablespoons sugar

2 teaspoons cinnamon

1/2 teaspoon nutmeg

24 whole cloves

Lemon-Honey Syrup (see directions)

Thaw dough at room temperature for two hours. Cut sheets in half crosswise. Cover with waxed paper and a damp towel. Butter the bottom of a 14x10-inch baking pan. Brush 10 sheets of phyllo with butter and line bottom of pan, overlapping when necessary. Combine nuts, sugar and spices. Sprinkle 1/3 of nut mixture over phyllo in pan. Drizzle with melted butter. Top with another 10 sheets, brushing each with melted butter. Repeat layers until nuts and phyllo are used up, ending with a layer of phyllo. Without cutting through bottom layer, cut into about 24 diamond-shaped pieces. Stick one whole clove into each piece. Bake at 350° for 50 to 55 minutes. Finish cutting all the way through and cool completely. Pour warm Lemon-Honey Syrup over top. Serves 24.

Lemon-Honey Syrup: In a medium pan, combine 1 cup sugar, 1 cup water and 1/2 lemon, sliced. Boil gently for 15 minutes. Remove lemon slices. Add 2 tablespoons honey and stir well.

Kurt F. Somerville

Residency: Wellesley Hills, Massachusetts

Age: 21

Height: 6'6"

Weight: 215

School: Dartmouth College

Training hours per week: 24

Toffee Ice Cream Pie and Sauce

1 9-inch graham cracker crust or vanilla wafer crust

1/2 gallon vanilla ice cream

1 cup coarsely chopped Heath candy bars

1 1/2 cups sugar

1 8-ounce can evaporated milk

1/4 cup butter

1/4 cup light corn syrup

Dash of salt

Spoon ice cream into pie shell. Sprinkle half of the Heath bars between layers of ice cream. Freeze until serving time. To make sauce, combine sugar, milk, butter, syrup and salt in a medium saucepan. Boil for one minute, stirring constantly. Remove from heat. Stir in remaining Heath bars until melted. Cool, stirring occasionally. Serve over slices of pie. Serves eight.

Gregg Stone

Residency: Cambridge, Massachusetts

Age: 26

Height: 6'3½"

Weight: 180

School: Harvard College '75, Harvard Law School '79

Training hours per week: 26

New England Codfish Balls

1 pound salt cod

Water

4 large potatoes, peeled

1 egg

1 pint light cream

Oil for deep frying

Cover cod with cold water and soak overnight. Drain. In a large pan, cover cod with fresh water and bring to a boil. (If too salty, drain and repeat boiling.) Add potatoes to cod and water. Boil until potatoes are soft. Drain. Mash cod and potatoes together. Beat in egg and cream at high speed until mixture is fluffy. Chill. Heat four to five inches of oil in deep fryer or heavy pan to 350°. Remove cod mixture from refrigerator. Swirl onto fork; do not shape into packed balls. Drop into oil. Ball will sink to bottom and rise to surface after a few seconds. Balls are done when medium brown. Remove from fat and drain. Serve hot. Serves four to six.

Contributors	Recipes

Gregg Stone

Broiled Bluefish

1 4 to 5 pound bluefish, cleaned and filletted

1/2 cup mayonnaise

1/4 cup lemon juice

Freshly ground black pepper

Place filets on a lightly greased broiler rack or a pan that will allow for maximum drainage of fat. Combine mayonnaise with lemon juice and brush on fish. Season liberally with pepper. Place in preheated broiler, about six inches from flame, for 15 to 25 minutes, depending on the thickness of the filet. Do not turn. It is done when slightly charred on top and meat is white all the way through. Serves two.

Nancy Storrs

Residency: Philadelphia, Pennsylvania

Age: 29

Height: 5'8"

Weight: 168

School: Bradford Junior College '71, Williams College '73

Training hours per week: 25

Easy Apple Cake

1 cup sugar

1/3 cup butter

1 egg

1 cup flour

1/2 teaspoon salt

1/2 teaspoon cinnamon

1/2 teaspoon nutmeg

1/2 teaspoon baking powder

1/2 teaspoon baking soda

3 cups peeled, cubed apples

1/4 cup coarsley chopped walnuts

Grease a 9x9-inch cake pan. Line with waxed paper. Grease and flour waxed paper. In a medium bowl, cream sugar and butter. Beat in egg. Combine dry ingredients and mix well. Stir in apples and nuts. Turn into prepared pan. Bake at 350° for 45 minutes. Cool in pan. Remove from pan and peel off paper. Serves eight.

Vegetable Quiche

1 unbaked 9-inch pie shell

2 onions, thinly sliced

2 tablespoons butter

1 10-12-ounce package frozen chopped broccoli, cooked and drained

1/4 cup butter

1/4 cup flour

1 cup milk

1/2 teaspoon onion salt

1/8 teaspoon pepper

1/2 teaspoon dill or basil

1½ cups shredded Cheddar or Swiss cheese

4 eggs, beaten

1/2 cup grated Parmesan or Cheddar cheese

Prick pie crust and bake at 450° for 10 to 12 minutes. Saute onions with butter in small skillet until soft. Set aside. In a large pan, melt butter. Stir in flour. Gradually stir in milk, onion salt, pepper, dill and cook over low heat, stirring constantly, until thick. Remove from heat and stir in cheese until melted. Stir in eggs, broccoli and onions. Pour into pie crust. Bake at 350° for 30 minutes or until firm. Sprinkle with remaining cheese and return to oven for five minutes. Let set 10 minutes before slicing. Serves six to eight.

Contributors	Recipes

Tom Woodman

Residency: Newtown, Pennsylvania

Age: 23

Height: 6'5"

Weight: 220

School: Oregon State University

Training hours per week: 23

Oatmeal Cookies

1 cup brown sugar

1/2 cup white sugar

1 cup butter or margarine

2 eggs

2 teaspoons vanilla

4 tablespoons milk

2 cups flour

1½ cups oatmeal

1 teaspoon baking soda

1/2 teaspoon salt

2 teaspoons cinnamon

In a medium bowl, cream sugars with butter. Beat in eggs, vanilla and milk. Stir in dry ingredients. Drop from a teaspoon onto a greased cookie sheet. Bake at 350° for about 12 minutes. Makes about four dozen cookies.

15
Shooting

Event Days:

Sunday,
July 20, 1980

Monday,
July 21, 1980

Tuesday,
July 22, 1980

Wednesday,
July 23, 1980

Thursday,
July 24, 1980

Friday,
July 25, 1980

Saturday,
July 26, 1980

Contributors:

Lanny Robert Bassham
Kurt Henderson Fitz-Randolph
Rod Fitz-Randolph, Jr.
David William Kimes
Melvin P. Makin
Steve F. Reiter
L. Michael Theimer
Lones W. Wigger, Jr.

Shooting ranks fifth among the Olympic sports for USA sports success; 71 gold medalists have acquired 104 gold medals. This sport is one of three for which the competition is open to women on the same footing as the men. The first woman to represent the USA in the Olympics was Margaret Murdock at Montreal. She was deprived of a gold medal in the three-position, small bore rifle when an apparent deadlock was broken by referral to international federation rules calling for a "count back." Thus the gold medal went to Lanny Bassham, USA, and Ms. Murdock received the silver.

International shooting competition for the USA dates from 1871 when a group of National Guard officers formed the National Rifle Association of America to engage the Ulster Rifle Club of Ireland.

In the Olympics pistol competition there are two events—free pistol and rapid fire pistol. The rifle competition consists of the small bore rifle, prone and the small bore rifle, three position, and the moving target. In addition there is shotgun competition in both skeetshooting and trapshooting under international rules. Don Haldeman was the '76 trapshooting victor.

In the rapid fire pistol, Lt. Col. Bill McMillan, USMC (ret) has been a member of the last six Olympic teams and is a candidate for an unprecedented (for any American) seventh team in 1980. He was the 1960 gold medalist in the rapid fire pistol.

Contributors	Recipes

Lanny Robert Bassham

Residency: New Braunfels, Texas

Age: 32

Height: 5'9"

Weight: 165

School: University of Texas at Arlington

Training hours per week: 15

Fay's Chocolate Meringue Pie

1 baked 9-inch pie crust

1 cup sugar

4 tablespoons flour

1/4 teaspoon salt

1/3 cup cocoa

2 cups milk

3 eggs, separated

1 tablespoon butter

1 tablespoon vanilla

1/4 cup sugar

1/2 teaspoon vanilla

In a medium pan, combine flour, salt, cocoa. Gradually stir in milk. Cover over medium heat, stirring constantly, until thick. Remove from heat and stir in egg yolks, butter and 1 tablespoon vanilla. Pour into pie crust. In a medium bowl with clean beaters, beat egg whites with sugar until stiff. Fold in vanilla. Cover pie filling with meringue. Bake at 400° for about five minutes or until meringue begins to turn light brown. Serves six to eight.

Kurt Henderson Fitz-Randolph

Residency: Palm Bay, Florida

Age: 18

Height: 160

Weight: 6'3"

School: Tennessee Technological University

Training hours per week: 15

Bourbon Balls

1 cup ground pecans

3 cups ground vanilla wafers

1 cup powdered sugar

3 tablespoons light corn syrup

1/2 cup bourbon

To grind pecans and vanilla wafers, put through the fine blade of a food grinder, or use an electric blender. In a large bowl, combine all ingredients and mix until well blended. Roll into balls the size of a nickel. Roll in additional powdered sugar. Store in a tightly covered container in the refrigerator. Makes about four dozen balls.

Chicken Soup

3 quarts water

1 pound boney chicken parts (backs, necks, wings, etc.)

1 tablespoon salt

1/2 cup chopped celery

1/2 cup raw rice

1 egg, beaten well

In a large kettle, bring water to a boil. Add chicken parts, cover, and simmer until chicken is tender, about one hour. Remove chicken. Add salt, celery and rice. Simmer until celery is tender and rice is done, about 30 minutes. Meanwhile, discard chicken skin and bones, but chop any usable meat and return to kettle. Just before serving, slowly pour egg into soup through wire strainer to form "egg drops." Serves eight.

Rod Fitz-Randolph, Jr.

Residency: Palm Bay, Florida

Age: 20

Height: 6'1"

Weight: 155

School: Tennessee Technological University

Training hours per week: 10

Date Nut Roll

2 cups (about 1/2 pound) vanilla wafer crumbs

1 cup chopped dates

1 cup chopped pecans

1/2 cup sweetened condensed milk

1 tablespoon lemon juice

1½ tablespoons brandy or bourbon, or 1/2 teaspoon vanilla and 4 teaspoons water

Whipped cream

Maraschino cherries

In a large bowl, combine crumbs, dates and pecans. In a separate bowl, combine milk, lemon juice, brandy. Add to date mixture, mix well and knead with hands until well blended. Shape into a roll. Wrap in waxed paper and refrigerate 12 hours or more. Slice. Top each slice with whipped cream and a cherry. Serves eight or more.

Contributors	Recipes

Rod Fitz-Randolph, Jr.

USA Spaghetti

1 tablespoon vegetable oil

1 large onion, chopped

1 large green pepper, chopped

1 pound ground beef

1 16-ounce can tomatoes

1 10¾-ounce can condensed tomato soup

1 10¾-ounce can condensed cream of mushroom soup

1 pound sharp cheese

2 bay leaves

1 teaspoon thyme

1 teaspoon pepper

2 teaspoons salt

1 12-ounce package vermicelli or spaghetti

In a large skillet, saute onion and pepper in oil. Remove from skillet and set aside. In same skillet, brown ground beef. Add onion and pepper to ground beef, along with tomatoes and soups. Bring to a boil and simmer, uncovered. Meanwhile, grate cheese. Add cheese, bay leaves, thyme, pepper and salt. Simmer for 30 minutes. Cook vermicelli according to package directions. Drain. Serve with meat sauce. Vermicelli and sauce may be combined and baked in a casserole, too. Serves four to six.

Rice Casserole

1 cup raw rice

1/2 cup butter or margarine

2 10¾-ounce cans condensed beef broth

1 tablespoon chopped onion

1 tablespoon chopped green pepper

1 tablespoon chopped pimiento

1 tablespoon slivered almonds (optional)

1 tablespoon chopped mushrooms (optional)

Combine all ingredients in a 2-quart casserole and cover. Bake at 350° for 30 minutes. Stir with a fork and return to oven for 30 more minutes, or until liquid is absorbed and rice is tender. Serves four.

David William Kimes

Residency: Monterey Park, California

Age: 38

Height: 5'9"

Weight: 150

School: Orange Coast College, 1960; University of California, Berkeley, 1962

Training hours per week: 20

Carne Con Chile

1 pork or beef roast, about 5 pounds

3 4-ounce cans green chiles, seeded and diced, or 12 fresh green chiles, roasted, peeled, seeded and diced

1 small onion, minced

6 to 8 fresh tomatoes, peeled and chopped, or 2 16-ounce cans whole tomatoes, chopped

1 tablespoon garlic salt

2 tablespoons salt

Cut meat into bite-size pieces and brown in a large kettle or Dutch oven, using fat from meat or vegetable oil if necessary. (If using pork, drain off excess fat.) Add remaining ingredients. (If using fresh tomatoes, add 2 cups water.) Bring to a boil, reduce heat and simmer for 20 to 30 minutes. Serves 10 to 12.

Contributors	Recipes

David William Kimes

Hot Spiced Wine

1 quart claret or burgundy

3/4 cup sugar

4 to 5 sticks cinnamon

5 to 10 whole cloves

1 cup water

1 sliced apple

1 peeled, sliced orange

Combine all ingredients in a large pan. Heat slowly, stirring occasionally. Heat only until steaming; do not simmer or boil. Cover and keep hot; flavor improves if kept hot for an hour or more. Serve in cups. Serves four to six.

Quick Baked Chicken

1 roasting chicken or capon, about 4 pounds

Tarragon

Garlic salt

Pepper

Rinse chicken, remove giblets and pat dry. Sprinkle liberally inside and out with tarragon, garlic salt and pepper. If desired, wash giblets and place inside chicken. Place breast-side up on a rack in a covered roasting pan. Bake at 450° for 1 to 1¼ hours. For crispy chicken, remove cover during last 10 minutes of baking. Serves four to six.

Melvin P. Makin

Residency: Aumsville, Oregon
Age: 38
Height: 5'8"
Weight: 150
Training hours per week: 12

Apple Crisp

2 cups thinly sliced apples

1/3 cup water

1/2 teaspoon cinnamon

1/4 cup butter

1/2 cup brown sugar

1/3 cup flour

Arrange apples in a buttered 8x8-inch baking dish. Pour water over apples and sprinkle with cinnamon. In a small bowl, with fingers or pastry blender, cut butter into brown sugar and flour until crumbly. Sprinkle over apples. Bake at 400° for 30 minutes or until apples are tender and top is golden brown. Serve warm or cold, plain, with whipped cream or ice cream. Serves six to eight.

Great-Great-Grandmother's Suet Pudding

1¾ cups flour

1 teaspoon salt

1 teaspoon cinnamon

1 cup raisins

1 cup currants

1 cup ground suet

1/2 teaspoon baking soda

1/2 cup molasses

1 cup milk

Custard Sauce:

1/2 cup butter or margarine

2 cups sugar

2 tablespoons flour

2 eggs

In a large bowl, combine flour, salt, cinnamon, raisins, currants and suet. Mix well. Dissolve soda in molasses. Stir into batter. Stir in milk and mix well. Turn into greased and floured 1½-quart pudding mold with tight lid. Place in large saucepan. Add boiling water to pan to reach halfway up side of mold. Cover and steam (simmer) for four hours. Just before pudding is ready, prepare Custard Sauce. Combine butter and sugar in top of double boiler. Stir in flour and eggs. Cook over hot water, stirring constantly, until thick and smooth. Unmold pudding and serve hot. Pass sauce. Serves eight.

Steve F. Reiter

Residency: Daly City, California

Age: 37

Height: 5'7"

Weight: 185

School: Mt. Angel Seminary (Oregon) Balboa High School (San Francisco)

Training hours per week: 16

Fillet of Sole Palm Beach

1/2 cup peeled, chopped tomato

1 pound fresh mushrooms, sliced

1 medium yellow onion, chopped

3 tablespoons butter

1/2 teaspoon basil

1/2 teaspoon thyme

1/4 teaspoon salt

1/4 teaspoon white pepper

2 cups cooked white rice

1 pound small shrimp, cleaned and shelled (or broken shrimp)

8 fillets of sole

8 slices bacon

8 large slices Monterey Jack cheese

In a large skillet, saute tomato, mushrooms and onion in butter until limp. Stir in seasonings, rice and shrimp. Cool. Place about 1/2 cup stuffing on each fillet. Roll up. Wrap each rolled fillet in bacon and secure with a toothpick. Place rolls in one large baking dish or individual casseroles. Top each roll with a cheese slice. Bake at 400° for 15 minutes or until fish turns white and flakes easily with a fork. Serves eight.

Spinach Salad

1½ pounds fresh spinach

1/2 pound fresh bean sprouts

1 6-ounce can water chestnuts, drained and sliced

5 slices bacon, cooked and crumbled

2 hard-boiled eggs, grated or sieved

2/3 cup vegetable oil

1/3 cup catsup

1/3 cup sugar

1/3 cup wine vinegar

2 teaspoons Worcestershire sauce

Salt and pepper to taste

Clean spinach and tear into bite-size pieces. Place spinach, sprouts, water chestnuts, bacon and eggs in a large salad bowl. Combine remaining ingredients in a pint jar and shake well. Pour over salad and toss. Serves eight.

Contributors	Recipes

L. Michael Theimer

Residency: Iowa Park, Texas

Age: 29

Height: 6'2"

Weight: 175

School: Midwestern State University, Wichita Falls, Texas

Training hours per week: one weekend per month

Roast Beef Hash

1/2 cup chopped onion

1 tablespoon butter or margarine

1/4 cup vegetable oil

1 pound frozen hash brown potatoes (chunked, not shredded, from a 2 pound bag)

1 cup diced leftover roast beef

1 cup or 1 8-ounce can beef gravy

Salt, pepper and seasoned salt

In a large skillet, saute onion in butter and oil until tender. Add potatoes and mix. Cover and cook over very low heat until completely thawed. Stir in remaining ingredients. Season to taste. Heat through. Serves two.

Butterscotch Pound Cake

1 yellow cake mix, two-layer size

2 3⅛-ounce packages instant butterscotch pudding mix

4 eggs

2/3 cup vegetable oil

2/3 cup water

1 cup pecans (optional)

Butterscotch Glaze (see directions)

Combine all ingredients in a large bowl and beat until well combined. Bake in a greased and floured bundt pan or 10-inch tube pan at 375° for 35 minutes. Cool in pan 15 minutes. Top with Butterscotch Glaze. Serves 12.

Butterscotch Glaze: In a small pan, melt 1 6-oz. package butterscotch chips with enough water to reach desired thickness. Pour over cake and allow to drip down sides. Makes enough to glaze one bundt cake.

Lones W. Wigger, Jr.

Residency: Carter, Montana

Age: 41

Height: 5'7"

Weight: 180

School: Montana State University

Training hours per week: 8

Easy Sugar Cookies

1 cup powdered sugar

1 cup granulated sugar

1 cup butter or margarine

1 cup vegetable oil

2 eggs

1 teaspoon vanilla

1 teaspoon salt

1 teaspoon baking soda

1 teaspoon cream of tartar

4¼ cups flour

In a large bowl, cream sugars with butter. Beat in oil. Add eggs, one at a time, beating well after each addition. Mix in remaining ingredients until well blended. Chill dough. With hands, roll into small balls and place on greased cookie sheet. Flatten with the bottom of a greased drinking glass dipped in sugar. Bake at 350° for 10 minutes. Makes about eight dozen.

Crusty Topped Cauliflower

1 large head fresh cauliflower

1/2 cup mayonnaise

2 teaspoons Dijon mustard

1/2 to 3/4 cup grated Cheddar cheese

In a large pan with a lid, cook cauliflower whole in a small amount of boiling water for about 20 minutes or until tender. Drain well. Place in a flat pan or casserole. Combine mayonnaise and mustard and spread over cauliflower. Sprinkle with cheese. Bake at 350° for 10 minutes or until cheese melts. Serves six.

16
Soccer Football

Event Days:

Sunday,
July 20, 1980

Monday,
July 21, 1980

Tuesday,
July 22, 1980

Wednesday,
July 23, 1980

Thursday,
July 24, 1980

Friday,
July 25, 1980

Sunday,
July 27, 1980

Tuesday,
July 29, 1980

Friday,
August 1, 1980

Saturday,
August 2, 1980

Contributors:

Larry Michael Hulcer
Perry Van der Beck

Spectator-wise, as well as the number of nations entering the pre-Olympic qualifying tournaments, soccer is the No. 1 sport in the Olympic Games. Since pre-Olympic qualifying tournaments were inaugurated, the USA has qualified only once for the Olympic Games tournament in 1972 at Munich.

While soccer was introduced to the program in 1908, the USA first entered soccer competition in 1924 at Paris. The team was eliminated in the second round.

Because of the "internationality" of the sport, in recent Olympic Games, preliminary games have been assigned to three or four cities outside of the host city. Of course, in accordance with Olympic protocol the final games must be played in the host city. The most successful USA soccer team in the Olympic Games was in 1956 when the squad reached the quarter-final round.

Among the Eastern European nations, Yugoslavia placed second in 1948, in 1952 and 1956 before winning all the marbles at Rome in 1960 by defeating Denmark 3–1. 1976 Olympic competition was almost decimated by the last-minute withdrawal of three African nations—Zambia, Nigeria and Ghana—forcing the cancellation of nine scheduled matches in the preliminary rounds. East Germany capped its successes of the Games of the XXI Olympiad by defeating Poland 3–1 for the gold medal.

Contributors	Recipes

Larry Michael Hulcer

Residency: Florissant, Missouri
Age: 21
Height: 5'10"
Weight: 165
School: St. Louis University
Training hours per week: 18

Dot's Polish Hot Potato Salad

10 medium red potatoes, boiled in their jackets

1 large green pepper, diced

1 large yellow onion, diced

1/2 pound bacon, diced and fried crisp

Salt and pepper to taste

1/4 cup water

3/4 cup white vinegar

1/4 cup sugar

1/4 cup cornstarch

2 cups water

2 tablespoons prepared mustard

Sliced hard-boiled eggs (optional)

Peel and slice potatoes. In a large bowl, alternate layers of potatoes, pepper, onion, and bacon until all are used. Add 1/4 cup water to the bacon drippings in a large skillet and bring to a boil. Add vinegar and sugar, mix well and bring to a boil again. Mix cornstarch with water until smooth and stir into boiling mixture. Stirring constantly, bring to a boil again. Remove from heat. Stir in mustard. Pour over salad. Toss gently until all potatoes are coated. Sprinkle with additional bacon bits and garnish with sliced eggs, if desired. Serves 12 or more.

Perry Van Der Beck

Residency: Tampa, Florida
Age: 19
Height: 5'11"
Weight: 154
School: St. Thomas Aquinas High School
Training hours per week: 20

Early American Sweet Potatoes

1 26-ounce can sweet potatoes, or three to four fresh sweet potatoes, cooked and mashed

3/4 cup sugar

2 eggs, beaten

1/4 cup butter or margarine

Topping:

1/3 cup butter or margarine

3/4 cup sugar

1 cup pecans

1/3 cup flour

Drain sweet potatoes; reserve liquid. Mash potatoes and add sugar, eggs and butter. Mix well, adding just enough reserved liquid to moisten. Place in a 1½-quart buttered casserole. In a small pan, melt butter. Stir in sugar. Stir in flour and nuts. Sprinkle over potatoes. Bake at 350° for about 30 minutes or until heated through and lightly browned on top. Serves four to six.

Hash Brown Omelet

4 slices bacon

2 cups cooked, shredded potatoes (frozen hash browns may be used)

1/4 cup chopped onion

1/4 cup chopped green pepper

4 eggs

1/2 teaspoon salt

1/4 cup milk

Dash of pepper

1 cup shredded sharp American or Cheddar cheese

In a 10 to 12-inch skillet, cook bacon until crisp. Remove bacon, crumble and set aside. Combine potatoes, onion and green pepper. Add to bacon drippings in skillet, patting into place to cover bottom of pan. Cook over low heat, without stirring, until bottom is crisp and lightly browned. Beat together eggs, salt, milk, and pepper. Pour over potatoes. Top with shredded cheese. Cover and cook over low heat until eggs are set. Loosen omelet and fold in half. Serves four.

17
Swimming

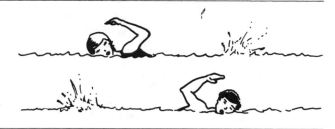

Event Days:

Sunday, July 20, 1980	Saturday, July 26, 1980
Monday, July 21, 1980	Sunday, July 27, 1980
Tuesday, July 22, 1980	
Wednesday, July 23, 1980	
Thursday, July 24, 1980	

Contributors:

Michael Lee Bruner	Tim Shaw
Deana Kim Dunson	Jill Sterkel
Stephanie Elkins	Sue Walsh
Bill Forrester	
Ambrose Gaines IV	
Robert W. Hackett	
Nancy Lynn Hogshead	
Robert S. Jackson	
Kimberly Lineham	
Scot Matsuda	

Since Charles Daniels won our first title in St. Louis, in 1904 with his "American Crawl," American men and women have accumulated 222 gold medals. In the last three Olympic Games the USA men's teams have won more medals (gold, silver, and bronze) than *all* the other nations put together.

The USA women dominated the women's swimming in 1968 and 1972 but yielded supremacy to East Germany at Montreal.

Mark Spitz is tied for the most gold medals earned in the Modern Olympic Games, nine (along with Larisa Latynina, USSR gymnast). Mark swam on two winning USA relay teams at Mexico before garnering seven (four in freestyle and butterfly individual races and three in relay races) in Munich. Don Schollander won four gold medals as high school graduate in

1964 at Tokyo and collected a fifth on a winning relay team in Mexico following his final year at Yale University.

Two Americans have won five gold medals: Schollander and John Weissmuller, 1924. Deborah Meyer, in 1968, won three individual gold medals (100m, 200m, 400m freestyle) and Sandra Neilson collected the 100m freestyle diadem, also in Mexico, along with two relay gold medals.

The hero of the USA swimming forces in Montreal was John Naber of the University of Southern California. He won two individual backstroke titles in world record time and was a member of two winning relay quartets. He also earned one silver medal.

Michael Lee Bruner

*Residency: Los Altos,
California*

Age: 22

Height: 5'10"

Weight: 165

School: Stanford University

Training hours per week: 33

Petti De Polla Memosa

3 whole broiler-fryer chicken
  breasts, halved, skinned and
  boned

2 eggs, beaten

1½ teaspoons salt

1/4 teaspoon white pepper

1/2 cup flour

6 tablespoons butter

6 slices prosciutto (Italian ham)

6 slices Mozzarella cheese

1/2 cup chicken broth

Pound breasts thin between sheets of waxed paper.
Beat eggs with salt and pepper. Dip meat in egg
mixture, then in flour. In a large skillet, melt butter
and brown chicken on both sides, about 8 minutes
per side. Place a ham slice on each piece of chicken.
Top with cheese slices. Add broth, cover and simmer
for five minutes. Serves six.

Caesar Salad

4 bread sticks, broken into
  bite-size pieces

1/2 cup olive oil

2 cloves garlic, minced

1 head romaine

1/4 teaspoon freshly ground
  black pepper

1 egg

3 tablespoons wine vinegar

6 anchovies, chopped

1 tablespoon chopped capers

1/4 cup grated Parmesan
  cheese

In a small bowl, soak bread in half the olive oil with
garlic. Break lettuce into large bowl. Season with
pepper. Pour on remaining oil. Toss. Break raw egg
into bowl. Toss. Add vinegar, anchovies and capers.
Toss. Sprinkle with cheese and marinated bread.
Serve immediately. Serves four.

Baked Fish Au Gratin

1 pound fish fillets

1 10¾-ounce can cream of
  celery soup

1/2 cup shredded mild cheese

Freshly ground black pepper

Spread fillets in a shallow baking pan. Pour soup
over fish. Sprinkle with pepper and cheese. Bake at
375° for 45 minutes. (To use same recipe with
chicken, eliminate cheese and add 1 clove garlic,
minced, and some chopped parsley. Bake at 350° for
one hour.) Serves four.

Deana Kim Dunson

Residency: Gainesville, Florida

Age: 21

Height: 5'7"

Weight: 135

School: University of Florida

Training hours per week: 22

Ethel's Sugar Cookies

1/2 cup vegetable shortening,
  softened

1/4 cup butter or margarine,
  softened

1 cup sugar

2 eggs

1/2 teaspoon vanilla

2 1/2 cups flour

1 teaspoon baking powder

1 teaspoon salt

In a medium mixing bowl, cream shortening, butter
and sugar. Beat in eggs. Combine dry ingredients
and stir into creamed mixture. Chill dough one hour.
Roll out onto floured surface and cut into shapes.
Place on lightly greased cookie sheet. Bake at 400°
for six to eight minutes or until edges are lightly
browned. Makes about four dozen cookies.

Contributors	Recipes

Deana Kim Dunson

Christmas Divinity

2 cups sugar
1/2 cup light corn syrup
1/2 cup water
Pinch of salt
2 egg whites
1 teaspoon vanilla
1/2 cup chopped nuts (optional)

Place sugar, corn syrup and water in a medium saucepan. Stir over low heat until sugar is dissolved. Cook without stirring until firm ball stage (252°) is reached. Just before syrup reaches firm ball, beat egg whites with salt until stiff, but not dry. With a clean damp cloth, wipe crystals from pouring lip of pan. Pour syrup in a very fine stream over egg whites, beating constantly while pouring. Do not scrape bottom of pan. Continue to beat until mixture holds shape. Fold in vanilla and nuts. Working quickly, drop from the tip of a spoon onto waxed paper. Or, turn out into an oiled shallow pan and cut into one-inch squares. Makes about 60 pieces.

Lasagna

1 to 1½ pounds ground beef
Garlic powder
Salt and pepper
1 packet (about 1½ ounces) spaghetti sauce seasoning mix
1 6-ounce can tomato paste
1 8-ounce package lasagna noodles
1 to 1½ pounds sharp Cheddar cheese
1 pint Ricotta cheese or cottage cheese
2 6-ounce packages sliced Mozzarella cheese

In a large skillet, brown meat. Drain fat. Season to taste with garlic powder, salt and pepper. Following package directions for spaghetti sauce, add seasoning mix and tomato paste. Cook noodles according to package directions. Grease a 13x9-inch pan. Line pan with noodles. Add alternating layers of meat sauce, sharp Cheddar cheese, Ricotta cheese, Mozzarella and noodles, ending with a layer of sauce topped with Mozzarella. Bake at 350° for 30 minutes. Let set for 10 minutes before cutting into squares. Serves six.

Stephanie Elkins

Residency: Gainesville, Florida
Age: 15
Height: 5'6½"
Weight: 125
School: Buchholz High School
Training hours per week: 22

Schachlick

8 slices bacon
4 small onions, sliced
1 pound beef sirloin, cut into cubes
1 pound beef liver cut into cubes
Salt and pepper
Worcestershire sauce
2 cups quick-cooking rice, cooked
Ketchup
Curry powder

In a large heavy skillet, fry bacon until crisp. Set aside. Saute onions, sirloin and liver in bacon fat until onions are tender and meat has reached desired degree of doneness. Season with salt, pepper and Worcestershire to taste. Serve over hot cooked rice, topped with ketchup, a dash of curry and crumbled bacon. Serves four to six.

Contributors	Recipes

Stephanie Elkins

Wiener Schnitzel

4 pork cutlets

2 eggs

1/2 cup dry bread crumbs

1 lemon, sliced

In a shallow dish, beat eggs. Spread crumbs on a plate or piece of waxed paper. Dip cutlets in egg, then coat on both sides with crumbs. In a heavy skillet over medium heat, fry in oil until golden brown on both sides. Serve topped with a lemon slice. Serves four.

Cheese Cake

1 9-inch graham cracker pie crust

4 large eggs

1½ cups sugar

3 8-ounce packages cream cheese, softened

Pinch of salt

1 teaspoon vanilla

1 cup sour cream

1 tablespoon sugar

In a medium bowl, beat eggs and sugar until thick and lemon-colored. In another bowl, beat cream cheese, salt and vanilla until creamy. Add cheese mixture to eggs, one spoonful at a time, while continuing to beat until well blended. Pour into pie shell. Bake at 325° for 45 minutes or until set. Combine sour cream and sugar. Spread over cheesecake. Run under broiler for five minutes to set topping. Chill and serve. Serves eight.

Bill Forrester

Residency: Hilton Head, South Carolina

Age: 21

Height: 5'11"

Weight: 170

School: Auburn University

Training hours per week: 8

Broccoli Main Dish

1½ to 2 pounds fresh broccoli

2 to 3 eggs, beaten

2 to 3 cups cottage cheese

1/4 to 1/2 cup minced green onion

1/4 to 1/2 cup shredded Cheddar cheese

3/4 cup whole wheat bread crumbs or bran

1/4 cup vegetable oil

1/4 cup grated Parmesan cheese

Chop broccoli and steam for five minutes, or until tender-crisp. Lay broccoli in a large casserole or 13x9-inch baking dish. Combine eggs, cottage cheese, onion and Cheddar cheese; pour over broccoli. Combine oil, crumbs and Parmesan cheese; sprinkle over cheese layer. Bake at 350° for 25 minutes. Serves four to six.

Granola

3 cups rolled oats

1/2 cup shredded or flaked coconut

1/2 cup sesame seeds

1/2 cup soy milk powder

1/2 cup chopped almonds

1/2 cup chopped pecans or other nuts or seeds

1/2 cup vegetable oil

1/2 cup honey

1/2 cup water

Combine dry ingredients in a 13x9-inch pan or a large roasting pan. Combine oil, honey and water and pour over oat mixture. Stir to combine well. Bake at 275° for 1½ to 2 hours. After the first hour, stir at 15 minute intervals until golden brown. Do not over-brown. Cool. (When cool, granola will be crunchy.) Store in a covered container in a cool, dry place. Makes about six cups granola.

Contributors	Recipes

Bill Forrester

Date-Apple Cookies

1 cup pitted dates
1/2 cup water
1 cup peeled, shredded raw apple
3/4 cup oil
1/2 cup chopped walnuts
1/2 teaspoon salt
1 teaspoon vanilla
3 cups rolled oats

In a medium saucepan, combine dates and water. Cook over medium heat, mashing and stirring until smooth. Add apple and oil and beat until smooth and oil is emulsified. Add remaining ingredients. Mix well. Let stand 10 minutes or until moisture is absorbed. Beat briskly. Drop from teaspoon onto ungreased cookie sheet. Bake at 375° for 25 minutes or until browned. Makes about three dozen cookies.

Ambrose Gaines IV ("Rowdy")

Residency: Winter Haven, Florida
Age: 20
Height: 6'1"
Weight: 160
School: Auburn University
Training hours per week: 24

Pineapple Burgers with Spicy Sauce

2 pineapple rings
1/2 pound ground beef
1/2 cup brown sugar
1/2 cup catsup
2 tablespoons prepared mustard

Drain pineapple well. Divide meat into four thin patties. Place a pineapple ring between two patties, sealing edges. Place patties on rack or broiling pan six inches from heat. Broil about five minutes. Turn and broil five more minutes. Meanwhile, combine brown sugar, catsup and mustard in a small saucepan; bring to a boil and simmer for two to three minutes. Pour spicy sauce over burgers. Serves two.

Calcutta Curry

3 tablespoons butter or margarine
1/4 chopped onion
1/4 cup chopped celery
1 2-ounce can sliced mushrooms, drained
1½ teaspoons curry powder
1/2 teaspoon salt
2 tablespoons apple juice
1/4 cup chicken broth or bouillon
1½ cups half and half or light cream
2 tablespoons cornstarch
1/4 cup water
1 6-ounce package frozen snow crab, thawed
Hot cooked rice
Raisins, peanuts and coconut (optional)

In a medium saucepan, melt butter. Saute onion, celery, mushrooms, curry powder and salt until onion is tender. Stir in apple juice, chicken broth and cream. Simmer for five minutes, stirring occasionally. Combine cornstarch and water, mix well and stir into curry mixture. Cook over medium heat, stirring constantly, for about five minutes or until thick. Stir in crab and heat through. Serve over hot cooked rice. If desired, garnish with raisins, peanuts and coconut. Serves four.

Contributors	Recipes

Ambrose Gaines IV ("Rowdy")

Butterscotch Krunchies

1 6-ounce package butterscotch chips

1/2 cup peanut butter

1 5-ounce can chow mein noodles

In a small saucepan over low heat, melt butterscotch chips and peanut butter, stirring constantly, until smooth. In a large bowl, combine butterscotch mixture with noodles. Drop by teaspoonsful onto a foil-lined cookie sheet. Or, spread into a foil-lined 9-inch square pan. Refrigerate. Makes about three dozen pieces of candy.

Robert William Hackett, Jr.

Residency: Cambridge, Massachusetts

Age: 19

Height: 6'2"

Weight: 190

School: Harvard College

Training hours per week: 22

Chicken Cacciatore

1 2½ to 3 pound broiler-fryer chicken, cut up

Oil to cover bottom of pan

3 cloves garlic, minced

1 can (2 pounds 3 ounces) whole peeled tomatoes

1 cup water

1/4 cup chopped fresh parsley (preferably flat Italian type)

In a large skillet or Dutch oven, brown garlic in oil. Add chicken and brown on both sides. Puree tomatoes with juice in electric blender. Add tomatoes, water and parsley to chicken. Cover and simmer for 45 minutes to one hour or until chicken is fork-tender. Serves four.

Nancy Lynn Hogshead

Residency: Jacksonville, Florida

Age: 16

Height: 5'8"

Weight: 136

School: Jacksonville Episcopal High School

Training hours per week: 25

High Fiber Banana Nut Bread

3/4 cup honey

2 eggs

1 cup butter or margarine, softened

1/2 cup milk

1 teaspoon vinegar

1 teaspoon baking soda

1 cup mashed bananas

1 cup bran

2¼ cups whole wheat flour

2 teaspoons baking powder

1 to 2 cups chopped nuts

In a medium mixing bowl, cream honey, eggs and butter. Add vinegar and baking soda to milk and stir into creamed mixture. Beat in mashed bananas. Stir in bran, flour and baking powder until well combined. Stir in nuts. Turn into one large greased loaf pan and bake at 325° for 1½ hours. Makes one large loaf.

Nancy Lynn Hogshead

Kitchen Sink Cookies

2 eggs

1/4 cup honey

1/4 cup molasses

1/4 cup melted butter or
  margarine

1 cup whole wheat flour

1/4 cup soy flour

1⅓ cups rolled oats

3/4 cup unsweetened flaked
  coconut

1/4 cup skim milk powder

1/2 teaspoon salt

1 teaspoon cinnamon

1/2 teaspoon ginger

2/3 cup raisins

2/3 cup chocolate chips

1/4 cup chopped peanuts

1/3 cup sunflower seeds

In a large mixing bowl, cream eggs, honey, molasses and melted butter. Mix in remaining ingredients. If mixture seems too dry, add a small amount of milk. Drop from a teaspoon onto an oiled cookie sheet. Bake at 350° for 10 to 12 minutes. Makes about four dozen cookies.

Great Granola

1 cup sesame seeds

14 cups rolled oats

1 cup peanuts

1 cup cashews

1 cup mixed dried fruit,
  chopped

2 cups raisins

2 cups unsweetened flaked
  coconut

2 cups honey

1⅓ cups oil

2 tablespoons vanilla

1/2 teaspoon salt

Combine all dry ingredients in a large roasting pan. In a medium saucepan, heat honey, oil, vanilla and salt until mixture is thin and well combined. Pour over dry mixture, stirring and tossing until ingredients are well coated. Makes about 1½ gallons granola. Store in a covered container in a cool, dry place.

Robert S. Jackson

*Residency: San Jose,
California*

Age: 21

Height: 6'4"

Weight: 205

School: University of Arizona

Training hours per week: 18

Lasagna

1 8-ounce package lasagna
  noodles

2 tablespoons vegetable oil

2 cloves garlic, minced

1 medium onion, chopped

1 pound ground beef

2½ teaspoons salt

1/2 teaspoon pepper

1/2 teaspoon rosemary

1/4 teaspoon oregano

1 tablespoon chopped parsley

2 6-ounce cans tomato paste

1½ cups hot water

2 cups cottage cheese

2 eggs, beaten

1/4 cup grated Parmesan
  cheese

1/2 pound grated Mozzarella
  cheese

Cook noodles according to package directions. Meanwhile, heat oil in a large skillet. Cook garlic and onion until soft. Add beef, salt, pepper, rosemary, oregano and parsley and cook until crumbly. Stir in tomato paste and hot water. Simmer for five minutes. In a medium bowl, beat together eggs, cottage cheese and Parmesan cheese. In a 13x9-inch baking dish, place a thin layer of meat sauce. Top with half the noodles, all the cottage cheese mixture and half the Mozzarella. Repeat with half the remaining meat sauce and the remaining noodles. Top with remaining sauce and cheese. Bake at 350° for 40 minutes. Let set for about 10 minutes before cutting. Serves six to eight.

Choco-Chip Bites

3/4 cup butter, softened

1/2 cup brown sugar

1/2 cup granulated sugar

3 eggs, separated

1 teaspoon vanilla

2 cups flour

1 teaspoon baking powder

1/4 teaspoon baking soda

1/4 teaspoon salt

1 6-ounce package chocolate
  chips

1 cup flaked coconut

3/4 cup chopped nuts

1 cup brown sugar

Cream butter, brown sugar, white sugar, egg yolks and vanilla. Combine flour, baking powder, soda and salt and stir into creamed mixture until well blended. Spread or pat into a greased 13x9-inch baking pan. Sprinkle with chocolate chips, coconut and nuts. In a medium bowl, beat egg whites until frothy. Add brown sugar and beat until stiff but not dry. Spread over chocolate chip layer. Bake at 350° for 35 minutes. Cool. Cut into bars. Makes about three dozen.

Kimberly Lineham

Residency: Sarasota, Florida

Age: 16

Height: 5'5"

Weight: 114

School: Riverview High School

Training hours per week: 28

Cheddar Cheese and Egg Souffle

5 slices buttered bread, cubed

1 pound sharp Cheddar
  cheese, grated

4 eggs, beaten

2 cups milk

1/2 teaspoon salt

1/2 teaspoon dry mustard

Dash of pepper

In a buttered two-quart baking dish, alternate layers of bread cubes and cheese. Beat together eggs, milk, salt, mustard and pepper. Pour egg mixture over bread and cheese. Cover and refrigerate overnight. Bake at 350° for one hour. If desired, one cup diced ham or some crumbled bacon may be added to the bread and cheese. Serves four to six.

Kimberly Lineham

Sour Cream Cake

1/2 cup butter, softened

1 cup sugar

2 eggs, beaten

1 teaspoon baking soda

1 cup sour cream

1½ cups sifted flour

1½ teaspoons baking powder

1 teaspoon vanilla

1/4 cup sugar

1 teaspoon cinnamon

1/2 cup chopped nuts

In a medium mixing bowl, cream butter and sugar. Add eggs and beat until smooth. Mix soda into sour cream. Beat into creamed mixture. Add flour and baking powder, beating until smooth. Stir in vanilla. Pour half of batter into a greased and floured 10-inch tube pan. In a small bowl, combine sugar, cinnamon and nuts. Sprinkle half of nut mixture over batter in pan. Pour remaining batter into pan. Top with remaining nut mixture. Bake at 350° for 45 minutes. Cool on rack for 15 minutes before removing from pan. Serves 12.

Rome Casserole

1/2 pound spaghetti or noodles

1 tablespoon butter or margarine

1½ pounds ground chuck and/or bulk Italian sausage

Salt and pepper

2 8-ounce cans tomato sauce or 2 cups spaghetti sauce

1 cup cottage cheese

1 8-ounce package cream cheese, softened

1/4 cup sour cream

1/4 cup chopped onion

1 teaspoon minced green pepper (optional)

2 tablespoons melted butter or margarine

Cook noodles according to package directions and set aside. In a large skillet, saute beef and/or sausage in butter until brown. Stir in tomato sauce. Salt and pepper to taste. In a separate bowl, combine cottage cheese, cream cheese, sour cream, chopped onion and green pepper. Place half the noodles in a two-quart casserole and cover with cheese mixture. Cover with remaining noodles. Drizzle with melted butter. Cover with meat sauce. Do not mix. Refrigerate until chilled. Bake at 375° for 45 minutes. If desired, sprinkle with Parmesan cheese. Serves four to six.

Scot Matsuda

Residency: Garden Grove, California

Age: 17

Height: 5'8"

Weight: 145

School: Tustin High School

Training hours per week: 26

Red Cake

1/2 cup vegetable shortening

1½ cups sugar

2 eggs

2 teaspoons red food coloring

2 teaspoons cocoa

2¼ cups sifted cake flour

1 teaspoon salt

1 cup buttermilk

1 teaspoon baking soda

1 teaspoon vinegar

Butter Frosting (see directions)

In a medium mixing bowl, cream shortening and sugar. Beat in eggs. Stir in coloring and cocoa. Combine flour with salt and add alternately with buttermilk, beating well after each addition. Combine soda with vinegar and carefully fold into batter. Pour into two greased and floured 9-inch layer cake pans. Bake at 350° for 35 to 40 minutes, or until surface springs back when lightly touched with fingertip. Cook in pans on racks. Remove from pans and frost with Butter Frosting. Serves 12.

Butter Frosting: Combine 3 tablespoons flour with 1 cup milk in a double boiler. Cook over hot water, stirring constantly, until thick. Cover and let cool. In a medium mixing bowl, cream 1 cup butter with 1 cup sugar and 1 teaspoon vanilla. Add cooled custard and beat well. Makes enough to fill and frost a 9-inch layer cake.

Contributors	Recipes

Scot Matsuda

W.L.A.'s Favorite Chocolate Cake

1½ cups water

3/4 cup vegetable oil

3 1-ounce squares
   unsweetened chocolate

3 cups flour

1 teaspoon salt

2 teaspoons baking soda

3 large eggs

2½ cups sugar

1 cup sour cream

1½ teaspoons vanilla

Easy Chocolate Frosting
   (see directions)

Chopped walnuts (optional)

In a double boiler over medium heat, combine water, oil and chocolate and cook, stirring constantly, until chocolate is melted and mixture is combined. Set aside. Sift together flour, salt and soda. Set aside. In a large mixing bowl, beat eggs and gradually add sugar. Beat well. Add sour cream and vanilla. Beat well. With mixer set at lowest speed, gradually add 1/3 of the flour mixture, alternately with the chocolate mixture, ending with the flour mixture. Do not overbeat; mix only until flour is blended. Grease and flour a 9x13-inch pan. Spread batter in pan. Bake at 350° for 40 to 45 minutes. Cool. Frost with Easy Chocolate Frosting and sprinkle with chopped nuts, if desired. Serves 12 or more.

Easy Chocolate Frosting: In a double boiler over medium heat, combine 2 1-ounce squares unsweetened chocolate with 1 14-ounce can sweetened condensed milk. Stir constantly and cook about 10 minutes, until chocolate is melted and mixture is thick. (If too thick, thin with hot water.) Cool. Stir in 1/4 teaspoon vanilla. Makes enough to frost a 13x9-inch cake.

Won Ton

1 pound peeled, deveined
   frozen shrimp, cooked and
   finely chopped

2 green onions, finely chopped

1 hard-boiled egg, finely
   chopped

1 7-ounce can water chestnuts,
   finely chopped

1/2 teaspoon monosodium
   glutamate (msg)

Salt and pepper to taste

1 1-pound package won ton
   skins

Oil for deep-fat frying

Combine all ingredients except won ton skins. Place a teaspoonful of shrimp mixture in the center of each won ton skin. Fold over one corner to form a triangle. Moisten edges with water to seal. Heat oil in deep fryer to 375°, or heat about three inches of oil in a heavy Dutch oven. Fry won tons in deep fat until golden brown, turning once. Eat hot or cold. Makes about four dozen appetizers.

Tim Shaw

Residency: Tucson, Arizona
Age: 21
Height: 6'2"
Weight: 170
School: University of Arizona
Training hours per week: 24

Fudge Bars

3 6-ounce packages chocolate
   chips (3 cups)

1/2 cup margarine

1 5-ounce jar marshmallow
   creme

1 cup chopped nuts

4½ cups sugar

1 8-ounce can evaporated milk

In a large bowl, combine chips, margarine, marshmallow creme and nuts. In a large pan, combine sugar and milk. Bring to a boil and simmer, stirring constantly, for 10 minutes. Pour over chocolate chip mixture. Beat well by hand until chips and margarine are melted, or mix with electric mixer. Pour into a greased 13x9-inch pan. Refrigerate. Cut into small squares. Makes about five dozen pieces.

Contributors	Recipes

Jill Sterkel

Residency: Hacienda Heights, California

Age: 17

Height: 5'11"

Weight: 156

School: Glen A. Wilson High School

Training hours per week: 22

Sour Cream Brownies

1 cup butter or margarine
4 heaping tablespoons cocoa
1 cup water
2 cups sugar
1/2 teaspoon salt
2 cups flour
1 teaspoon baking soda
1/2 cup sour cream
2 eggs, beaten
Cocoa Frosting (see directions)

In a medium pan, heat butter, cocoa and water to boiling. Remove from heat and beat in sugar, salt, flour and soda. Beat in sour cream and eggs. Pour into a greased 13x9-inch pan. Bake at 375° for 20 minutes. Frost with Cocoa Frosting while still hot. Cool and cut into bars. Makes about three dozen.

Cocoa Frosting: During last five minutes of baking time, combine 6 tablespoons milk, 4 tablespoons cocoa and 1/4 cup margarine or butter in a medium pan. Heat to boiling, stirring frequently. Remove from heat and beat in 3 to 4 cups powdered sugar and 1 teaspoon vanilla. Spread on brownies while hot. If desired, sprinkle with nuts. Makes enough to frost a 13x9-inch pan of brownies.

Tamale Pie

1 pound ground beef
1 medium onion, chopped
1 16-ounce can creamed corn
1 cup sliced pitted ripe olives
1 10¾-ounce can condensed tomato soup
1/2 cup milk
1 can (about 14 ounces) tamales, cut up
1 cup grated cheese

In a large skillet, brown meat with onion. Combine remaining ingredients. Turn into a two-quart casserole and bake at 350° for about 30 minutes. Serves four to six.

Sue Walsh

Residency: Hamburg, New York

Age: 16

Height: 5'8"

Weight: 122

School: Mount Mercy Academy

Training hours per week: 15

Toll House Pan Cookies

1 cup butter or margarine, softened
3/4 cup brown sugar
1 teaspoon vanilla
2 eggs
2¼ cups flour
1 teaspoon baking soda
1 teaspoon salt
1 12-ounce package chocolate chips

In a medium mixing bowl, cream butter and brown sugar. Beat in vanilla and eggs. Combine flour, baking soda and salt. Gradually add flour mixture to creamed mixture. Mix well. Stir in chocolate chips. Spread in a greased 13x9-inch baking pan. Bake at 375° for 20 minutes. Cut into bars while still slightly warm. Makes about three dozen bars.

Sue Walsh

Banana Bread

1/2 cup vegetable shortening

1 cup sugar

2 eggs, beaten

2 ripe medium bananas, mashed

1 cup sifted cake flour

1 cup sifted all-purpose flour

1 teaspoon salt

1 teaspoon baking soda

2 tablespoons cold water

1 teaspoon vanilla

In a medium mixing bowl, cream shortening and sugar. Beat in eggs and bananas. Combine dry ingredients. Stir into creamed mixture. Mix in water and vanilla. Turn into a greased medium loaf pan. Bake at 350° for one hour. Do not cut until cool. Makes one loaf.

Brownies

1 cup sugar

1/2 cup vegetable shortening

2 eggs

1 teaspoon vanilla

3/4 cup sifted flour

1/2 teaspoon baking powder

1/2 teaspoon salt

2 1-ounce squares unsweetened baking chocolate

1 cup chopped nuts

In a medium mixing bowl, cream sugar with shortening. Beat in eggs and vanilla. Mix in dry ingredients. Melt chocolate over hot water. Stir chocolate and nuts into batter. Spread into a greased and floured 8-inch-square pan. Bake at 350° for 30 to 35 minutes. Cool. If desired, sprinkle with powdered sugar before cutting into squares. Makes about two dozen brownies.

18
Team Handball

Event Days:

Sunday,
July 20, 1980

Sunday,
July 27, 1980

Monday,
July 21, 1980

Monday,
July 28, 1980

Tuesday,
July 22, 1980

Tuesday,
July 29, 1980

Thursday,
July 24, 1980

Wednesday,
July 30, 1980

Saturday,
July 26, 1980

Contributors:

Mary Phyl Dwight
Carmen Sue Forest
William Johnson
Linda "Chick" Lillis
Carol Beth Lindsey
Cynthia Stinger
Joe Story
Mark Wright

Among Americans the least known and understood sport on the program for the Olympic Games is team handball. The game is now played indoors on a court about one-third larger than the one used for basketball and can be described as a combination-game employing the strategies of basketball (the ball is slightly larger than a "softball" but smaller than a volleyball), soccer and ice hockey. It is played with seven players on a side, by both men and women. The "goals" are comparable in size to ice hockey goals; more physical contact is permitted than in basketball; and all goals must be thrown and score one point.

At Munich the USA men's team finished 14th after defeating Spain in the first game involving the four lowest-ranked teams and then dropping a one-goal contest in the final minute to Denmark.

The USA team qualifying for the games in Montreal was far superior in both ability and experience but placed tenth out of eleven. The USA women's team did not qualify.

The four Eastern Europe teams dominated the women's play at Montreal with the USSR women capturing the first ever gold medal in the sport. For the men, the USSR scored a notable upset over the world championship Romanian team. The hero for the Soviets was goalie Mikhaill Istchenko.

Contributors	Recipes

Mary Phyl Dwight

Residency: Manhattan, Kansas

Age: 27

Height: 5'6"

Weight: 145

School: Southwest Missouri State University, 1974 B.S.; Kansas State University, 1975 M.S.

Training hours per week: 11

Watergate Salad

1 3-ounce package instant pistachio pudding mix

1 16-ounce can crushed pineapple, with juice

1 cup miniature marshmallows

1 9-ounce container frozen nondairy whipped topping

In a large bowl, mix dry pudding mix with pineapple and juice. Fold in marshmallows and whipped topping. Turn into an 11x7-inch glass pan. Chill. Serves six to eight.

Mom's Meat Loaf

2 pounds ground beef

1½ cups bread crumbs

1 cup milk

2 eggs

1 1⅞-ounce packet dry onion soup mix

Combine all ingredients in a large bowl. Mix with hands until bread crumbs are incorporated with meat to give a fine texture. Pack into a large loaf pan. Bake at 350° for one hour. Let set for 10 minutes before slicing. Serves six to eight.

Carmen Sue Forest

Residency: North Little Rock, Arkansas

Age: 23

Height: 5'10"

Weight: 160

School: Oklahoma State University, Master's Degree in Physical Education; University of Missouri-St. Louis, B.S. in Physical Education

Training hours per week: 17

Cheese Ball

2 8-ounce packages cream cheese, softened

1½ teaspoons Worcestershire sauce

1/2 teaspoon monosodium glutamate (msg)

3 green onions, chopped

1 4-ounce package dried beef

In a medium bowl, combine cheese, Worcestershire sauce and msg. Chop all but four slices of beef. Add chopped beef to cheese. Mix well with hands. Form into a ball. Wrap with remaining beef slices. Chill. Makes one cheese ball approximately five inches in diameter.

Cracked Wheat Bread

2 cups boiling water

1/2 cup sugar

2 teaspoons salt

2 tablespoons butter or margarine

2/3 cup warm water

2 teaspoons sugar

2 packets dry yeast

6 cups flour

1/3 cup cracked wheat

In a large bowl, combine boiling water, sugar, salt and butter. In a small bowl, combine warm water with sugar and yeast. When mixture in larger bowl has cooled to lukewarm, stir in yeast mixture. Add flour and cracked wheat, stirring to form a stiff dough. Turn out onto a floured surface and knead until smooth and elastic, adding more flour as necessary. Place in a greased bowl and let rise in a warm place until doubled, about 45 minutes. Punch down, shape into two loaves and place in two medium greased loaf pans. Let rise until doubled. Bake at 350° for 40 to 45 minutes. While loaves are still hot, rub crusts with butter. Makes two medium loaves.

Contributors	Recipes

Carmen Sue Forest

"Cracker Jack"

2 cups brown sugar

1/2 cup light corn syrup

1 cup margarine

1 teaspoon butter flavoring

1 teaspoon salt

6 quarts popped corn

Combine all ingredients except popped corn in a medium pan. Bring to a boil and boil five minutes. Pour over popped corn in a large roasting pan. Bake at 225° for 45 minutes, stirring two or three times. Cool. Makes six quarts "cracker jack."

William Johnson

Residency: Hewlett, New York

Age: 25

Height: 6'5"

Weight: 200

School: Adelphi University

Training hours per week: 20

Miniature Walnut Tarts

1 3-ounce package cream cheese, softened

1/2 cup butter, softened

1 cup flour

1 egg, beaten

3/4 cup brown sugar

1 cup chopped walnuts

1 tablespoon melted butter

1 teaspoon vanilla

In a small bowl, cut cheese and butter into flour until mixture is crumbly. With hands, line miniature muffin tins with pastry dough. Mix remaining ingredients together well and spoon into lined tins. Bake at 375° for 15 to 20 minutes or until filling is set. Makes 12 to 18 tarts.

Jolly Gelatin Gem Dessert

1 3-ounce package raspberry jello

1 3 -ounce package orange jello

2 3-ounce packages lime jello

Boiling water

1½ cups graham cracker crumbs

1/2 cup sugar

1/2 cup melted butter or margarine

1½ cups whipping cream

Dissolve each package of jello, in four separate containers, in 1½ cups boiling water. Pour red, orange and one of the green jello mixtures into three separate 8-inch square pans. Chill until firm. Cut into 1/2-inch cubes and lightly toss together. Meanwhile, let one container of green jello stand until mixture is the consistency of egg whites. Combine crumbs with 1/4 cup sugar and melted butter. Press into bottom and sides of a 9-inch springform pan. Chill. Whip cream and remaining sugar until stiff. Fold in thick gelatin. Fold in gelatin cubes. Pour into lined pan. Chill overnight or for four hours. Remove from pan. Serves eight to 12.

Zucchini Nut Bread

1 cup vegetable oil

2 cups sugar

3 eggs

2 cups grated zucchini

3 cups flour

1 teaspoon salt

1 teaspoon cinnamon

1 teaspoon baking soda

1 tablespoon vanilla

1 cup chopped nuts

In a large bowl, cream oil with sugar. Beat in eggs and zucchini. Combine dry ingredients and mix into batter until well blended. Stir in nuts and vanilla. Turn into two greased and floured medium loaf pans. Bake at 325° for one hour. Makes two medium loaves.

Linda "Chick" Lillis

Residency: Chicago, Illinois
Age: 24
Height: 5'5"
Weight: 130
School: Graduate Concordia Teachers College
Training hours per week: 30

Shrimp With Apricot Sauce

2 pounds fresh or frozen raw shrimp, thawed
2 eggs
1/2 cup milk
3/4 cup flour
2 tablespoons cornstarch
1 teaspoon baking powder
1 teaspoon salt
2 teaspoons vegetable oil
Oil for deep frying
Apricot Sauce (see directions)

Shell and devein shrimp, leaving tails on. Rinse and drain well. In a medium bowl, beat eggs. Beat in milk, flour, cornstarch, baking powder, salt and oil until smooth. In a deep fryer or heavy kettle, heat oil to 375°. Meanwhile, make Apricot Sauce. Dip shrimp in batter, coating thoroughly. Fry a few at a time until golden brown, about four minutes. Drain. Serve with hot Apricot Sauce. Serves six.
   Apricot Sauce: In a small saucepan, stir 1/2 cup pineapple juice with 2 to 4 tablespoons dry mustard until smooth. Add 2 tablespoons soy sauce, 1 cup apricot jam, 2 teaspoons grated lemon peel and 1/4 cup lemon juice. Heat, stirring constantly, until jam melts. Makes about two cups sauce.

Peanut Banana Spread

1 3-ounce package cream cheese, softened
1/4 cup peanut butter
1 tablespoon honey
1 medium banana, mashed

Combine all ingredients and blend well. Spread between slices of bread for a sandwich. Or, substitute mashed avocado for banana and combine with slices of ham and Swiss cheese for broiled open-face sandwiches. Makes 1 cup spread.

Chicken Veronique

1 2½- to 3-pound broiler-fryer chicken, cut up
1/2 lemon
Salt
1/3 cup butter
1/3 cup sauterne or other dry white wine
1 cup seedless green grapes
Paprika

Rub chicken with lemon and sprinkle with salt. Let dry for 15 minutes. Heat butter in a large skillet until bubbly. Brown chicken, turning once. Add wine and stir to loosen brown bits. Spoon sauce over chicken. Cover and simmer until tender, about 30 minutes. Add grapes, heat through. Sprinkle with paprika; remove to a heated platter; pass sauce. Serves four.

Crunchy Peanut-Stuffed Hot Dogs

4 slices processed American cheese, chopped
1/4 cup prepared mustard
1/4 cup chopped peanuts
1 pound hot dogs
12 slices bacon
12 hot dog buns

Combine cheese, mustard and peanuts. Slit each hot dog almost all the way through. Stuff each hot dog with cheese mixture. Wrap with bacon and secure with toothpicks. Grill over hot coals or broil until done, turning occasionally, for five to 10 minutes. Serve on buns. Serves six or more.

Contributors	Recipes

Linda "Chick" Lillis

Avocado Bacon Sandwich

1/4 cup buttermilk

1/2 cup mayonnaise

2 tablespoons chopped onion

1/2 teaspoon Worcestershire sauce

Dash of garlic salt

1/2 cup (2 ounces) crumbled blue cheese

6 slices rye bread, toasted

Leaf lettuce

12 slices bacon, cooked crisp

3 medium avocados, peeled and sliced

1 lemon, cut in six wedges

Place buttermilk, mayonnaise, onion, Worcestershire and garlic salt in electric blender. Add half the cheese. Blend until smooth. Stir in remaining cheese. Spread each piece of toast generously with spread. Top each with lettuce, two slices bacon, avocado slices. Drizzle with remaining dressing. Garnish with lemon wedges. Serves six.

Carol Beth Lindsey

Residency: Martinsburg, West Virginia

Age: 23

Height: 5'7½"

Weight: 145

School: Purdue University

Training hours per week: 12

Trondheim Surprise

1 medium carrot, chopped

1 medium onion, chopped

2 stalks celery, chopped

1 leek, chopped

1 pound ground beef

1 tablespoon butter

Salt and pepper

1½ to 2 cups ketchup

1/4 cup cream or milk

1 teaspoon Italian seasoning or poultry seasoning

1 to 2 teaspoons curry powder

Salt and pepper

Hot cooked noodles or spaghetti

In a large skillet, saute vegetables and ground beef in butter, breaking up beef. Season with salt and pepper. Combine remaining ingredients and pour over meat. Simmer for 10 to 15 minutes, adding more water if desired. Correct seasoning with salt and pepper if necessary. Serve over noodles or spaghetti. Serves four.

Cynthia Stinger

Residency: Lawrenceville, New Jersey

Age: 20

Height: 5'8½"

Weight: 140

School: Davis & Elkins College

Training hours per week: 24

Coleslaw

3/4 cup sugar

1 teaspoon dry mustard

1/2 teaspoon salt

1/4 teaspoon paprika

3 eggs, beaten

1/2 cup vinegar

1/2 cup water

Pat of butter

1 medium head cabbage, shredded

In a medium pan, combine dry ingredients. Stir in beaten eggs. Add vinegar and water. Over medium heat, stirring constantly, bring to a boil. Do not allow to boil. Remove from heat immediately. Stir in butter. Cool to room temperature. Pour over shredded cabbage. Chill. Serves six to eight.

Cynthia Stinger

Onion Lover's Twist

1 packet dry yeast
1/4 cup warm water
4 cups flour
1/4 cup sugar
1/2 cup hot water
1/2 cup milk
1/2 cup margarine, softened
1 egg
Onion Filling (see directions)

In large mixing bowl, dissolve yeast in warm water. Add two cups flour, sugar, water, milk, margarine and egg. Blend at low speed until moistened. Beat at medium speed for two minutes. Stir in remaining flour by hand to form soft dough. Cover and let rise in a warm place until doubled, 45 minutes to one hour. Stir down. Toss on a floured board until no longer sticky. Roll out to an 18x12-inch rectangle. Spread with filling (below). Cut lengthwise into three strips, for one large loaf. (For two shorter loaves, cut strips in half crosswise.) Starting with the longer side, roll up each strip. Seal edges and ends. On a greased cookie sheet, braid three rolls together. (If making two loaves, repeat.) Cover. Let rise until doubled. Bake at 350° for 45 minutes to one hour or until golden. Serve warm or cold.

Onion Filling: In a medium pan, melt 1/4 cup margarine. Add 1 cup finely chopped onion (or 1/4 cup instant minced onion), 1 tablespoon grated Parmesan cheese, 1 tablespoon sesame or poppy seeds, 1 teaspoon garlic salt and 1 teaspoon paprika. Mix well.

Joe Story

Residency: Salem, Oregon
Age: 26
Height: 5'7"
Weight: 160
School: Willamette University (1975 graduate)
Training hours per week: 28

Teriyaki Kabob Pupus

1 pound sirloin or rib eye steak, cut 3/4-inch thick
1 16-ounce can pineapple chunks
1/4 cup soy sauce
1 tablespoon sugar
1/2 to 1 teaspoon grated ginger root
1 clove garlic, minced
16 water chestnuts
16 stuffed green olives

Cut meat into 16 pieces. Make a marinating sauce by combining 1/2 cup syrup from canned pineapple, soy sauce, sugar, ginger and garlic. Marinate meat for one hour or longer, turning frequently. Using shish kebab skewers, alternate cubes of meat, pineapple and water chestnuts. Broil three inches from heat for five minutes. Turn and broil other side for five minutes or until meat reaches desired degree of doneness. Garnish ends of skewers with olives. Serves three to four.

Mark Wright

Residency: Pacific Palisades, California
Age: 28
Height: 6'5"
Weight: 225
Training hours per week: 15

Mexican Flank Steak

2 beef flank steaks, scored (1 pound each)
3/4 teaspoon salt
1/8 teaspoon garlic salt
1/8 teaspoon pepper
1 15-ounce can tamales in sauce
2 tablespoons cooking oil
1¼ cups boiling water
1 8-oune can tomato sauce (1 cup)
dash bottled hot pepper sauce

Pound meat well on both sides; sprinkle with salt, garlic salt and pepper. Unwrap tamales; place in center of steaks, and roll as for a jelly roll. Brown the rolls in hot oil in a heavy skillet. (Electric skillet 350°.) Drain excess fat. Combine remaining ingredients. Pour over meat. Reduce heat. Cover; simmer till tender, basting occasionally, 1/4 to 1¼ hours. Before serving skim off fat. Makes 6 to 8 servings.

19

Volleyball

Event Days:

Sunday,
July 20, 1980

Monday,
July 21, 1980

Tuesday,
July 22, 1980

Wednesday,
July 23, 1980

Thursday,
July 24, 1980

Friday,
July 25, 1980

Saturday,
July 26, 1980

Sunday,
July 27, 1980

Monday,
July 28, 1980

Tuesday,
July 29, 1980

Wednesday,
July 30, 1980

Friday,
August 1, 1980

Contributors:

Douglas P. Beal
Rita Crockett
Debra L. Landreth
Diane McCormick
David E. Olbright

In 1895, William G. Morgan, the athletic director of the Holyoke (Mass.) YMCA, developed new indoor game by stringing a tennis net across his gymnasium, took the bladder out of the soccer ball, and called the game "Mintonette." At a YMCA physical directors' conference at Springfield (Mass.) College in 1896, Professor Alfred T. Halstead renamed the game "volleyball".

The sport was introduced in the 1964 Olympic Games at Tokyo. In the men's competition the order of finish was the USSR, Czechoslovakia and Japan. The host country, Japan, won the women's title, followed by the USSR and Poland.

At one epic-game at Montreal (Poland defeating the USSR for the men's title) not a spectator stirred for more than four hours during the hectic action at the Forum and the TV cameras outside of the USA stayed with the match. Japan blasted the USSR 3–0 for the women's gold medal by the incredible scores of 15–7, 15–8, and, finally, 15–2.

As a result of lack of success in international volleyball, the U.S. Volleyball Association in 1976 established permanent training quarters for the national men's and women's teams. Rated among the top players in the world are Patty Dowdell, Debbie Green, and Flo Hyman from the current USA national team.

Douglas P. Beal

Residency: Dayton, Ohio
Age: 31
Height: 6'2"
Weight: 190
School: Ohio State University
Training hours per week: 25

Boeuf Bourguignon

1/3 pound salt pork or bacon, diced

2 pounds beef stew meat

1 pound fresh mushrooms, whole or sliced

1 small onion, chopped

1 10¾-ounce can beef consomme

3 tablespoons tomato paste

Salt and pepper to taste

1/2 teaspoon marjoram

1/2 teaspoon basil

1 cup dry red wine

Hot cooked noodles

In a large skillet, brown salt pork or bacon. Remove with a slotted spoon and set aside. Brown beef, mushrooms and onion in drippings. Drain off excess fat. If salt pork was used, cut out any meaty parts and add to beef. If bacon was used, add crumbled bacon to beef. Stir in consomme, tomato paste and seasonings. Cover and simmer for 30 minutes. Add wine and simmer for 1½ hours, adding more wine or water if necessary. Serve over hot buttered noodles. Serves four to six.

Rita Crockett

Residency: Colorado Springs, Colorado
Age: 21
Height: 5'8½"
Weight: 138
School: University of Houston
Training hours per week: 34½

Spinach Salad

1 pound fresh spinach

4 to 6 bacon slices

1/2 pound fresh mushrooms, sliced

3 tablespoons finely chopped green onion

3 hard-boiled eggs, cut in wedges

Salt and pepper to taste

1/4 teaspoon sugar

3 ounces crumbled blue cheese

1/4 cup cider vinegar

Wash spinach: remove stems and tear into bite-size pieces. Place in a large salad bowl. Fry bacon until crisp; drain, cool and crumble over spinach. Saute mushrooms in bacon fat. Add both mushrooms and fat to spinach. Add remaining ingredients to spinach. Toss and serve. Serves six to eight.

Carrot Cake

2 cups sugar

1/4 cup oil

4 eggs

1 teaspoon vanilla

1 cup raisins

1/4 cup coarsely chopped walnuts

3 cups flour

2 teaspoons baking soda

2 teaspoons baking powder

2 teaspoons cinnamon

1/2 teaspoon salt

3 cups grated raw carrots

Cream Cheese Frosting (see directions)

In a large bowl, cream sugar with oil. Add eggs one at a time, beating after each addition. Beat in vanilla. In another bowl, toss raisins and nuts with 2 tablespoons flour and set aside. Combine remaining flour and dry ingredients. Stir dry ingredients into batter alternately with carrots. Stir in raisin mixture. Turn into a greased 10-inch tube pan. Bake at 350° for 1 hour and 15 minutes. Cool in pan on rack for 10 minutes. Remove from pan. Cool. Frost. Serves 12.

Cream Cheese Frosting: Beat together 1 3-ounce package cream cheese, 2 tablespoons light corn syrup, 1/2 teaspoons vanilla and 2 to 3 cups powdered sugar. Makes enough to frost one tube or bundt cake.

Contributors	Recipes

Rita Crockett

Jalapeno Cheese Dip

1/2 pound processed American cheese food

1 16-ounce can stewed or whole tomatoes with peppers

Canned Jalapeno peppers, drained and sliced

Tortilla chips

Cut cheese into cubes and place in double boiler. Stir constantly over hot water until melted and smooth. Add tomatoes, using only enough juice to give the desired thickness. Add as many peppers as necessary to give the desired degree of hotness. Serve warm with tortilla chips for dipping. Makes two to three cups dip.

Debra L. Landreth

Residency: Colorado Springs, Colorado

Age: 22

Height: 5'8"

Weight: 150

School: University of Southern California

Training hours per week: 35

Vegetable Dip

1 cup mayonnaise

1 cup sour cream

1 tablespoon dill

1 tablespoon chopped chives

1 tablespoon beau monde seasoning

1 teaspoon minced parsley

Combine all ingredients until well blended. Serve as a dip with fresh raw vegetables. Makes two cups.

Vegetable Soup

1 leek, diced

1 onion, diced

2 cups cut green beans or 1 10-ounce package frozen green beans

2 cups diced carrots

2 cups diced potatoes

2 cups diced tomatoes

2½ quarts boiling water

1 tablespoon salt

2 cups diced zucchini

2 cloves garlic, minced

1 tablespoon dried basil or 2 tablespoons fresh basil, minced

Pinch of salt

2 tablespoons tomato paste

1/4 cup grated Parmesan cheese

1/4 cup olive oil

In a large kettle, combine leek, onion, beans, carrots, potatoes, tomatoes, boiling water and salt. (If frozen vegetables are being used, add later as indicated.) Cover and simmer for 45 minutes. Add zucchini and any frozen vegetables. In a small bowl, make a paste of garlic, basil, salt, tomato paste and cheese. With a fork or wire whisk, beat in olive oil, a little at a time. Stir one or two ladles of hot soup into tomato paste mixture. Stir well and add to soup, stirring again. Simmer for five minutes. Serve with additional Parmesan cheese, if desired. Serves eight to 10.

Contributors	Recipes

Debra L. Landreth

Peanut Butter Munchies

1/2 cup peanut butter

1/2 cup honey

1/2 cup noninstant skim milk powder

1/8 teaspoon vanilla

1/2 cup granola

1/2 cup carob chips

In a medium bowl, combine peanut butter, honey, milk powder and vanilla. Mix well. Mixture will be sticky. With hands, roll into bite-size balls. Combine granola and carob chips in a small bowl. Roll balls in granola mixture. Chill. Store in refrigerator. Makes about three dozen balls.

Diane McCormick

Residency: Charleroi, Pennsylvania

Age: 28

Height: 5'11½"

Weight: 140

School: Indiana University of Pennsylvania

Training hours per week: 34

Pennsylvania Dutch Cake

1 cup quick-cooking oatmeal

1½ cups water

1 teaspoon salt

1/2 cup butter or margarine

1 cup white sugar

1 cup brown sugar

2 eggs

1 teaspoon baking soda

1 teaspoon cinnamon

1½ cups flour

1 cup chopped walnuts

6 tablespoons butter or margarine

3/4 cup brown sugar

1 cup flaked coconut

1 cup chopped walnuts

1 teaspoon vanilla

Cook oatmeal in water and salt as for cereal. Cover and remove from heat. In a large bowl, cream butter with sugars. Beat in eggs. Beat in soda and cinnamon. Add oatmeal mixture alternately with flour, mixing well after each addition. Stir in nuts. Turn into a greased and floured 13x9-inch pan. With a pastry blender, cut butter into brown sugar. Blend in remaining ingredients. Crumble over top of cake. Bake at 350° for 45 minutes. Serves 12.

Spanish Rice

2 tablespoons butter or margarine

1 cup raw rice

4 large onions, chopped

1 pound ground beef

2 16-ounce cans tomatoes

2 cups water

2 large green peppers, diced

Salt and sugar to taste

In a large skillet, brown rice, onions and beef in butter until meat is crumbly. Mix in remaining ingredients. Turn into a large casserole or 13x9-inch baking pan. Bake, covered at 350° to 400° for 1½ hours or until liquid is absorbed and rice is tender. Serves four to six.

Contributors	Recipes

Diane McCormick

Apple Dumplings

Pastry for a double pie crust

10 to 12 small baking apples, or 5 to 6 large apples

Sugar

Cinnamon

Butter

Sauce:
1/2 cup brown sugar

1/2 cup white sugar

1 tablespoon flour

2 tablespoons butter

Pinch of salt

1½ cups boiling water

Peel and core apples. If apples are small, you will use a whole one in each dumpling. If they are large, you will use a half. Roll out dough and cut into squares large enough to cover apples. Place an apple in the center of each square. In the center of the apple, place a tablespoon of sugar, a dash of cinnamon and a small chunk of butter. Fold up corners of dough and fasten by pressing together. Place seam-side-down in a 13x9-inch baking dish. Bake at 375° for 30 minutes. Meanwhile, combine sugars and flour for sauce in a medium pan. Add remaining ingredients and cook slowly, stirring constantly, until sugar dissolves, butter melts and mixture thickens slightly. Pour sauce over dumplings and continue to bake for 30 more minutes. Or, continue to bake dumplings, without sauce, and serve sauce separately at the table. Makes 10 to 12 dumplings.

Good Pie Crust Mix

4 cups flour

1½ cups vegetable shortening

2 teaspoons salt

In a large bowl, using a pastry blender or two knives, cut shortening into dry ingredients until mixture resembles coarse meal. Store in a tightly covered container in the refrigerator. For a one-crust pie, combine 1 cup mix with 2 tablespoons cold water. For a two-crust pie, combine 1½ cups mix with 3½ tablespoons cold water. For a baked pie shell, prick all over with a fork and bake at 475° for 10 to 12 minutes. For most two-crust fruit pies, bake at 475° until crust begins to brown, then reduce heat to 375°; total baking time should be about 55 minutes.

David E. Olbright

Residency: Dayton, Ohio
Age: 26
Height: 6'1"
Weight: 175
School: UCLA
Training hours per week: 25

Orange-Tarragon Chicken

1 2½ to 3-pound broiler-fryer chicken, cut up

1/2 cup orange juice

Grated rind of one orange

1/4 cup melted butter or margarine

2 teaspoons tarragon

Salt and pepper to taste

Arrange chicken pieces, skin-side-up in a 13x9-inch baking pan. Bake at 400° for 15 minutes. Reduce heat to 350°. Combine remaining ingredients. Brush chicken liberally with this mixture several times during remaining cooking time, about 45 minutes or until chicken is fork-tender. Serves four.

David E. Olbright

Willa Mae's Pineapple Ice Box Dessert

1 ⅓ cups graham cracker crumbs (1 packet, crushed)

1/4 cup melted butter or margarine

1/4 cup sugar

Filling:
1 cup sugar

3 egg yolks

1/3 cup butter or margarine

1 tablespoon cream

1 cup well-drained crushed pineapple

1/4 cup chopped nuts

1/4 cup maraschino cherries, chopped

Whipped cream or nondairy whipped topping

To make crust, combine all ingredients. Reserve 3 tablespoons for topping. Pat remainder into the bottom of an 8x8-inch baking pan or over the bottom and sides of a 9-inch pie pan. Bake at 400° for 10 minutes.

To make filling, in a medium pan beat sugar and egg yolks together. Stir in butter, cream and pineapple. Cook over low heat, stirring constantly, until thick. Pour over crust. Top with nuts and cherries. Spread with whipped cream. Sprinkle with reserved crumbs. Chill 12 hours before serving. Serves eight.

20
Water Polo

Event Days:

Sunday, July 20, 1980	Friday, July 25, 1980
Monday, July 21, 1980	Saturday, July 26, 1980
Tuesday, July 22, 1980	Monday, July 28, 1980
Thursday, July 24, 1980	Tuesday, July 29, 1980

Contributors:

Thomas James Belfanti
Christopher Taylor Dorst
Gary Figueroa
John A. Gansel
Jack D. Graham, Jr.
Russell A. Hafferkamp
Joseph M. Vargas

England, the home of bare knuckle fighting, came up with an even rougher sport in 1870 when the game of water polo was "born".

Today, under "reformed rules" the game is one of skillful ball handling with a minimum of mayhem.

The USA failed to qualify for the 1976 Olympic tournament for the only time in the history of sport but water polo in the USA appears to be on its way back internationally after we finished a "solid" fifth in the 1978 World Water Polo Championships. Thus the USA has an automatic qualifying berth for the 1980 Games at Moscow.

Sure, the USA won the 1904 water polo competition in St. Louis. Why not? All teams were USA club teams so we landed all three medals. The USA garnered bronze medals in 1924 (Johnny

Weissmuller doubled in swimming and water polo that year), 1932, and 1972 at Munich.

In the early Olympic tournaments Great Britain won the 1900, 1908, 1912, and 1920 and has failed to medal since. After Hungary won the silver medal in 1928, they captured the gold medal in 1932, 1936, 1952, 1956 and 1964.

Yugoslavia defeated the USSR for the gold at Mexico in 1968. At Munich, the USSR and Hungary played a 3–3 deadlock, but the gold went to the USSR because they had outscored their opponents. Then at Montreal, Hungary regained the title and Italy captured the silver.

Contributors	Recipes

Thomas James Belfanti

Residency: Walnut Creek, California

Age: 25

Height: 5'11"

Weight: 175

School: University California at Berkeley

Training hours per week: 30

Barbecue Steak Western

3½ pounds top round steak, cut 2 inches thick

1/2 cup vegetable oil

1/2 cup finely chopped onion

1/3 cup lemon juice

2 tablespoons catsup

1 tablespoon Worcestershire sauce

1 tablespoon prepared horseradish

1 tablespoon paprika

1 clove garlic, minced

2 bay leaves

Place steak in a glass or stainless steel baking pan. Combine remaining ingredients and pour over steak. Cover and refrigerate overnight; turn meat once or twice. Lift steak from marinade and drain briefly. Place on greased grill four to six inches above a solid bed of low glowing coals. Turn every 10 minutes until desired degree of doneness is reached. Serves six to eight.

Lemon Meringue Pie

1 9-inch baked pie shell

1½ cups sugar

1/3 cup plus 1 tablespoon cornstarch

3 egg yolks, slightly beaten

2 teaspoons grated lemon peel

1/2 cup lemon juice

1½ cups water

3 tablespoons butter or margarine

3 egg whites

1/4 teaspoon cream of tartar

6 tablespoons sugar

1/2 teaspoon vanilla

In a medium saucepan, combine sugar and cornstarch. Stir in egg yolks along with lemon peel and juice. Gradually stir in water. Over medium heat, stirring constantly, cook until thick. Stir in butter until melted. Pour into pie shell. In a medium mixing bowl with clean beaters, beat egg whites until foamy. Add cream of tartar and beat until soft peaks form. Gradually add sugar, one tablespoon at a time, and continue to beat until stiff peaks form. Fold in vanilla. Mound onto pie, sealing edges. Bake at 450° for about five minutes or until peaks or meringue are golden brown. Cool. Serves six to eight.

Barbecued Ham Slice

1 6-ounce packet Italian salad dressing mix

1/4 cup catsup

1 tablespoon vegetable oil

1 tablespoon vinegar

1 fully-cooked smoked ham slice, cut 1 inch thick

In a small bowl, combine dressing mix, catsup, oil and vinegar. Set oven control at broil or 550°. Diagonally slash outer edge of fat at one-inch intervals to prevent curling. Broil three inches from heat for 10 minutes or until light brown. Brush with catsup mixture during last minute. Turn; broil six minutes more, brushing with catsup mixture during last minute. Serves four.

Christopher Taylor Dorst

Residency: Atherton, California

Age: 22

Height: 6'4"

Weight: 195

School: Standford University, AB, 1977

Training hours per week: 23

Captain Whidbey's Biscuits

6 cups flour

1/4 cup baking powder

1/2 cup skim milk powder

1/4 cup sugar

2 teaspoons salt

2 teaspoons cream of tartar

2 cups vegetable shortening

1½ cups water

In a large mixing bowl, combine all dry ingredients. With pastry blender or two knives, cut in shortening until mixture resembles coarse crumbs. With a fork, stir in water. Knead eight to 10 times. On a floured surface, roll into a 13x9-inch rectangle, about 3/4-inch thick. Cut into 1½-inch squares. Place on a greased cookie sheet about 1/2-inch apart. Bake at 400° for about 30 minutes or until light golden brown. May be frozen, unbaked, for up to three months. Bake frozen biscuits at the same time and temperature as unfrozen. Makes about 4½ dozen biscuits.

Delicious Potatoes

6 medium potatoes, cooked, peeled and grated

2 cups grated Cheddar cheese

2 cups sour cream

1/2 cup chopped green onion

1/2 cup melted butter or margarine

Salt and pepper

Combine all ingredients. Turn into a two-quart buttered casserole or baking dish. Salt and pepper to taste. Bake at 200° for one hour. Serves eight.

Easy Hot Fudge Sauce

2 1-ounce squares unsweetened chocolate

1/3 cup light corn syrup

In a small saucepan over low heat, heat chocolate and corn syrup, stirring constantly, until chocolate is melted and mixture is well combined. Serve hot over ice cream. Makes about 1/2 cup sauce, enough for two sundaes.

No Knead Bread

6 cups warm water

1/2 cup vegetable oil

5 pounds flour

1 cup sugar

2 tablespoons salt

1 cup skim milk powder

2 packets dry yeast

Combine dry ingredients in a large mixing bowl. Add warm water and oil. Mix well with hands. Cover, set in a warm, draft-free place and let rise for three hours. Punch down. Shape into five medium greased loaf pans. Let rise in a warm place for 1½ hours. Bake at 350° for 45 minutes. Makes five medium loaves.

Gary Figueroa

Residency: Newport Beach, California

Age: 22

Height: 6'

Weight: 170

School: University of California at Irvine

Training hours per week: 17

Juevos Enchiladas

2 tablespoons butter

8–12 tortillas

6 eggs

1/4 pound shredded Cheddar cheese

Salsa

In a skillet over high heat, soften tortillas in butter, allowing one to two tortillas per person. Place tortillas on oven-proof plates. Fry eggs. Place eggs on tortillas. Sprinkle with cheese and salsa. Run under broiler until cheese melts. Serves four to six.

Green Chile Enchiladas

2 10¾-ounce cans cream of mushroom soup

1 7-ounce can chopped green chiles

2–3 tablespoons vegetable oil

16 corn tortillas

1/2 cup chopped green onions

1/2 to 3/4 pound shredded Cheddar cheese

Shredded lettuce

Sour cream

Hot sauce

In a medium pan, warm soup and chiles. Heat oil in a skillet over high heat. Quickly fry a tortilla in oil until it is soft. (Fry only about 30 seconds; tortilla shouldn't be crispy.) Place tortilla on oven-proof plate. Top with soup mixture, lettuce, cheese and onions. Repeat layers, using four tortillas in all. Repeat on separate plates for each serving. Place plates in oven and bake at 350° for five to 10 minutes or until heated through. Garnish with sour cream and hot sauce. Serves four.

Red Chile Burritos

2 to 2½ pounds round steak, cubed

2 tablespoons vegetable oil

1 28-ounce can red chili sauce

1 19-ounce can enchilada sauce

2 to 4 tablespoons salsa ranchera (very hot salsa)

1 17-ounce can refried beans

1/4 cup flour

10–12 12-inch flour tortillas

1/2 pound grated Cheddar cheese

In a heavy 5-quart pan, brown steak cubes in oil. Add red chili sauce, enchilada sauce and salsa ranchera. Simmer, covered for 1½ hours or until meat is tender, stirring occasionally. To thicken sauce, stir in refried beans. Sift flour into sauce gradually, stirring constantly. To assemble burritos, place one to two tortillas on an oven-proof plate. Spoon filling down center and roll up. Spoon sauce lightly over top. Sprinkle with cheese. Place under broiler for two to three minutes to melt cheese. Serve immediately. Serves six.

John A. Gansel

Residency: Stanford, California
Age: 20
Height: 6'3"
Weight: 185
School: Stanford University
Training hours per week: 6

Over-Nite Fruit Salad

1 16-ounce can pineapple chunks

2 tablespoons flour

Dash of salt

1/4 to 1/2 cup sugar

1 egg

1 9-ounce container frozen nondairy whipped topping, or the equivalent of the dried whipped topping mix, prepared

3 to 4 applies, cored and sliced

3 to 4 oranges, peeled and cut into chunks

2 cups miniature marshmallows

1 16-ounce can fruit cocktail, drained

In a medium pan, combine juice from pineapple chunks, flour, salt, sugar and egg. Stir well and bring to a boil. Cool and pour over pineapple chunks and remaining ingredients. Any combination of fruit may be used. Chill overnight. Serves eight.

Egg and Ham Brunch Bake

6 to 7 slices bread, cubed

1 pound diced cooked ham

1/2 pound sharp Cheddar cheese, shredded

3 eggs, beaten

2 cups milk

1/2 teaspoon dry mustard

1/2 teaspoon salt

1/2 cup melted butter or margarine

In a greased 13x9-inch pan, combine bread cubes and ham. Sprinkle with shredded cheese. Beat together remaining ingredients and pour over casserole. Drizzle with melted butter. Cover and refrigerate overnight. Bake at 325° for one hour, uncovered. Allow to set for about 10 minutes before cutting into squares. Serves eight.

Jack D. Graham, Jr.

Residency: Brimonton, Washington
Age: 18
Height: 6'2"
Weight: 180
School: University of Southern California
Training hours per week: 25

Cheese Cake

15 double graham crackers, crushed

1/2 cup butter or margarine, melted

1/2 cup sugar

4 3-ounce packages cream cheese, softened

2 tablespoons milk

1/2 cup sugar

1 teaspoon vanilla

3 eggs, beaten

1/2 cup sugar

1/2 teaspoon vanilla

In a medium bowl, combine graham cracker crumbs with butter and sugar. Mix well; pour into a 9-inch pie pan. With hands, pat to line bottom and sides of pan. Beat together cheese and milk until smooth. Beat in sugar, vanilla and eggs. Pour into pie shell. Bake at 350° for 20 minutes or until center is firm. Cool for 20 minutes. Meanwhile, preheat oven to 475° and mix sugar with vanilla. Sprinkle over top of cheese cake. Bake at 475° for nine minutes or until lightly browned. Cool. Refrigerate. Serves eight.

Contributors	Recipes

Jack D. Graham, Jr.

Cheese Relenos

2 4-ounce cans whole green chilies

1 to 1½ pounds mild Cheddar cheese, shredded

3 eggs

3 cups milk

1 cup biscuit mix

Drain chilies; remove seeds. Arrange chilies to cover bottom of a lightly greased 13x9-inch baking pan. Cover with cheese. In a medium bowl, beat eggs. Beat in milk. Add biscuit mix gradually, beating constantly, until smooth. Pour over cheese. Bake at 350° for 30 to 40 minutes or until top is lightly browned and knife inserted in center comes out clean. Serves six to eight.

Russell A. Hafferkamp

Residency: San Diego, California

Age: 24

Height: 6'4"

Weight: 200

Schools: University of California, Santa Barbara–BA, San Diego State University–BA

Training hours per week: 20

Zucchini Boats

4 zucchini, about 8 inches long

1 cup finely chopped onion

3/4 cup butter

2 tablespoons tamari soy sauce

1½ pounds Ricotta cheese

1/2 cup grated Parmesan cheese

1/2 cup chopped walnuts

Salt and pepper to taste

Trim zucchini and slice in half lengthwise. Steam for 10 to 15 minutes or until just tender. Scoop out pulp and reserve. In a large skillet, saute onion with butter and soy sauce until limp. Add zucchini pulp and simmer for five minutes. Remove from heat and stir in cheeses, nuts, salt and pepper. Stuff zucchini shells with mixture, mounding up. Place in a buttered baking dish and bake at 400° for 15 minutes or until heated through. If desired, sprinkle with additional Parmesan cheese. Serves six to eight.

Joseph M. Vargas

Residency: Hacienda Heights, California

Age: 23

Height: 6'3"

Weight: 201

School: UCLA

Training hours per week: 50

Sweet-Sour Chicken A La Russe

1 2½ to 3-pound broiler-fryer chicken, cut up

1 8-ounce bottle Russian salad dressing

1 1⅞-ounce packet dry onion soup mix

3/4 cup apricot-pineapple preserves

In a medium bowl, combine dressing, soup mix and preserves. Dip each chicken piece in mixture, generously coating. Place chicken, skin-side-up, in a single layer in a 13x9-inch baking pan. Bake at 350° for 1½ hours or until fork-tender and glazed. Serves four.

Green Chili Eggs

1 8-ounce can green chilies

1 pound grated Monterey Jack cheese

12 eggs

2 cups sour cream

Drain chilies and pat dry. Remove as many seeds as possible. Layer chilies with cheese in a buttered 13x9-inch baking dish. Beat eggs with sour cream. Pour over chili-cheese mixture. Bake at 350° for 30 minutes or until puffy and light golden brown on top. Serves eight to 10.

21
Weightlifting

Event Days:

Sunday, July 20, 1980	Saturday, July 26, 1980
Monday, July 21, 1980	Sunday, July 27, 1980
Tuesday, July 22, 1980	Monday, July 28, 1980
Wednesday, July 23, 1980	Tuesday, July 29, 1980
Thursday, July 24, 1980	Wednesday, July 30, 1980

Contributors:

Guy A. Carlton
David Jones
Michael Karchut
Paul James Salisbury
Kurt N. Setterberg
Stewart B. Thornburgh
Donnie Warner

Between 1932 and 1960 the United States of America was internationally preeminent in the sport of weightlifting. Yet, publicity for our weightlifters such as two-time Olympic heavyweight champion John Davis of Brooklyn (1948, 1952), the achievements of monstrous Paul Anderson (1956 champion), the career of Hawaii's Tommy Kono (winner of two gold and one silver medals in the Olympics in three different weight classes), can scarcely be found in newspaper clippings anywhere in the USA.

Compare this with the acclaim and prerequisites for the Soviet heavyweight gold medalists—Yury Vlasov, Leonid Zhabotinsky and two-time Olympic and seven-time world champion, Vasily Alexeev.

Followers of weight lifting find it one of the most fascinating of all sports on the Olympic program.

"Gamesmanship" plays as much a role in deciding finish places as the bulging muscles and sports skills of the lifters. The "plotting" of coaches and managers plays a key part in helping one lifter "out psyche" his opponent.

There are ten different weight classes on the program for Moscow, ranging from the flyweights (114 pounds) to the super heavyweights (those above 242 pounds).

Awards are made on the basis of the total weight lifted for the two Olympic-style lifts—the two-hand snatch and the two-hand clean and jerk. Each lifter is given three "attempts" in each lift.

Contributors	Recipes

Guy A. Carlton

Residency: La Place, Illinois
Age: 25
Height: 6'
Weight: 220
School: Eastern Illinois
*   University*
Training hours per week: 10

Round Steak and Vegetables

3 pounds beef round steak,
   about 1/2-inch thick
Seasoned flour
1 16-ounce can tomatoes, or 4
   fresh tomatoes
3 large green peppers
4 or 5 large carrots
4 large potatoes
2 4-ounce cans mushrooms

Cut steak into serving-size pieces. Dredge in seasoned flour. In a large heavy skillet or Dutch oven, brown meat in a minimum amount of oil or fat. Meanwhile, prepare vegetables by cutting into bite-size chunks. Add all remaining ingredients to steak in pan. Cover and simmer for 45 minutes to 1 hour, adding more water if necessary. Serves six to eight.

Many Layer Salad

1 head lettuce, chopped
1 small onion, diced
1 cup diced celery
4 hard-boiled eggs, sliced
1 10-ounce package frozen
   peas
1 small head cauliflower or 1
   10-ounce package frozen
   cauliflower, broken into small
   pieces
1/2 cup diced green peppers
2 cups mayonnaise
2 tablespoons sugar
1/4 cup grated Parmesan
   cheese
7 slices bacon, cooked crisp
   and crumbled

In a large ceramic or glass bowl or flat dish, place half of the lettuce in a layer. Choosing at least four of the next six ingredients, place more layers. (Peas and cauliflower should be used frozen; do not thaw.) Top with remaining lettuce. Spread with mayonnaise. Sprinkle with sugar, cheese and crumbled bacon. Cover and refrigerate for 24 hours. Toss gently before serving. Serves eight.

Pumpkin Bread

3½ cups cooked, mashed
   pumpkin, or 1 29-ounce can
   pumpkin
1 cup vegetable oil
4 cups sugar
1 teaspoon cloves
1 teaspoon cinnamon
1 teaspoon salt
5 cups flour
1 teaspoon soda

In a large bowl, cream pumpkin with oil and sugar. Add remaining dry ingredients and mix well. Turn into three medium greased loaf pans. Bake at 350° for one hour and 15 minutes. Cool in pans for a few minutes before removing. Makes three medium loaves.

Contributors	Recipes

Guy A. Carlton

Jelly-Butter Cookies

1 cup butter, softened
3/4 cup sugar
3 egg yolks
1 teaspoon vanilla
2½ cups flour
Tart jelly

In a medium bowl, cream butter with sugar. Beat in egg yolks and vanilla. Mix in flour until well blended. Dough will be stiff. With hands, form into small balls and place on ungreased cookie sheets. With tip of index finger, depress center. Fill depression with a small amount of jelly. Bake at 375° for seven to 10 minutes. Makes about three dozen.

David Jones

Residency: Eastman, Georgia
Age: 30
Height: 5'4"
Weight: 148¾
School: Georgia Southern College
Training hours per week: 11

Marinated Bean Salad

1 16-ounce can green beans
1 16-ounce can wax beans
1 16-ounce can kidney beans
1 16-ounce can peas
1 small onion, chopped
1 green pepper, chopped
1 stalk celery, diced
1 tablespoon diced pimiento
2 cups sugar
1½ cups white vinegar
1/2 cup water
1 tablespoon salt

Drain beans and peas and combine with remaining vegetables in a large bowl or refrigerator container. In a medium pan, combine remaining ingredients and bring to a boil, stirring to dissolve sugar. Pour hot syrup over beans. Toss lightly. Chill in refrigerator for 24 hours before serving. Serves 12.

Sweet and Sour Chicken

1 2½ to 3-pound broiler-fryer chicken, cut up
Seasoned flour
1/4 cup vegetable oil
1/2 cup cider vinegar
3 tablespoons brown sugar
1/3 cup chopped sweet gherkins
1 tablespoon Worcestershire sauce
1 tablespoon ketchup

Coat chicken with seasoned flour. In a large skillet, brown chicken in oil. Transfer chicken to a 13x9-inch baking pan. (Or, if skillet is oven-proof, leave in skillet.) In a small bowl, combine remaining ingredients. Brush over chicken. Cover chicken and bake at 350° for 30 minutes or until fork-tender. Serves four.

David Jones

Skillet Chops and Beans

4 pork chops

1 tablespoon vegetable oil

4 slices onion

Salt and pepper to taste

2 stalks celery, sliced

1/4 cup water

1 16-ounce can pork and beans

2 tablespoons prepared mustard

2 tablespoons ketchup

In a large skillet, brown chops in oil. Top each chop with an onion slice. Sprinkle with salt and pepper. Scatter sliced celery over chops. Add water. Cover and simmer for 45 minutes or until chops are tender. Combine remaining ingredients, add to chops and heat through. Serves four.

Michael Karchut

Residency: Calumet City, Illinois

Age: 34

Height: 5'6"

Weight: 182

School: Case Inst. of Tech., Cleveland, Ohio

Training hours per week: 10

Prune Cake

2 cups sugar

1 cup vegetable oil

3 eggs

1 cup buttermilk

1 teaspoon vanilla

2 cups flour

1 teaspoon baking soda

1 teaspoon salt

1 teaspoon nutmeg

1 teaspoon cinnamon

1/4 to 1/2 teaspoon allspice

1 cup chopped nuts

1 cup pitted, cooked prunes

Buttermilk Topping (see directions)

In a large bowl, cream sugar and oil. Beat in eggs, buttermilk and vanilla. Combine remaining dry ingredients and add to batter. Mix well. Fold in nuts and prunes. Turn into a greased 13x9-inch pan. Bake at 350° for 45 to 50 minutes. While cake is hot, pierce top with fork and spoon on Buttermilk Topping until absorbed. Serves 12.

Buttermilk Topping: In a medium pan, combine 1 cup sugar, 1 cup buttermilk, 1/2 cup butter and 1 teaspoon baking soda. Stir well and bring to a rolling boil. Makes enough to top a 13x9-inch cake.

Pound Cake Torte

1 6-ounce package semi-sweet chocolate chips

1/2 cup butter or margarine

1/4 cup water

4 egg yolks, slightly beaten

2 tablespoons sifted powdered sugar

1 teaspoon vanilla

1 12-ounce purchased pound cake

In a heavy pan, melt chocolate chips with butter and water, stirring until blended. Cool slightly. Add yolks, sugar and vanilla and stir until smooth. Chill until spreadable, about one hour. Slice cake horizontally into six layers. Spread chocolate mixture between layers and over top and sides. Chill one hour before slicing. Serves eight.

Contributors	Recipes

Michael Karchut

Corn Saute

6 ears fresh corn

6 tablespoons butter or margarine

1/2 cup chopped onion

1 cup diced green pepper

1 teaspoon salt

1/4 teaspoon pepper

Cut corn from cob and set aside. In a large skillet, melt butter and saute onion and green pepper for three minutes. Add corn, salt and pepper. Cook and stir for three minutes. Serves four.

Paul James Salisbury

Residency: Altamont, New York

Age: 31

Height: 5'7"

Weight: 198

School: Hudson Valley Community College, Troy, New York

Training hours per week: 20

Bean Sprout Salad

2 cups fresh bean sprouts

1/4 cup vegetable oil

2 tablespoons lemon juice or cider vinegar

2 tablespoons tamari soy sauce

1/4 teaspoon sea salt

1/4 cup finely chopped scallions

2 tablespoons sesame seeds

1 clove garlic, minced or pressed

1 tablespoon chopped chives

2 tablespoons chopped parsley

1/8 teaspoon grated ginger root (optional)

Place sprouts in a medium bowl. Combine remaining ingredients. Pour over sprouts. Toss lightly. Chill and serve. Serves four.

Diane's Fig Potassium Pick-Up Bars

2 cups ground figs

1/2 cup ground raisins

1/4 cup sunflower seeds

1/2 cup fresh orange juice

1/4 cup carob powder

1/4 cup wheat germ

1/2 cup unsweetened flaked coconut

In a large bowl, using hands if necessary, combine all ingredients except coconut and mix well. Press firmly into a metal ice cube tray, without the dividers. Chill well. Cut into bars and roll in coconut. Wrap individually in waxed paper or plastic and store in refrigerator. Makes eight to 10 bars.

Frozen Banana Surprise

3 cups water

3 ripe bananas

6 tablespoons whey powder

1 tablespoon brewer's yeast

1/4 cup honey

1/2 cup nuts, broken

Combine all ingredients in electric blender and blend until smooth. Pour into two or three ice cube trays. Freeze until firm. Remove cubes and wrap individually in waxed paper or plastic. Return to freezer. Makes about three dozen cubes.

Contributors	Recipes

Kurt N. Setterberg

Residency: Masury, Ohio
Age: 26
Height: 5'11"
Weight: 215
Training hours per week: 8

High-Protein Milkshake

2 cups milk
3 raw eggs
1 tablespoon instant cocoa mix
1/4 cup skim milk powder

Combine all ingredients in electric blender and blend until smooth and foamy. Serves one to two.

Stewart B. Thornburgh

Residency: Charleston, Illinois
Age: 18
Height: 5'9"
Weight: 132
School: Lake Land College
Training hours per week: 14

Lasagna

1 8-ounce package lasagna noodles
1 cup creamed cottage cheese
1 cup sour cream
1 tablespoon vegetable shortening
1 pound ground beef
1/2 cup chopped onion
1 16-ounce can tomato sauce
1 teaspoon garlic salt
1/2 teaspoon oregano
Dash of pepper
3/4 cup shredded Cheddar cheese

Cook lasagna according to package directions. Combine cottage cheese with sour cream and set aside. In a large skillet, brown ground beef in shortening with onion. Stir in tomato sauce, salt, oregano and pepper. Simmer for five minutes. Place a layer of noodles in the bottom of a 13x9-inch pan. Add a layer of cottage cheese mixture. Add half of meat sauce. Top with noodles, remainder of sauce and cheese. Bake at 350° for 45 minutes. Let set 10 minutes before cutting into squares. Serves six to eight.

Donnie Warner

Residency: York, Pennsylvania
Age: 20
Height: 5'3"
Weight: 145½
School: Wm. Penn Senior High
Training hours per week: 9

Bedtime Steamed Crackers

Saltines or butter crackers
1 tablespoon sugar
Pat of butter
1 cup milk
1/2 teaspoon cinnamon
Cinnamon or nutmeg

Half fill a cereal bowl with crackers. Dot with butter. Sprinkle with sugar. Scald milk. Add vanilla to milk and pour over crackers. Sprinkle with cinnamon. Cover bowl with a plate until crackers soak up milk and become soft. Serves one.

Corn Bread

1/2 cup vegetable shortening
1 cup sugar
2 eggs
1/4 teaspoon salt
4 teaspoons baking powder
1½ cups flour
1½ cups corn meal
1½ cups milk

Cream sugar and shortening in a large bowl. Beat in eggs. Combine dry ingredients and stir into batter alternately with milk. Pour into a 13x9-inch greased and floured baking pan. Bake at 375° for 30 minutes or until firm to the touch and pulling away from the sides of the pan. Serve with butter, or in a bowl with milk. Serves eight to 12.

22
Wrestling—
Freestyle–
Greco Roman

Event Days:

Sunday, July 20, 1980	Sunday, July 27, 1980
Monday, July 21, 1980	Monday, July 28, 1980
Tuesday, July 22, 1980	Tuesday, July 29, 1980
Wednesday, July 23, 1980	Wednesday, July 30, 1980
Thursday, July 24, 1980	Thursday, July 31, 1980

Contributors:

Russ Hellickson
John Patrick Hughes
Wilfredo Leiva, Jr.
Dan Mello
Thomas Minkel
Ben Peterson
William John Rosado
Craig Schoene
David Leslie Schultz

The present two styles of wrestling on the program for the Olympic Games (the classic Greco-Roman and the "Americanized" free-style) have been fixtures since 1908. The difference between the two styles is a simple one: in the classic Greco-Roman variety no holds are permitted below the waist; free-style permits leg holds which are considered important in the repertoire of every free-style grappler.

The USA has won 28 Olympic titles in free-style since 1908, but has never won a medal in Greco-Roman. In the last 24 years the Eastern European countries have risen to places of prominence in both styles of grappling.

Today, there is a time limit of nine minutes for each bout. However, in 1912, in the days before time limits, Max Klein of Czarist Russia took nearly 11 hours to win the middleweight silver medal from Finland's Alfred Asikainen. There are ten different weight classes, ranging from 105.5 pounds to the unlimited classes for wrestlers over 220 pounds. Each country is permitted to enter one man in each weight class for each style.

The only USA champion at Montreal was John Peterson in the 180-pound class. At Munich the USA placed three on the highest rung of the victory podium—Dan Gable, 149.5 pounds; Wayne Wells, 163 pounds; and, Ben Peterson, 198 pounds.

Contributors	Recipe

Russ Hellickson

Residency: Oregon, Wisconsin
Age: 30
Height: 5'11"
Weight: 220
School: University of Wisconsin
Training hours per week: 20

Pumpkin Bars

4 eggs

2 cups cooked, mashed pumpkin or 1 16-ounce can pumpkin

2 cups sugar

1 cup vegetable oil

2 cups flour

2 teaspoons baking powder

1/2 teaspoon salt

1 teaspoon baking soda

1½ teaspoons cinnamon

1/4 teaspoon nutmeg

1/4 teaspoon cloves

Cream Cheese Frosting (see directions)

In a large bowl, cream eggs, pumpkin, sugar and oil. Add dry ingredients and beat until smooth. Pour into a greased 15x11x1-inch jelly roll pan or cookie sheet. Bake at 350° for 30 minutes. Cool and frost with Cream Cheese Frosting. Cut into bars. Makes about five dozen bars.

Cream Cheese Frosting: Beat together 1 3-ounce package softened cream cheese, 1/3 cup softened butter, 1 tablespoon milk, 1 teaspoon vanilla and 2½ cups powdered sugar. Frost bars and top with chopped walnuts, if desired. Makes enough to frost a 15x11-inch cake or pan of bars.

Seven Layer Salad

1 small head lettuce, finely cut

1 10-ounce package frozen peas, unthawed

1/2 to 3/4 cup diced green pepper

1 small onion, chopped

3 to 4 grated carrots

2 to 3 stalks celery, sliced

2 cups mayonnaise

1 cup shredded Cheddar cheese

8 to 10 slices bacon, cooked and crumbled

In a large glass bowl, layer all ingredients, beginning with the lettuce and ending with the bacon. Cover and refrigerate for eight to 12 hours. Toss and serve. Serves eight or more.

John Patrick Hughes

Residency: Minneapolis, Minnesota
Age: 25
Height: 5'5"
Weight: 145
School: University of Minnesota
Training hours per week: 26

Mock Chow Mein

1 pound ground beef

1 cup chopped onions

1 cup sliced celery

2 cups raw rice

1 10¾-ounce can cream of mushroom soup

1 10¾-ounce can cream of celery soup

2 soup cans water

3 tablespoons soy sauce

In a large skillet, brown ground beef. Stir in remaining ingredients. Turn into a buttered 13x9-inch baking pan or a large casserole. Cover and bake at 350° for 1½ hours. Fluff with fork before serving. Serves six to eight.

Contributors	Recipes

John Patrick Hughes

Stefato

2 pounds beef stew meat, diced

1/4 cup olive oil

2 tablespoons cumin

1/4 cup wine vinegar

12 whole allspice

10 to 14 whole cloves

2 to 3 bay leaves

Juice and grated rind of half a lemon

8 to 9 medium onions, peeled

10 to 12 cloves garlic, peeled

Water

3 tomatoes, sliced, or 1 16-ounce can stewed tomatoes

1 6-ounce can tomato paste

1 pound fresh green beans, sliced

In a large kettle or Dutch oven, place stew meat. Cover with olive oil. Sprinkle with cumin, vinegar, allspice, cloves, bay leaves and lemon. Cover pan and let set while preparing onions and garlic. Add whole peeled onions and garlic cloves. Add enough water to half-cover the onions. Stir in remaining ingredients. Bring to a boil and boil for 15 minutes. Reduce heat, cover and simmer for 1½ hours. If gravy is too thin, thicken with flour or cornstarch, or continue to cook uncovered until desired consistency is reached. Season to taste with salt and pepper. Serve over rice, bread or riced potatoes. Serves four to six.

Wilfredo Leiva, Jr.

Residency: Camp Lejeune, North Carolina

Age: 19

Height: 5'2½"

Weight: 110

School: Christopher Columbus High School

Training hours per week: 30

Watergate Cake

1 white cake mix, 2-layer size

1 3-ounce package instant pistachio pudding mix

1 cup vegetable oil

3 eggs

1/2 cup chopped walnuts

1 cup club soda

Watergate Frosting (see directions)

In a large bowl, combine cake mix with pudding mix. Make a well in the center of the dry mixture and add oil, eggs, nuts and club soda. Beat for four minutes at medium speed and pour into a greased 13x9-inch baking pan, or a 10-inch bundt or tube pan. Bake at 350° for 40 minutes for a sheet cake, or 45 to 50 minutes for a bundt cake. Cool in bundt pan for 15 minutes before removing. Cool and frost with Watergate Frosting. Serves 12.

Watergate Frosting: Whip 1/2 cup milk with 1 envelope instant nondairy whipped topping mix until stiff. Add 1 3-ounce package instant pistachio pudding mix and beat for two more minutes. Makes enough to frost one 13x9-inch sheet cake or one bundt cake.

Mushroom Rice Pilaff

1/2 cup butter or margarine

1 small onion, chopped

1/2 pound fresh mushrooms, sliced

2 cups raw rice

3 10¾-ounce cans beef consomme

1/2 teaspoon salt

In a large skillet, saute onions and mushrooms in butter until soft. Add rice and cook for two more minutes, stirring constantly. Stir in consomme and salt. Turn into a buttered two-quart casserole. Cover and bake at 350° for 1½ to 2 hours, or until rice is done and liquid is absorbed. Stir with a fork every 30 minutes during cooking period. Serves eight.

Contributors	Recipes

Dan Mello

Residency: Bakersfield, California

Age: 25

Height: 5'3"

Weight: 135

School: Portland State University

Training hours per week: 28

Chicken and Rice Casserole

1 10¾-ounce can cream of mushroom, chicken or celery soup

1 soup can water

1 cup raw rice

1 4-ounce can mushrooms (optional)

1 2½ to 3-pound broiler-fryer chicken, cut up

1 1⅞-ounce packet dry onion soup mix

In a large greased casserole or 11x7-inch baking dish, mix soup with water, rice and mushrooms. Place chicken pieces on rice mixture, skin-side-up. Sprinkle with onion soup mix. Cover and bake at 350° for one hour. Uncover and bake for 15 minutes more. Serves four.

Meat Loaf

3 pounds ground beef

1 pound ground pork

4 teaspoons salt

1 teaspoon onion salt

2 cups cracker crumbs

1 cup milk

2 eggs, beaten

Dash of pepper

1/2 teaspoon sage

Catsup

1 medium onion, chopped

Combine all ingredients, except catsup and onion, in a large bowl. Mix well with hands until thoroughly blended. Pack into a large loaf pan or casserole. Cover with catsup and sprinkle with onions. Cover and bake at 325° for 1 hour and 45 minutes. Let set for 10 minutes before slicing. Serves eight to 12.

Thomas Minkel

Residency: Mt. Pleasant, Michigan

Age: 29

Height: 5'8"

Weight: 150

School: Central Michigan University

Training hours per week: 28

Chicken A La Champion

1 2½ to 3-pound broiler-fryer chicken, cut up

1/4 cup vegetable oil

2 10¾-ounce cans cream soup (cream of chicken, mushroom, celery or onion)

In a large skillet, brown chicken in oil. Remove chicken from pan and drain off excess fat. Pour one can soup into pan and cook over low heat, scraping pan to loosen brown bits. Place chicken in soup mixture. Top with remaining can of soup. Cover and simmer for one hour or more. Serves four.

Ben Peterson

Residency: Watertown, Wisconsin

Age: 28

Height: 6'

Weight: 205

School: Iowa State University, Maranatha Baptist Bible College–Graduate School

Training hours per week: 15

Butterhorn Rolls

1 package dry yeast

1/2 cup warm water

1 tablespoon sugar

1 cup warm milk

1/2 cup melted margarine or butter

1/2 cup sugar

1 teaspoon salt

3 eggs, beaten

4 to 5 cups flour

Dissolve yeast in warm water with sugar. In a large bowl, combine milk, margarine, sugar, salt and eggs. Stir in yeast mixture. Stir in enough flour to form a soft dough. Cover and let raise in a warm place until doubled, about two to three hours. Divide dough in half. On a floured surface, roll out into a 12-inch circle. Cut into 16 wedges. Starting at the wide end, roll up each wedge. Place on buttered cookie sheets. Repeat with remaining dough. Let rise until almost doubled. Bake at 350° for 12 to 15 minutes. Makes 32 rolls.

Contributors	Recipes

Ben Peterson

Pizza Burgers

2 pounds ground beef

1 onion, chopped

1 6-ounce can tomato paste

1/2 teaspoon garlic salt

1 8-ounce can pizza sauce

6 to 8 stuffed green olives, sliced

1 teaspoon Italian seasoning or 1/2 teaspoon oregano and 1/2 teaspoon basil

2 cups shredded Mozzarella cheese

8 to 10 hamburger buns

In a large skillet, brown beef with onion. Drain off excess fat. Stir in remaining ingredients, except cheese. Cover and simmer for 30 minutes. Sprinkle with cheese and continue to cook until cheese melts. Serve on toasted hamburger buns. Serves eight to 10.

William John Rosado

Residency: Tempe, Arizona

Age: 23

Height: 5'

Weight: 120

School: Arizona State

Training hours per week: 24

Pepper Steak

1 pound beef round steak

1 small onion, sliced

1 small green pepper, sliced

1/2 cup vinegar

Garlic salt

1 tablespoon vegetable oil

1 8-ounce can tomato sauce

Slice steak into one-inch strips. Marinate meat, onion and green pepper in vinegar, with garlic salt to taste, for one hour. Heat oil in skillet or wok over very high heat. Drain meat and vegetables. Stir-fry onions and peppers for one minute. Add meat and stir-fry to medium rare. Add tomato sauce, mix well, bring to a boil and cook for one minute. Serves two.

Island Spaghetti Sauce

1/4 cup olive oil

1/4 of a green pepper, sliced

1 teaspoon sugar

1 24-ounce can whole tomatoes, mashed

1 12-ounce can tomato paste

3 cups water

1 small onion, sliced

Garlic salt

Oregano

1 pound fresh mushrooms, sliced

2 pounds ground beef

In a large pot, saute green pepper in olive oil and sugar. Add tomatoes, tomato paste, water and onion. Add garlic salt and oregano to taste. Bring to a boil, cover and simmer one hour. Add mushrooms and simmer two more hours. Brown ground beef in a large skillet, drain off excess fat and add to sauce. Simmer one more hour. Serves eight.

Craig Schoene

Residency: Eugene, Oregon

Age: 20

Height: 6'4"

Weight: 240

School: University of Oregon

Training hours per week: 28

Post Weigh-In Omelet

5 eggs

Salt and pepper

Dash of Tabasco sauce

1/2 to 1 cup chopped ham

Monterey Jack cheese

In a large bowl, combine eggs, salt, pepper and Tabasco. Beat well with a fork or wire whisk. Beat in ham. Pour into a hot, well-greased skillet or omelet pan. Reduce heat to medium. Lay slices of cheese over half of omelet. As cheese melts and egg mixture begins to set, fold omelet in half. Continue to cook over low heat until eggs are set. Serves two, or one hungry athlete.

David Leslie Schultz

Residency: Los Angeles, California

Age: 19

Height: 5 '8½"

Weight: 170

School: UCLA

Training hours per week: 20

Blintzes

Crepes:

4 cups flour

4 teaspoons salt

16 eggs, beaten

5⅓ cups milk

3 tablespoons melted butter, margarine or oil

Filling:

8 cups (4 pounds) Ricotta cheese or low-fat cottage cheese

8 egg yolks

1/2 cup sugar

2 teaspoons cinnamon

4 teaspoons vanilla

Topping:

Strawberry jam

Sour cream

Cinnamon-Sugar mixture

In a large bowl, combine flour with salt. Mix eggs with milk and melted butter. Add half of egg mixture to flour, beating until smooth. Add remaining egg mixture and beat until smooth. Set aside. Combine all filling ingredients in a large bowl, mix until well blended and set aside. Ladle 1/4 to 1/3 cup batter into a hot, greased skillet or 9-inch crepe pan. Swirl pan so batter covers bottom. Cook until mixture is set and edges are brown. Remove crepe. Place about 3 tablespoons filling on cooked side of crepe. Fold crepe, tucking in edges, to form a square, rectangular or triangular packet. When all blintzes are assembled, fry in butter on both sides until lightly browned. Serve with jam, sour cream and a sprinkle of sugar-cinnamon. (Filled blintzes may be frozen and then fried, unthawed, until heated through and lightly browned.) Makes about 60 blintzes.

23

Yachting

Event Days:

Monday,
July 21, 1980

Monday,
July 28, 1980

Tuesday,
July 22, 1980

Tuesday,
July 29, 1980

Wednesday,
July 23, 1980

Thursday,
July 24, 1980

Sunday,
July 27, 1980

Contributors:

Tom Blackaller
Dennis Conner
Harry C. Melges, Jr. (Bud)
David Ullman

Adverse weather conditions forced the cancellation of the scheduled yachting races in 1896. Thus, the sport was first held during the 1900 Games. But it was not until 1928 that the USA made its debut in yachting competition, placing sixth in both the 6- and 8-meter classes and tenth in the Dinghy class.

At Los Angeles in 1932 the USA earned gold medals in the Star Class and the 8-meter class, and finished second in the 6-meter class. The last gold medal for the USA was in 1972 at the Kiel, West Germany, regatta where Harry Melges skippered the Soling Class entry, finishing no lower than third in any of the six races.

Usually there are five or six different classes included in the Olympic Games regatta. There was an astronomical 15 classes in 1920 in Belgium.

The International Yacht Racing Union (IYRU) reviews the regatta-classes quadrennially and makes revisions. For example, at Tallin in 1980 the Star Class will be returned to the Olympic Games after an absence in 1976, the class in which the USA has enjoyed its greatest success over the years.

Perhaps the most successful of all Olympic sailors is Denmark's Paul Elvstrom, skipper of winning boats in four successive regattas—1948, 1952, 1956, and 1960.

At Kingston, Ontario, in 1976 the USA won two silver medals and a bronze. This was the best performance for the USA since medaling in all classes in 1964 in Japan.

Contributors	Recipes

Tom Blackaller

Residency: Alameda, California
Age: 39
Height: 6'2"
Weight: 205

Nutty Chicken Salad

3 cups cooked brown rice

2 cups diced cooked chicken

1/2 cup diced celery

2 green onions, chopped

1/2 cup diced green pepper

1/4 cup Italian salad dressing, regular or low-calorie

1/2 cup mayonnaise or plain yogurt

1/2 cup cashew pieces

Combine rice, chicken, celery, green onions and green pepper in a large bowl. In a small bowl, combine dressing and mayonnaise. Add to rice mixture and stir gently. Chill for two hours. Serve on lettuce, topped with cashews. Serves six to eight.

Pineapple Nut Bread

1/2 cup currants or golden raisins

1¾ cups flour

1/2 teaspoon salt

1/2 teaspoon cinnamon

2 teaspoons baking powder

1/4 teaspoon baking soda

3/4 cup sugar

3 tablespoons butter, softened

2 eggs

3/4 cup chopped walnuts

1 8-ounce can crushed pineapple, with juice

Rinse currants or raisins in hot water to plump. Let stand 10 minutes; drain well. Combine flour, salt, cinnamon, baking powder and soda; set aside. In a medium bowl, cream sugar with butter. Beat in eggs one at a time. Stir in currants or raisins and walnuts. Mix in half the pineapple with half the flour; repeat. Pour into a greased 9x5x3-inch loaf pan or a one-dozen-size muffin tin. Bake at 350° for 60 minutes for loaf, 25 minutes for muffins. Cool loaf in pan for 10 minutes before removing. Makes one large loaf or one dozen muffins.

Dennis Conner

Residency: San Diego, California
Age: 36
Height: 6'1"
Weight: 220
School: San Diego State

Huevos Rancheros

1 16-ounce can whole tomatoes

1 4-ounce can diced green chilies, drained

1 medium onion, chopped

Eggs

Tortillas

Refried beans

Combine tomatoes, chilies and onions. Refrigerate overnight. Place tomato mixture in a medium skillet. Heat to boiling. Reduce heat to simmer. Break one to two eggs per person into a small bowl and ease into simmering sauce. Poach eggs to desired degree of doneness. Meanwhile, fry tortillas. To serve, place a spoonful of refrijoles on a hot tortilla, top with one or two eggs and some sauce. Serves four to six.

Contributors	Recipes

Harry C. Melges, Jr. (Bud)

Residency: Zenda, Wisconsin
Age: 49
Height: 6 '
Weight: 195

Glazed Wild Ducks With Wine Sauce

4 wild ducks, about 2 pounds each, dressed
2 apples, cored and chopped
2 onions, chopped
4 strips bacon, cut in half
Sauce:
1/2 cup currant jelly
1/4 cup Port wine
1/4 cup catsup
1/2 teaspoon Worcestershire sauce
1/8 teaspoon freshly ground black pepper
2 tablespoons butter

Rinse ducks in cold water and pat dry. Combine apples and onions and place in body cavities of ducks, dividing mixture evenly among ducks. Place birds breast-up on a rack in a roasting pan. Lay two pieces of bacon over the breast of each duck. Bake at 450° for 15 minutes; reduce heat to 350° and bake for 45 minutes, brushing with glaze every 15 minutes. Increase cooking time for larger birds or according to your preference. Serves four.
  Wine Sauce: Combine all ingredients in a small pan. Bring to a boil over low heat, stirring constantly. Remove from heat. Use to baste duck during cooking. Serve remaining sauce hot, with duck. Also good with venison.

Chicken Divan

4 whole broiler-fryer chicken breasts
2 10-ounce packages frozen broccoli spears
2 10¾-ounce cans cream of chicken soup
1/4 cup lemon juice
1¼ cups mayonnaise
1/4 teaspoon paprika
1/2 cup shredded sharp Cheddar cheese
1/2 cup dry bread crumbs
2 tablespoons melted butter

In a medium pan, boil chicken breasts for about 30 minutes. Discard skin and bones. Break meat into pieces. Cook broccoli according to package directions. Cover bottom of a greased 13x9-inch baking pan with broccoli. Top with chicken. Combine soup, mayonnaise, lemon juice and paprika and pour over chicken. Sprinkle with cheese. Mix crumbs with butter and sprinkle over cheese. Bake at 350° for 30 minutes or until heated through. Serves four to six.

David Ullman

Residency: Newport Beach, California
Age: 33
Height: 5'5"
Weight: 125
School: Orange Coast College
Training hours per week: 10

Poached Salmon Steaks

4 chicken bouillon cubes or 4 teaspoons instant bouillon
1½ cups water
4 fresh salmon or halibut steaks
1/2 cup chopped green onion
1/2 teaspoon dill
Pepper
2 tablespoons minced parsley
Lemon wedges

In a large skillet, dissolve bouillon in water. Place steaks in water. Sprinkle with onion, dill and pepper. Cover, bring to a boil and simmer for about 10 minutes or until fish flakes easily with a fork. Sprinkle with parsley and serve with lemon wedges. Serves four.

David Ullman

Sesame Sea Bass

2 pounds sea bass fillets

3/4 teaspoon salt

1/2 cup butter or margarine

2 tablespoons minced green onions

1/2 teaspoon freshly ground black pepper

3 tablespoons toasted sesame seeds

Minced parsley

Lemon wedges

Wipe fish with damp cloth. Sprinkle both sides with salt. Arrange in a single layer in a buttered baking pan. Melt butter and stir in onions, pepper and sesame seeds. Drizzle over fish. Bake at 350° for 15 to 20 minutes or until fish flakes easily with a fork. Baste occasionally with pan drippings. Sprinkle with parsley and serve with lemon wedges. Serves four.

Bibliography

We have included below some personal information about the athletes who have graciously taken time from their intensive training schedules and many competitions to contribute to this book. All are working long hours to prove themselves worthy representatives of the United States in the 1980 Olympic Games in Moscow. Each is a champion in his or her own right. We want to express our gratitude to these men and women for making the effort to share a bit of themselves with all of us. All eyes will be on the 1980 Olympic Games . . . All America will be cheering on our nation's athletes as they try for new highs.

Acosta, Israel (Boxing); Milwaukee, Wis.; Age 23; 5′3″; 106 lbs.; page 30

Adams, Judi (Archery); Phoenix, Ariz.; Age 19; 6′0″; 110 lbs.; page 12

Anderson, Heidi A. (Gymnastics); Furlong, Penn.; Age 16; 4′11″; 86 lbs.; page 70

Barron, Brett Dewey (Judo); San Mateo, Calif.; Age 19; 5′10″; 172 lbs.; pages 80-81

Barton, Bruce (Canoe & Kayak) 1976 Olympics; Homer, Mich.; Age 21; 5′11″; 160 lbs.; page 34

Barton, Greg (Canoe & Kayak); Homer, Mich.; Age 19; 5′9″; 160 lbs.; page 34

Bassham, Lanny Robert (Shooting); 1972 Olympics, Silver; 1976 Olympics, Gold; New Braunfels, Tex.; Age 32; 5′9″; 165 lbs.; page 102

Beal, Douglas P. (Volleyball); Dayton, Ohio; Age 31; 6′2″; 190 lbs.; page 128

Beasley, Genia Gail (Basketball); Benson, N.C.; Age 20; 6′2″; 155 lbs.; page 24

Bednar, Richard Lee (Archery); Suffield, Ohio; Age 21; 5′10″; 160 lbs.; page 12

Belfanti, Thomas James (Water Polo); Walnut Creek, Calif.; Age 25; 5′11″; 175 lbs.; page 134

Belger, Mark (Athletics Track and Field) 1976 Olympics (alternate); Arlington, Mass.; Age 22; 5′11″; 150 lbs.; page 18

Blackaller, Tom (Yachting); Alameda, Calif.; Age 39; 6′2″; 205 lbs.; page 152

Blazejowski, Carol (Basketball); Fairview, N.Y.; Age 22; 5′10″; 150 lbs.; page 25

Boggs, Philip G. (Diving) 1976 Olympics, Gold— Springboard; Ann Arbor, Mich.; Age 29; 5′5″; 129 lbs.; page 44

Bradley, Jeff (Cycling); Davenport, Ia.; Age 17; 6′0″; 160 lbs.; page 38

Briley, Melissa (Diving); 1976 Olympics, Bronze—10 meter dive; Miami, Fla.; Age 22; 5′3″; 110 lbs.; page 44

Brown, Carol P. (Rowing); 1976 Olympics, Bronze—8 w/cox; Seattle, Wash.; Age 25; 5′7½″; 148 lbs.; page 92

Bruner, Michael Lee (Swimming); 1976 Olympics; Los Altos, Calif.; Age 22; 5′10″; 165 lbs.; page 110

Bumphus, Johnny (Boxing); Nashville, Tenn.; Age 18; 5′11″; 139 lbs.; pages 30-31

Bungum, Brian P. (Diving); Bloomington, Minn.; Age 23; 5′8½″; 148 lbs.; pages 44-45

Burley, Michael E. (Modern Penthathlon); 1976 Olympics; Austin, Tex.; Age 26; 6′0″; 145 lbs.; page 88

Canary, Christa (Gymnastics); Northbrook, Ill.; Age 16; 5′1″; 90 lbs.; pages 70-71

Carlton, Guy A. (Weightlifting); LaPlace, Ill.; Age 25; 6′0″; 220 lbs.; pages 140-41

Cashin, Richard Marshall, Jr. (Rowing); 1976 Olympics— Team; Boston, Mass.; Age 25; 6′5″; 205 lbs.; page 93

Cassello, Jackie (Gymnastics); Silver Spring, Md.; Age 13; 4′7″; 70 lbs.; page 71

Cheeseman, Gwen W. (Field Hockey); West Chester, Penn.; Age 27; 5′2″; 121 lbs.; page 62

Coffee, Jerome (Boxing); Nashville, Tenn.; Age 20; 5′7″; 112 lbs. pages 31-32

Conner, Bart (Gymnastics); 1976 Olympics; Norman, Okla.; Age 20; 5′5″; 120 lbs.; page 72

Conner, Dennis (Yachting); San Diego, Calif.; Age 36; 6′1″; 220 lbs.; page 152

Cragg, Robert (Diving); 1976 Olympics; Ann Arbor, Mich.; Age 25; 6′1″; 180 lbs.; pages 45-46

Crawford, Cosema E. (Rowing); Westgate, Washington, D.C.; Age 23; 6′½″; 163 lbs.; page 93

Crockett, Rita (Volleyball); Colorado Springs, Colo.; Age 21; 5′8½″; 138 lbs.; pages 128-29

D'Asaro, Gay K. (Fencing); 1976 Olympics; San Jose, Calif.; Age 24; 5′9″; 135 lbs.; page 58

Daubenspeck, Irene (Archery); Phoenix, Ariz.; Age 25; 5′5″; 160 lbs.; page 12

DeFrantz, Anita L. (Rowing); Philadelphia, Penn.; Age 26; 5′11″; 155 lbs.; page 94

Demgen, Gregory J. (Cycling); LaCrosse, Wis.; Age 18; 5′10″; 155 lbs.; pages 38-39

DiGrazia, Derek (Equestrian); S. Hamiton, Mass.; Age 23; 6′0″; 150 lbs.; page 52

Doberstein, Kurt (Canoe & Kayak); Lombard, Ill.; Age 23; 6′2″; 180 lbs.; page 35

Donaghy, Bruce (Cycling); Emmaus, Penn.; Age 19; 5′11″; 173 lbs.; page 39

Doran, Barbara (Field Hockey); New York, N.Y.; Age 25; 5′5″; 125 lbs.; pages 62-63

Dorst, Christopher Taylor (Water Polo); Atherton, Calif.; Age 22; 6′4″; 195 lbs.; page 135

Dragan, Linda Murray (Canoe & Kayak); 1972 and 1976 Olympics; Washington, D.C.; Age 26; 5′6″; 140 lbs.; pages 35-36

Dunson, Deana Kim (Swimming); Gainesville, Fla.; Age 21; 5′7″; 135 lbs.; pages 110-11

Dwight, Mary Phyl (Team Handball); Manhattan, Kans.; Age 27; 5′6″; 145 lbs.; page 122

Elkins, Stephanie (Swimming); Gainesville, Fla.; Age 15; 5′6½″; 125 lbs.; pages 111-12

Figueroa, Gary (Water Polo); Newport Beach, Calif.; Age 22; 6′0″; 170 lbs.; page 136

Fitzgerald, John D. (Modern Pentathlon); 1972 and 1976 Olympics; San Antonio, Tex.; Age 30; 6′1″; 170 lbs.; page 88

Fitz-Randolph, Kurt Henderson (Shooting); Palm Bay, Fla.; Age 18; 6′3″; 160 lbs.; page 102

Fitz-Randolph, Rod, Jr. (Shooting); Palm Bay, Fla.; Age 20; 6′1″; 155 lbs.; pages 102-103

Forest, Carmen Sue (Team Handball); North Little Rock, Ark.; Age 23; 5′10″; 160 lbs.; pages 122-23

Forrester, Bill (Swimming); 1976 Olympics; Hilton Head, S.C.; Age 21; 5′11″; 170 lbs.; pages 112-13

Gaines, Ambrose, IV ("Rowdy") (Swimming); Winter Haven, Fla.; Age 20; 6′1″; 160 lbs.; pages 113-14

Gansel, John A. (Water Polo); Stanford, Calif.; Age 20 6′3″; 185 lbs.; page 137

Garlich, Greg Alan (Diving); Kirkwood, Mo.; Age 23; 5′9″; 155 lbs.; page 46

Girven, Paula Darcel (Athletics Track and Field); Dale City, Va.; Age 21; 5'9"; 136 lbs.; pages 18-19

Glenesk, Neil (Modern Pentathlon); San Antonio, Tex.; Age 26; 5'6"; 135 lbs.; page 89

Gminski, Michael Thomas (Basketball); Monroe, Conn.; Age 19; 6'11"; 245 lbs.; page 25

Gorski, Mark Brian (Cycling); Itasca, Ill.; Age 19; 6'2"; 175 lbs.; page 40

Graham, Jack D., Jr. (Water Polo); Brimonton, Wash.; Age 18; 6'2"; 180 lbs.; pages 137-38

Gregg, R. Scott (Field Hockey); Whitehall, Penn.; Age 24; 6'2"; 165 lbs.; page 63

Grylls, David M. (Cycling); Grosse Pointe, Mich.; Age 21; 6'½"; 175 lbs.; page 40

Gurney, Hilda (Equestrian); 1976 Olympics, Bronze—Team; Woodland Hills, Calif.; Age 35; 5'6"; 138 lbs.; page 52

Hackett, Robert William, Jr. (Swimming); 1976 Olympics, Silver; Cambridge, Mass.; Age 19; 6'2"; 190 lbs.; page 114

Hafferkamp, Russell A.; San Diego, Calif.; Age 24; 6'4"; 200 lbs.; page 138

Hartung, James N.; Omaha, Neb.; Age 18; 5'5"; 135 lbs.; pages 72-73

Hatton, Hollis Straley (Rowing); Philadelphia, Penn.; Age 30; 5'5"; 105 lbs.; pages 94-95

Hellickson, Russ (Wrestling); 1976 Olympics, Silver; Oregon, Wis.; Age 30; 5'11"; 220 lbs.; page 146

Hills, Elizabeth (Rowing); 1976 Olympics; Hingham, Mass.; Age 24; 5'10"; 155 lbs.; page 95

Hogshead, Nancy Lynn (Swimming); Jacksonville, Fla.; Age 16; 5'8"; 136 lbs.; pages 114-15;

Hooks, Charles L. (Judo); Granger, Ind.; Age 40; 6'2"; 238 lbs.; pages 81-82

Howard, Alexsandra P. (Equestrian); El Granada, Calif.; Age 37; 5'5½"; 124 lbs.; page 53

Huber, Mike (Equestrian); S. Hamilton, Mass.; Age 18; 6'0"; 140 lbs.; page 54

Hughes, John Patrick (Wrestling); Minneapolis, Minn.; Age 25; 5'5"; 145 lbs.; pages 146-47

Hulcer, Larry Michael (Soccer); Florissant, Mo.; Age 21; 5'10"; 165 lbs.; page 108

Iqbal, Manzar M. (Field Hockey); Livermore, Calif.; Age 20; 5'9"; 143 lbs.; page 64

Jackson, Clinton (Boxing); Nashville, Tenn.; Age 24; 5'11½"; 160 lbs.; page 32

Jackson, Robert S. (Swimming); 1976 Olympics; San Jose, Calif.; Age 21; 6'4"; 205 lbs.; page 116

Johnson, Hewlett V. (Field Hockey); Yonkers, N.Y.; Age 29; 6'0"; 165 lbs.; page 65

Johnson, Lynette R. (Archery); Cypress, Calif.; Age 21; 5'6"; 145 lbs.; page 13

Johnson, William (Team Handball); Hewlett, N.Y.; Age 25; 6'5"; 200 lbs.; page 123

Jones, David (Weightlifting); Eastman, Ga.; Age 30; 5'4"; 148¾ lbs.; pages 141-42

Jonston-Ono, Teimoc (Judo); 1976 Olympics; New York, N.Y.; Age 23; 6'0"; 174 lbs.; page 82

Karchut, Michael (Weightlifting); Calumet City, Ill.; Age 34; 5'6"; 182 lbs.; pages 142-43

Kardos, Linda (Gymnastics); Bethel Park, Penn.; Age 16; 4'11"; 80 lbs.; page 73

Kennedy, James Edward (Diving); Knoxville, Tenn.; Age 25; 5'5½"; 138 lbs.; pages 46-47

Kimes, David William (Shooting); Monterey Park, Calif.; Age 38; 5'9"; 150 lbs.; pages 103-104

King, Albert (Basketball); College Park, Md.; Age 19; 6'6"; 197 lbs.; page 26

Knudson, Wendy Koenig (Athletics Track and Field); 1972 and 1976 Olympics; Logan, Utah; Age 23; 5'7½"; 122 lbs.; pages 19-20

Kovach, John (Field Hockey); Chevy Chase, Md.; Age 22; 6'0"; 180 lbs.; pages 65-66

Landreth, Debra L. (Volleyball); Colorado Springs, Colo.; Age 22; 5'8"; 150 lbs.; pages 129-30

Leiva, Wilfredo, Jr. (Wrestling); Camp Lejeune, N.C.; Age 19; 5'2½"; 110 lbs.; page 147

Lekach, Stanley V. (Fencing); Upton, N.Y.; Age 32; 5'10"; 155 lbs. pages 59-60

Lieberman, Nancy (Basketball); Norfolk, Va.; Age 20; 5'10"; 150 lbs.; page 26

Lillis, Linda "Chick" (Team Handball); Chicago, Ill.; Age 24; 5'5"; 130 lbs.; pages 124-25

Lind, Joan (Rowing); 1976 Olympics, Silver—Womens' Single Sculls; Long Beach, Calif.; Age 26; 5'9"; 144 lbs.; page 96

Lindsey, Carol Beth (Team Handball); Martinsburg, W. Va.; Age 23; 5'7½"; 145 lbs.; page 125

Lineham, Kimberly (Swimming); Sarasota, Fla.; Age 16; 5'5"; 114 lbs.; pages 116-17

Liquori, Martin (Athletics Track and Field); 1968 Olympics; Gainesville, Fla.; Age 29; 6'0"; 145 lbs.; page 20

Losey, Gregory (Modern Pentathlon); San Antonio, Tex.; Age 29; 6'2"; 180 lbs.; page 89

Louganis, Gregory E. (Diving); 1976 Olympics, Silver— 10 meter dive; El Cajon, Calif.; Age 19; 5'9"; 145 lbs.; pages 47-48

McCormick, Diane (Volleyball); Charleroi, Penn.; Age 28; 5'11½"; 140 lbs.; pages 130-31

McKinney, Richard L. (Archery); Muncie, Ind.; Age 25; 5'6"; 120 lbs.; page 14

Makin, Melvin P. (Shooting); Aumsville, Ore.; Age 38; 5'8"; 150 lbs.; page 104;

Martin, Thomas Gerard (Judo); Stockton, Calif.; Age 22; 5'11"; pages 82-83

Maruyama, Paul K. (Judo); Monument, Colo.; Age 37; 5'6"; 154 lbs.; page 84

Matsuda, Scot (Swimming); Garden Grove, Calif.; Age 17; 5'8"; 145 lbs.; pages 117-18

Matz, Michael (Equestrian); Plymouth Meeting, Penn.; Age 28; 5'10"; 150 lbs.; pages 54-55

Melges, Harry C., Jr. (Bud) (Yachting); 1964 Olympics, Bronze; 1972 Olympics, Gold; Zenda, Wis.; Age 49; 6'0"; 195 lbs.; page 153

Mello, Dan (Wrestling); Bakersfield, Calif.; Age 25; 5'3"; 135 lbs.; page 148

Miller, Anita C. (Field Hockey); Irvine, Calif.; Age 27; 5'8"; 130 lbs.; pages 66-67

Minkel, Thomas (Wrestling); Mt. Pleasant, Mich.; Age 29; 5'8"; 150 lbs.; page 148

Mount, George Lewis (Cycling); 1976 Olympics; Berkeley, Calif.; Age 23; 5'10"; 140 lbs.; page 41

Nakasone, Keith (Judo); San Jose, Calif.; Age 23; 5'6"; 143 lbs.; pages 84-85

Nonna, John (Fencing); 1972 and 1976 Olympics (alternate); Pleasantville, N.Y.; Age 30; 5'11"; 170 lbs.; page 60

Olbright, David E. (Volleyball); Dayton, Ohio; Age 26; 6'1"; 175 lbs.; pages 131-32

Pace, Darrell O. (Archery); 1976 Olympics, Gold Medal; Cincinnati, Ohio; Age 22; 6'0"; 150 lbs.; pages 14-15

Page, Scott (Archery); Fallbrook, Calif.; Age 23; 5'10"; 145 lbs.; pages 15-16

Peterson, Ben (Wrestling) 1972 Olympics, Gold; 1976 Olympics, Silver; Watertown, Wis.; Age 28; 6'0"; 205 lbs.; pages 148-49

Potter, Cynthia Ann (Diving); 1976 Olympics, Bronze—3 meter dive; Dallas, Tex.; Age 28; 5'1½"; 98 lbs.; page 48

Prehn, Thomas A. (Cycling); Annapolis, Md.; Age 21; 5'8½"; 140 lbs.; page 42

Purdy, William D. (Rowing); Liverpool, N.Y.: Age 21; 6'5"; 200 lbs.; pages 97-98

Pyfer, Leslie (Gymnastics); Eugene, Ore.; Age 16; 5'2"; 90 lbs.; page 74

Ramos, Alex (Boxing); Bronx, N.Y.; Age 18; 5'10"; 165 lbs.; page 32

Randhawa, Bikramjit Singh (Field Hockey); Hercules, Calif.; Age 26; 5'11½"; 165 lbs.; page 67

Reiter, Steve F. (Shooting); Daly City, Calif.; Age 37; 5'7"; 185 lbs.; page 105

Riddick, Steve (Athletics Track and Field); 1976 Olympics, Gold—4 by 100 relay; Philadelphia, Penn.; Age 27; 6'3½"; 175 lbs.; pages 20-21

Robinson, Clifford Trent (Basketball); Los Angeles, Calif.; Age 18; 6'10"; 220 lbs.; page 26

Rosado, William John (Wrestling); 1976 Olympics; Tempe, Ariz.; Age 23; 5'0"; 120 lbs.; page 149

Salazar, Alberto (Athletics Track and Field); Eugene, Ore.; Age 20; 6'0"; 142 lbs.; page 21

Salisbury, Paul James (Weightlifting); Altamont, N.Y.; Age 31; 5'7"; 198 lbs.; page 143

Saylor, John (Judo); Lucas, Ohio; Age 25; 6'1"; 228 lbs.; page 85

Schoene, Craig (Wrestling); Eugene, Ore.; Age 20; 6'4"; 240 lbs.; page 149

Schultz, David Leslie (Wrestling); Los Angeles, Calif.; Age 19; 5'8½"; 170 lbs.; page 150

Schwandt, Rhonda (Gymnastics); Los Alamitos, Calif.; Age 15; 4'11½"; 110 lbs.; page 75

Scott, Steven Michael (Athletics Track and Field); Irvine, Calif.; Age 22; 6'1"; 160 lbs. page 22

Setterberg, Kurt N. (Weightlifting); Masury, Ohio; Age 26; 5'11"; 215 lbs.; page 144

Shaw, Tim (Swimming); 1976 Olympics, Silver—400 meter freestyle; Tucson, Ariz.; Age 21; 6'2"; 170 lbs.; page 118

Shine, Michael L. (Athletics Track and Field); 1976 Olympics, Silver—400 meter hurdles; Youngsville, Penn.; Age 25; 6'0"; 168 lbs.; page 22

Somerville, Kurt F. (Rowing); Wellesley Hills, Mass.; Age 21; 6'6"; 215 lbs.; page 98

Sterkel, Jill (Swimming); 1976 Olympics, Gold—4 by 100 freestyle relay; Hacienda Heights, Calif.; Age 17; 5'11"; 156 lbs.; page 119

Stetina, Wayne (Cycling); 1972 and 1976 Olympics; Indianapolis, Ind.; Age 25; 6'0"; 165 lbs.; page 42

Stinger, Cynthia (Team Handball); Lawrenceville, N.J.; Age 20; 5'8½"; 140 lbs.; pages 125-26

Stockebrand, Gwen (Equestrian); Santa Rosa, Calif.; Age 24; 5'5½"; 125 lbs.; pages 55-56

Stone, Gregg (Rowing); Cambridge, Mass.; Age 26; 6'3½"; 180 lbs.; pages 98-99

Storrs, Nancy (Rowing); 1976 Olympics—Team; Philadelphia, Penn.; Age 29; 5'8"; 168 lbs.; page 99

Story, Joe (Team Handball); Salem, Ore.; Age 26; 5'7"; 160 lbs.; page 126

Swain, Michael L. (Judo); Bridgewater, N.J.; Age 18; 5'10"; 143 lbs.; page 85

Theimer, L. Michael (Shooting); 1976 Olympics; Iowa Park, Tex.; Age 29; 6'2"; 175 lbs.; page 106

Thomas, Kurt B. (Gymnastics); 1976 Olympics; Terre Haute, Ind.; Age 22; 5'5"; 127 lbs.; pages 75-76

Thornburgh, Stewart B. (Weightlifting); Charleston, Ill.; Age 18; 5'9"; 132 lbs.; page 144

Turner, Ann (Canoe & Kayak); Wasco, Ill.; Age 22; 5'9"; 143 lbs.; page 36

Ullman, David (Yachting); Newport Beach, Calif.; Age 33; 5'5"; 125 lbs.; pages 153-54

Valentine, Darnell (Basketball); Lawrence, Kans.; Age 20; 6'2"; 180 lbs.; page 26

Van Der Beck, Perry (Soccer); Tampa, Fla.; Age 19; 5'11"; 154 lbs.; page 108

Vandeweghe, Ernest "Kiki" (Basketball); Los Angeles, Calif.; Age 20; 6'8"; 225 lbs.; page 27

Vargas, Joseph M. (Water Polo); Hacienda Heights, Calif.; Age 23; 6'3"; 201 lbs.; page 138

Vidmar, Peter (Gymnastics); Los Angeles, Calif.; Age 17; 5'5"; 127 lbs.; page 76

Virts, Mark (Diving); Austin, Tex.; Age 24; 5'7"; 140 lbs.; page 49

Vosler, Kent (Diving); 1976 Olympics; Columbus, Ohio; Age 23; 5'5"; 138 lbs.; page 50

Walsh, Sue (Swimming); Hamburg, N.Y.; Age 16; 5'8"; 122 lbs.; pages 119-20

Warlick, Holly (Basketball); Knoxville, Tenn.; Age 20; 5'7"; 128 lbs.; page 28

Warner, Donnie (Weightlifting); York, Penn.; Age 20; 5'3"; 145½ lbs.; page 144

Weinstein, Barb (Diving); Cincinnati, Ohio; Age 20; 5'3"; 104 lbs.; page 50

Weinstein, Jayne Jennifer (Gymnastics); Eugene, Ore.; Age 15; 5'0"; 85 lbs.; pages 76-77

White, Nancy Pitkin (Field Hockey); McLean, Va.; Age 20; 5'10"; 145 lbs.; page 68

Wigger, Lones W., Jr. (Shooting); 1964 Olympics, Gold—Smallbore rifle, 3-position; Silver—Smallbore rifle, English Match; 1968 Olympics; 1972 Olympics, Gold—300 meter free rifle 3-position; Carter, Mont.; Age 41; 5'7"; 180 lbs.; page 106

Wilson, Michael Gower (Gymnastics); Moore, Okla.; Age 22; 5'5"; 125 lbs.; page 77

Wilson, Tory (Gymnastics); Lawton, Okla.; Age 15; 5'0"; 94 lbs.; pages 77-78

Wofford, James C. (Equestrian); 1968 Olympics, Silver—Team; 1972 Olympics, Silver—Team; Upperville, Va.; Age 34; 5'8"; 150 lbs.; page 56

Woodman, Tom (Rowing); Newtown, Penn.; Age 23; 6'5"; 220 lbs.; page 100

Wright, Mark (Team Handball); Pacific Palisades, Calif.; Age 28; 6'5"; 225 lbs.; page 126

Zang, Linda L. (Equestrian); Davidsonville, Md.; Age 31; 5'6"; 130 lbs.; page 56

Sour Cream Brownies, 119
Sugar Cookies, 76
Toll House Pan Cookies, 119

DESSERTS

Apple Crisp, 104
Apple Dumplings, 131
Baklava, 98
Best-Ever Chocolate Mousse, 55
Brownies, 120
Butter-Rum Bananas, 53
Cheese Cake, 50, 112, 137
Cherry Delight, 12
Chocolate Nut Waffles w/Ice Cream
    Topping, 36
Cranberry Gelatin Mold, 39
Date Nut Roll, 102
Easy Hot Fudge Sauce, 135
Fitz's Lemon Icebox Cake, 88
Frozen Banana Surprise, 143
Grandma's Jello, 35
Grape Krem, 36
Great-Great-Grandmother's
    Suet Pudding, 104
Greg's Hot Fudge Sauce, 40
Jolly Gelatin Gem Dessert, 123
Kristiana Kringel, 64
Miniature Walnut Tarts, 123
Orange Whip Dessert, 92
Peach Cobbler, 56
Philadelphia Cheese Cake, 41
Pineapple Casserole, 85
Pineapple-Orange Jello, 71
Polly's Cream, 40
Pound Cake Torte, 142
Strawberry Supreme, 76
Three Minute Yogurt Pie, 70
Willa Mae's Pineapple Ice Box
    Dessert, 132

MEATS

Baked Pork Chops, 34
Barbecued Ham Slice, 134
Barbecue Steak Western, 134
Beef Sprout Patties, 73
Crunchy Peanut-Stuffed
    Hot Dogs, 124
Hawaiian Broil Flank Steak, 68
Island Spaghetti Sauce, 149
Joe's Special, 85
Meat Loaf, 148
Meat Loaf w/Cheesey
    Tomato Sauce, 32
Mexican Flank Steak, 126
Mock Chow Mein, 146
Mom's Meat Loaf, 122
Mushroom Savory T-Bone Steak, 82
Oven Pot Roast, 31

Pepper Steak, 149
P.G.'s Roast Beef, 18
Pineapple Burgers with
    Spicy Sauce, 113
Pizza Burgers, 149
Pro Burgers, 39
Round Steak and Vegetables, 140
Skillet Chops and Beans, 142
Spaghetti Sauce, 80
Sweet and Sour Pork, 34
Trondheim Surprise, 125
Veal Saute, 25
Veal Scaloppini with Marsala, 20
Wiener Schnitzel, 112

MISCELLANEOUS

Avocado Bacon Sandwich, 125
Bagel Sandwiches, 77
B & M Beans, 78
Bar-B-Q Sauce, 88
The Basic Quiche w/Variations, 44
Blintzes, 150
Brown Rice Burgers, 25
Chile Quiche, 44
Corn Saute, 143
Crab Quiche, 89
Cranberry Coffee Ring, 96
Crunchy Peanut-Stuffed
    Hot Dogs, 124
Delicious Potatoes, 135
Early American Sweet Potatoes, 108
Fruit Cereal, 18
Glazed Wild Ducks
    w/wine sauce, 153
Green Chile Enchiladas, 136
Green Tomato Mince Meat, 19
Hash Brown Omelet, 108
Homemade Noodles, 67
Hot Tuna-Filled Finger Rolls, 73
Island Spaghetti Sauce, 149
Juevos Enchiladas, 136
Loo Son Ngou Yuk, 58
The Morning After Breakfast, 18
Mushroom Rice Pilaff, 147
Peanut Banana Spread, 124
Quiche Lorraine, 63
Quick Homemade Pizza, 38
Red Chile Burritos, 136
Rice Cooked in Chicken Stock, 59
Salad Sandwich Surprise, 89
Shrimp Quiche, 83
Spaghetti Sauce, 80
Teriyaki Kabob Pupus, 126
Vegetable Sukiyaki, 50
Vegetarian Tostados, 41
Zucchini Quiche, 48

PASTRY AND PIES

Cream Cheese Foldovers, 27
Elephant Ears, 27
Fay's Chocolate Meringue Pie, 102
Glazed Strawberry Pie, 34
Good Pie Crust Mix, 131
Lemon Meringue Pie, 134
Miniature Walnut Tarts, 123
Old Fashioned Pumpkin Pie, 65
Pecan Pie, 56
Southern Fruit Pie, 26
Sugar Cream Pie, 75
Toffee Ice Cream Pie and Sauce, 98

POULTRY, FISH & EGGS

Baked Fish au Gratin, 110
Baked Stuffed Chicken Breasts, 73
The Basic Quiche w/Variations, 44
The Basic Souffle w/Variations, 45
Braised Fish, 55
Broiled Bluefish, 99
Calcutta Curry, 113
Cheddar Cheese and
    Egg Souffle, 116
Cheese and Bacon Puff, 72
Cheese Bake Judy, 85
Cheeseman's Stir-Fried Chicken, 62
Cheese Relenos, 138
Chicken a la Champion, 148
Chicken and Rice Casserole, 148
Chicken Cacciatore, 114
Chicken Divan, 153
Chicken Surprise, 26
Chicken Veronique, 124
Chile Quiche, 44
Crab Hot Dish, 84
Crock Pot Barbecued Chicken, 20
Cuban Chicken with Rice, 21
Egg and Ham Brunch Bake, 137
Fillet of Sole Palm Beach, 105
Garden Chicken, 32
Green Chili Eggs, 138
Halibut Stroganoff, 21
Huevos Rancheros, 152
Italian Style Fried Chicken, 66
Italian Style Stuffed Chicken
    Breasts, 76
Juevos Enchiladas, 136
New England Codfish Balls, 98
Omelet, 49
Orange-Tarragon Chicken, 131
Peanut Butter Omelet, 46
Petti De Polla Memosa, 110
Poached Salmon Steaks, 153
Post Weigh-in Omelet, 149
Quiche Lorraine, 63
Quiche Taste Treat, 40
Quick Baked Chicken, 104

Sesame Sea Bass, 154
Shrimp Tempura, 78
Shrimp with Apricot Sauce, 124
Sliced Marinated Chicken Breasts
Sauteed, 60
Sweet and Sour Chicken, 55, 141
Sweet-Sour Chicken a la Russe, 138
Turkey or Chicken Rice Salad, 64

SALADS

Avocado Salad, 15
Bean Sprout Salad, 143
Caesar Salad, 110
Coleslaw, 125
Cranberry Gelatin Mold, 39
Dot's Polish Hot Potato Salad, 108
Italian Salad, 81
Jello Salad, 70
Many Layer Salad, 140
Marinated Bean Salad, 141
Nutty Chicken Salad, 152
Over-nite Fruit Salad, 137
Parkie's French Dressing, 88
Rascal Salad, 66
Sesame Citrus Dressing, 72
Seven Layer Salad, 146
Special Salad, 72
Spinach Salad, 35, 105, 128
Spinach Salad w/Hot Bacon
Dressing, 50

Taco Salad, 31
Turkey or Chicken Rice Salad, 64
Watergate Salad, 122

SNACKS

Bedtime Steamed Crackers, 144
"Cracker Jack," 123
Diane's Fig Potassium Pick-Up
Bars, 143
Frozen Banana Surprise, 143
Granola, 81, 85, 112
Great Granola, 115
Honey Popcorn Crunch, 42
Peanut Butter Munchies, 130

SOUPS & STEWS

Boeuf Bourguignon, 128
Canadian Cheese Soup, 35
Carne Con Chile, 103
Cashew Chili, 97
Chicken Soup, 102
Cincinatti Chili, 14
Coach Stop Chili, 56
Country Stew, 22
Dumplings, 28
Fish Broth, 65
Fish Chowder, 83
Hamburger Soup, 74
Homemade Chili, 32

Homemade Vegetable Soup, 31
P.G.'s Stew, 19
Quick Beef Stroganoff, 80
Round Steak and Vegetables, 140
Stefato, 147
Veal Saute, 25
Vegetable Soup, 63, 129
Venison Stew, 63

VEGETABLES

Baked Stuffed Squash, 14
Broccoli Casserole, 76, 92
Broccoli Main Dish, 112
Corn Saute, 143
Carottes Marinees, 60
Crusty Topped Cauliflower, 106
Green Bean and Mushroom
Casserole, 66
Green Bean Casserole, 70
Green Beans Deluxe, 74
Layered Vegetable Cheese Bake, 49
Margie's Beans, 92
Pea and Mushrooom Curry, 64
Stuffed Cabbage Rolls, 78
Stuffed Green Peppers, 54
Vegetable Quiche, 99
Vegetable Sukiyaki, 50
Zucchini Boats, 138
Zucchini Supreme, 92